W9-AVB-478

# TEACHING AND LEARNING STRATEGIES
# FOR
# THE THINKING CLASSROOM

# TEACHING AND LEARNING STRATEGIES

# FOR
# THE THINKING CLASSROOM

ALAN CRAWFORD, WENDY SAUL, SAMUEL R. MATHEWS,
AND JAMES MAKINSTER

A PUBLICATION OF
THE READING AND WRITING FOR
CRITICAL THINKING PROJECT
www.rwct.org

Published by:
The International Debate Education Association
400 West 59th Street
New York, NY  10019

Copyright © 2005 Open Society Institute

All rights reserved.  No part of this publication may be reproduced or
transmitted in any form or by any means, electronic or mechanical,
including photocopy, or any information storage and retrieval system,
without permission from the publisher.

ISBN: 1-932716-11-4
       978-1-932716-11-5

Library of Congress Cataloging-in-Publication Data

Crawford, Alan.
  Teaching and learning strategies for the thinking classroom / Alan Crawford, Wendy Saul, Samuel
R. Mathews.
     p. cm.
  Includes bibliographical references.
  ISBN 1-932716-11-4 (alk. paper)
  1.  Active learning. 2.  Effective teaching.  I. Saul, Wendy. II. Mathews, Samuel R. III. Title.
  LB1027.23.C72 2005
  371.102--dc22
  2005001668

Design by Fúzygrafik (fuzygrafik@yahoo.com)
Printed in the USA

# CONTENTS

# PREFACE

Many teachers realize that engaged teaching and active learning are desirable. Teaching that encourages students to ask questions and look for answers, to apply what they have learned in order to solve problems, to listen to each other and debate ideas politely and constructively—this is teaching students can use in their lives. But knowing that these things are important is not the same thing as knowing how to make them work in the classroom with a crowded curriculum, short class periods, and many students.

The staff development program **Teaching and Learning Strategies for the Thinking Classroom (The Thinking Classroom)** came about to satisfy the need in the schools for deeper learning, life-long learning—learning that students can use and that makes them not only better students but more productive members of society. And it also came about in order to teach "the small ideas," as one teacher called them. "The big ideas" are the lofty proclamations about how important active learning and critical thinking are. The "small ideas" are how to actually teach for active learning and critical thinking, in real classrooms.

**The Thinking Classroom** was inspired by the **Reading and Writing for Critical Thinking Project** (RWCT), and the present authors have long worked in that project. RWCT has worked with more than 40,000 teachers in 29 countries. The RWCT program was designed by Jeannie Steele, Charles Temple, Scott Walter, and Kurt Meredith, and was brought to life by 70 volunteer teacher-trainers from the United States, Canada, the United Kingdom, and Australia. Their numbers were multiplied tenfold by certified trainers in the 29 participating countries. The trainers were recruited and given administrative support by the International Reading Association. George Soros' Open Society Institute provided financial support, and the 29 Soros Foundation offices around the world gave the project a home. Quotations from teachers and students in the RWCT project are found throughout this book.

Trainers for the **The Thinking Classroom** program are available to go anywhere in the world.

For training activities in Europe and Central Asia, please contact the International RWCT Consortium, care of:

      Daiva Penkauskiene (daiva.dc@vpu.lt) or
      Maria Kovacs (mkovacs_rwct_ro@yahoo.com)

For training activities in other parts of the world, please contact:

      Critical Thinking International, Inc. (info@criticalthinkinginternational.org)

# SECTION 1:

# PRINCIPLES OF ACTIVE LEARNING AND CRITICAL THINKING

## THE MOST PRODUCTIVE TEACHING

Many teachers are seeking to change their practices to support reading and writing for critical thinking. They want to challenge their students not just to memorize, but to question, examine, create, solve, interpret, and debate the material in their courses. Such teaching is now widely recognized as "best practice." Studies show that active classes, so long as they are purposeful and well organized, are often the ones in which students learn the material most fully and usefully. Learning fully and usefully means that students can think about what they learn, apply it in real situations or toward further learning, and can continue to learn independently (Gardner 1993; Marzano 2001). Learning that can be used, learning that lasts is a far better investment of the teacher's time and the community's funds than learning that leaves students passive, that tires the teacher with its routine, and that is soon forgotten because it is not practiced or built upon.

---

My students have become more able to freely express themselves, to speak their thoughts. They also have become more attentive listeners to each other. They actively get involved in the creative process of knowledge building.

(Primary grade teacher from Armenia)

---

This guidebook is dedicated to the practice of lively teaching that results in reading and writing for critical thinking. It demonstrates and explains a well organized set of strategies for teaching that invites and supports learning. At the same time the guidebook presents a large set of teaching practices, it helps you, the reader, form judgments about teaching and learning so that you can use the right practices with the students you have, in the subject or subjects you teach.

This book will present strategies for teaching and learning that can be used from upper primary school right through secondary school. The approaches can be used with all subjects in the curriculum, including the study of crosscutting issues (important contemporary problems that do not easily fit into any one discipline).

## ORGANIZING INSTRUCTION FOR ACTIVE LEARNING

Some years ago, the Swiss psychologist Jean Piaget demonstrated that we learn by making sense of the world in terms of the concepts we already have. And in the process of making sense of the world, we change our old concepts, and thus expand our capacity for making even more sense of our future encounters with the world. For instance, before students can begin to appreciate a lesson on the Encounter of 1492, they need to have some knowledge of world geography, the importance of trade, and the culture of Europe in the late fifteenth century. Then, after they have studied the Encounter, they will have a more elaborated sense of world geography, the importance of trade, and the changes that cultures can exert on each other. Their elaborated concepts prepare them to inquire more easily into topics related to these.

In the 1970s and 1980s, cognitive psychologists extended Piaget's thinking into a way to approach teaching (Neisser 1976; Pearson and Anderson 1984). Because students learn by using the knowledge they already have (even though some of their concepts may be flawed; they may be incomplete or be little more than superstitions), teachers should begin a lesson by drawing out students' prior concepts, and getting them ready to learn by asking questions and setting purposes for learning.

Since students learn by making sense—that is, by exploring and inquiring—teachers should encourage students to inquire. And since inquiry is an activity that one can get good at, teachers should show students *how* to inquire, question, seek and examine information.

Finally, since the act of learning changes our old ideas and expands our capacity to learn new things, teachers should prod students to reflect on what they have learned, examine its implications, apply it in some useful way, and modify their old ways of thinking about the topic.

You will notice a pattern in the core lessons that follow in this guidebook. Each has three phases, corresponding to the activities of learning that Piaget and his followers identified.[1]

## THE ANTICIPATION PHASE
First, each lesson begins with a phase of **anticipation**, in which students are directed to think and ask questions about the topic they are about to study.

The Anticipation Phase serves to:

- call up the knowledge students already have
- informally assess what they already know, including misconceptions
- set purposes for learning
- focus attention on the topic
- provide a context for understanding new ideas

---

[1] In this guidebook we call the three phases of a lesson *Anticipation, Building Knowledge,* and *Consolidation* (in English these three terms are abbreviated as "ABC"). The Reading and Writing for Critical Thinking Project (See www.rwct.net) is based on a three-part teaching model that goes by the name of **Evocation, Realization of Meaning,** and **Reflection**, which were terms introduced by Jeannie Steele and Kurt Meredith (1997). The three-phase model was earlier called **Anticipation, Realization,** and **Contemplation** by Joseph Vaughn and Thomas Estes (1986).

## THE BUILDING KNOWLEDGE PHASE

After the lesson gets started, the teaching leads students to inquire, find out, make sense of the material, answer their prior questions, and find new questions and answer those, too. We call this second or middle phase of the lesson the **building knowledge phase.**

The Building Knowledge phase serves to:

- compare expectations with what is being learned
- revise expectations or raise new ones
- identify the main points
- monitor personal thinking
- make inferences about the material
- make personal connections to the lesson
- question the lesson

## THE CONSOLIDATION PHASE

Toward the end of the lesson, once students have come to understand the ideas of the lesson, there is still more to be done. Teachers want students to reflect on what they learned, ask what it means to them, reflect on how it changes what they thought, and ponder how they can use it. This phase of the lesson is called the **consolidation phase**.

The Consolidation Phase serves to:

- summarize the main ideas
- interpret the ideas
- share opinions
- make personal responses
- test out the ideas
- assess learning
- ask additional questions

Throughout this guidebook, we will refer again and again to these three phases of **anticipation, building knowledge,** and **consolidation.** The many teaching activities that will be presented in these pages will usually serve the purposes of one or another of these three phases of a lesson.

The ABC model is illustrated throughout the text with a simple triad of icons inspired by the different phases of the wheat plant's life cycle:

In the **anticipation phase**, a seed is planted in rich soil. The success of a lesson does not just depend on this "seed," however; it must also draw on knowledge the students already possess, just as the seed must draw on the nutrients in the soil.

The essential groundwork laid, the teacher proceeds to the **building knowledge phase**; the wheat seed sprouts roots and a plant grows.

The lesson concludes with the **consolidation phase**. The head of wheat is mature, and contains seeds of many other plants; so too the lesson can lead into many other activities.

These three icons are always shown together and in sequence, suggesting teachers build on what came before and keep in mind what may come next. The life-cycle of wheat, from seed to soil to plant and back to seed, also suggests the constant educational cycle of building on prior knowledge to move forward.

## THINKING CRITICALLY

The most successful classrooms are those that encourage students to think for themselves and engage in *critical thinking* (Halpern 1996; Kurland 1995; Unrau 1997). *Critical thinking* allows us to think about our own thoughts and the reasons behind our points of view. It means that we reflect on our own ways of making decisions or solving problems. Thinking like this means that our thoughts are consciously directed to some goal. Our thoughts and ideas are based not on our biases or prejudices but on logic and information we might gather and filter from many sources. As we think critically, we are always mindful of what and how we are thinking. When we detect an error or a different way to think about a problem, we explore it eagerly. Students who think critically are typically excited about their learning. They see challenges and opportunities for learning in even the most difficult intellectual tasks. These students are mindful of opportunities to use their critical thinking skills and typically engage these opportunities eagerly—whether in the classroom context or in the world of their own communities. These are the students who make teaching enjoyable and exciting.

One way that people who study and teach critical thinking and active learning (e.g., Anderson 2000) organize goals for teaching and learning is to create categories or types of questions and teaching objectives. The idea is that simply remembering some fact is a very "low level" question and objective. At the other end of the list is the "high level" act of creating new ideas or making new inferences. Below is a list that includes categories of questions and objectives that range from the lowest level (remembering) to the highest level (creating).

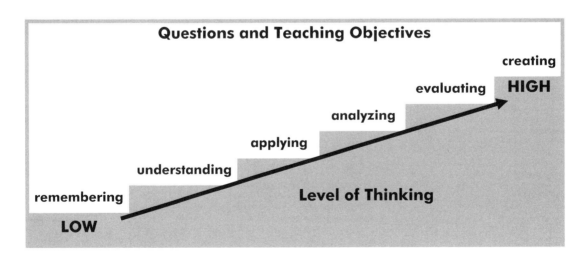

While there is a need to work at all levels, by going beyond questions that require simple memory or recall, we, as teachers, help students tap higher levels of critical thinking, even as they develop factual knowledge. Asking high-level questions and achieving the higher level objectives require that teachers restructure classrooms so that they support the practice of critical thinking. Recently edu-cators and educational researchers have provided some guidelines for restructuring classrooms along these lines (Herrenkohl 1998; Herrenkohl 1999). In such classrooms active learning and critical thinking are valued and encouraged by teachers and students. Discussions among students and between students and teachers are frequent, civil, and lively. Many times, discussions follow a question that arises from either a student or the teacher. The level, type, and structure of questions are important to the discussions that follow. They support higher levels of complexity in students' critical thinking. This section provides a description of various levels and types of questions and models and guidelines for classroom discussion.

When we speak of *levels of questions*, we are referring to the difference between questions that address details (such as names, dates, places, capitals of counties or provinces) and questions that address more complex ideas, such as the relationships between concepts or causes of some event or situation. *Low-level questions* ask about facts and details. Such questions might include the following examples:

- What is the year Mexico obtained its independence from Spain?
- What temperature is the freezing point of water at sea level?
- What is the name of Cervantes' best known literary work?
- On what continent is the Orinoco River?

It may be important for students to know these facts, but simply knowing them does not ensure that they will be able to use the facts to solve problems or make important decisions. Strategies that facilitate learning at lower levels include:

- Orally rehearsing a fact repeatedly
- Writing and rewriting the information
- Reading and rereading material to be remembered

While these strategies may help in the near future, they do not ensure memory for the information over a longer period. If the goal of education is to be able to not only remember facts, but also to use those facts to solve problems and make decisions, then students are best served when they are asked questions that require them to complete more complex, *higher order* critical thinking, using *higher order questions*.

*Higher order questions* are those that ask how or why something happens or how one event, object, or idea might be related to other events, objects, or ideas. These questions are phrased so that the person providing the answer must engage in *critical thinking*. That is, students might *use* facts and details in the process of answering the question, but they must go beyond the facts and details to construct a rationale for the response. With higher order questions, the person responding is *actively* asserting some position about causes or relationships. Questions phrased as *higher order questions* typically require the use of mental strategies associated with critical thinking.

*Higher order questions* encourage students to locate important information and use it to draw conclusions and make comparisons.

- How did Mexico's movement for independence from Spain impact people in neighboring countries?
- Why does water near bridges and in the cities freeze later in the winter than water in lakes located in rural areas?
- The Amazon River impacts many regions in Brazil. How is its impact different for those regions near the Atlantic coast and those in the central part of Brazil?

Questions like these might have more than one valid and plausible answer. These questions reflect a higher level of thinking beyond questions that simply request a repetition of facts.

The content of the question is important in promoting critical thinking, but so is the way it is asked. There are many strategies that teachers can use to make their questioning strategies even more effective (Gibbs 2001):

- Ask questions that invite more than one plausible answer.
- Provide wait time after asking a question to give less confident students an opportunity to formulate their responses.
- Ask follow-up questions, such as, "What can you add?" "What is your opinion, Margarita?"
- Provide feedback that neither confirms nor denies student responses. Then the discussion remains open. Examples are: "Interesting." "I hadn't thought about that before."
- Request a summary. "Who can make Jamila's point in different words?"
- Survey the other students. "Who agrees with Max?" "Who disagrees? Why?"
- Encourage students to direct questions to other students. "Ask Michel if he can add something to your response."
- Be the devil's advocate. "How would you feel if…?" "How would your answer change if…?"
- Use think-aloud. "How did you figure out that answer?"
- Call on all students, not only those who raise their hands. But move on quickly if a student chooses not to answer.
- Alert the students to possible answers. "There are many possible answers to this question."
- Change the perspective. "How would you feel about your answer if you were…?"
- Imagine. "What would happen if…?"
- Relate the response to something else. "How is (student's response) similar to _____?" "How is it different?"
- Transform the response in some way. "What if you changed (student's idea) to _____?" What if we combined Jamila's idea with Michel's idea?

Here, in this school I can share a secret with my teacher. We have team works and we have our own rights, which does not exist in other schools. Our school in comparison with other schools is a KING!

(Student from the Republic of Georgia)

## THE CLASSROOM ENVIRONMENT

Classrooms that invite students to learn actively and think critically have these features in common (Mathews 2003):

1. **Teachers and students share responsibility for the classroom climate.** For example, students may participate in developing class rules for conduct. Teachers invite students to take initiative—for example, by using cooperative learning strategies in which each student is assigned his or her own role to play in helping classmates learn. (See the Third Core Lesson: Cooperative Learning.)

2. **Teachers model thinking for students and support students as they share their thinking strategies.** Teachers demonstrate how a person thinks critically, not by propounding ideas as if everything that came out of their mouths was a certainty, but by approaching ideas tentatively, conditionally, and promoting respect for different points of view in their lessons. Students have open discussions with each other, and learn not only each other's ideas, but each other's ways of thinking. Teachers may question their own, their students, and others' conclusions and knowledge, and encourage students to do likewise.

3. **There is an atmosphere of inquiry and openness.** The teacher and students use high-level questions (That is, not just "What?" "Where?" and "When"; but *"Why?", "What if?"* and *"Why not?"*) as they analyze problems and make decisions. Students take certain roles in activities as they practice different kinds of thinking: they make predictions, gather information, organize the information, and question conclusions. Teachers show students ways to carry out tasks in the classroom, and they give students more corrective advice than criticism and evaluation.

4. **Students are given support, but just the right amount of it.** Teachers pay close attention to what students are learning and how they are thinking, investigating, and communicating as they go about learning. Students are taught to examine their own learning and to improve their own performance. Teachers vary the amount of guidance they give students, and offer them more independence as they show they are ready for it. There is an emotionally secure learning environment in which students feel free to try new tasks, and in which unsuccessful attempts may lead to eventual success.

5. **The arrangement of the space makes it easy and natural for the students to work together and talk to each other.** Traditional classrooms are arranged so they resemble ceremonial places, where the students sit in rows like an audience or a congregation, and the teacher sits in the front, often on an elevated plane, like the mayor or the priest. If we want to stress the idea that the students are important, that what they have to say is interesting and should be shared, then we should arrange the classroom space to allow for them to talk to each other, and to work

together. Shown below are some different ways to arrange classroom space, to help students interact with each other. Of course, whether or not you can use a given plan depends on the furniture you have in the classroom. The diagrams below provide suggestions.

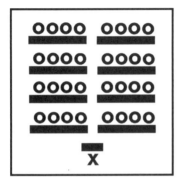

*This design is best for listening to the teacher, but it is not good for interaction among students. Teachers who want students to talk to each other* **avoid this arrangement***.*

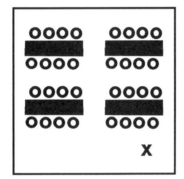

*This design is suitable for having small groups working together. Note that the teacher is not stationary during most group activities; rather he or she circulates around the room to observe the groups, answer questions, or offer guidance.*

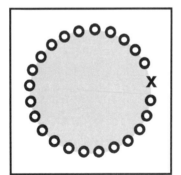

*This arrangement is suitable for a whole class meeting or discussion. Note that the teacher is one discussant among many.*

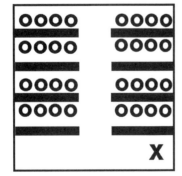

*This arrangement is used when students are seated on immovable benches. The students sitting in front of the desk turn around and work across the desk with the students behind them.*

## HOW TO MAKE THE MOST OF THIS LEARNING PROGRAM

Learning a new teaching method is like learning a new move in sports—you have to see it done, try it out in front of someone who knows how to do it, and get suggestions to improve your performance. The workshops are arranged just this way: you take part in a demonstration lesson as if you were a student, then you discuss the methods and learn how to conduct them, then you plan and teach a lesson using the method yourself. At the end of the workshop, you will design a real lesson to teach in your classroom, which you will teach after the workshop is over.

Section 2 of this guidebook contains core lessons that demonstrate teaching methods in action. Then they tell you how to carry out, step by step, the teaching methods that were demonstrated. After showing you how to teach each method used in the core lesson, the guide shows you several related teaching methods that can also be used to reach similar goals.

Section 3 outlines some general ideas about assessment and lesson planning as they apply to Reading and Writing for Critical Thinking methods. This section includes classroom management techniques and assessment rubrics, all based on the successful practices of different teachers at different grade levels and in different subjects.

Section 4, "Teaching In and Across the Disciplines," focuses on the application of RWCT methods on the teaching of literature, mathematics, science, art, and interdisciplinary, or "crosscutting," subjects.

Remember, you must try these methods out in order to learn to use them well. It is recommended that you use a new method many times before you decide if it works in your teaching. Not only must you get used to teaching with the method, but your students must get used to learning with it too.

Also, you should collaborate with other teachers. At least once each month, try to get together with one or more other teachers who are teaching with these new methods. Write down your questions and stories of your successes, and bring those to the meeting to discuss with others. Bring your lesson plans, and samples of the students' work. You are sure to find that you have good suggestions that will help your colleagues overcome problems they are having, and they will have suggestions that will help you too.

---

As a professional with a university degree and 30 years of teaching experience, I consider my participation in the project equivalent to completing another higher education degree.

(Teacher from Azerbaijan)

---

# SECTION 2:

# TEACHING METHODS AND STRATEGIES

Teaching is more than a set of methods. Teaching well means addressing a set of objectives, for a particular group of students, at a certain point in the school year, with certain resources, within a particular time frame, in a particular school and community setting. It means finding a balance between direct instruction and orchestrating the activities of individuals and groups of students. It means developing students' skills and strategies for learning, at the same time they learn the content of the curriculum.

Artful teachers approach the subject matter not as static knowledge or inert ideas, but as ways of knowing. Using ways of knowing—thinking within a discipline—means to command a set of concepts and a set of strategies for asking questions and creating knowledge. To think *across* disciplines means to identify problems, to ask the right questions, to bring the right knowledge to bear, to find the right solutions, and to apply the right measure of one's success.

Although teaching is more than a set of strategies, there are some teaching methods that should be part of every creative teacher's repertoire. Some of these are comprehensive strategies that can shape a whole lesson. Others can be combined to make a complete lesson plan.

## CORE LESSONS AND HOW TO READ THEM

In the pages that follow you will find eight **core lessons** described in detail. Each of these lessons sets out activities and teaching strategies chosen for each of the three phases—**anticipation**, **building knowledge**, and **consolidation**—that was described in the previous section. These lessons are scripted, almost as if they were plays, to give you an idea what the teacher and students say and do. If you are taking part in a workshop, it is likely that you will have a chance to take part in these lessons as if you were a student.

In the text of the script, each phase of a lesson will be indicated by the following icons:

 the *anticipation phase* of a lesson

 the *building knowledge phase*

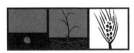 the *consolidation phase*

Each **Lesson** is followed by invitations for you to reflect on how they worked and what they achieved. Then the **Methods** are carefully described and their steps laid out so that you may follow them in teaching your own lessons. Finally, **Variations and Related Methods** that can be used to teach the same kind of lesson are described.

It is important to remember that some of these methods are better suited for one or more of the ABC phases. The ABC icons above are also used in the **Methods,** indicating which phase(s) the method can be used in. Some methods span several phases, or are suitable for more than one phase. For example:

 (This method is suitable for the anticipation and consolidation phase.)

Every method is presented in the same format to make it easier for you to use in actual lesson planning:

 **Rationale**—outline of the goals of the method and how it helps students learn.

 **Group Size**—the number of students most suitable to involve in this method.

 **Resources**—what materials are needed, if any.

 **Time Required**

 **Activity**—every step of the method, described in detail.

 **Assessment**—during and after the lesson, if appropriate or desired.

 **Reflections**—discussion of the method that will give the reader a better idea of how or why to use it.

 **Tips**—suggestions on how to conduct the method successfully, or addressing it to specific groups with different needs.

The following core lessons were designed to be used with any level of student and with any subject. Each core lesson was chosen to illustrate teaching for different aims.

FIRST CORE LESSON          **Learning Information from Text**

SECOND CORE LESSON         **Understanding Narrative Text**

THIRD CORE LESSON          **Cooperative Learning**

FOURTH CORE LESSON         **Conducting Discussions**

FIFTH CORE LESSON          **Writing and Inquiry**

SIXTH CORE LESSON          **Writing to Persuade**

SEVENTH CORE LESSON        **Understanding Arguments**

EIGHTH CORE LESSON         **Critical Listening**

# FIRST CORE LESSON: LEARNING INFORMATION FROM TEXT

This lesson shows you ways to help students learn from reading an informational text. The lesson follows the three-part format of anticipation, building knowledge, and consolidation that was presented in the first section this guidebook. The lesson will use the **Structured Overview** (Ausubel 1968), the **Know/Want to Know/Learn (K-W-L)** procedure (Ogle 1986), **Paired Reading/ Paired Summarizing** (Vaughn 1986), and the **Value Line** (Kagan 1997).

The text for this lesson is called "Elephants and Farmers," but the procedures in the lesson are meant to be used with any informational text that you have. This lesson is done here with sixth graders, but the procedures can be used with grades below that or up through the secondary level.

## HOW TO READ THIS LESSON

As you read the following demonstration lesson, please bear in mind that its purpose is to demonstrate teaching methods (and not to teach you about elephants!). Think about this lesson in two ways:

1. Imagine that you are a *student* who is participating in this lesson. What is your experience? What kind of thinking are you doing? What are you learning?

2. Then think yourself into the role of the *teacher* who is leading the lesson. What are you doing? Why are you doing it? How are you handling the three phases of the lesson—anticipation, building knowledge, and consolidation?

## LESSON

 **ANTICIPATION**

The teacher begins with a **Structured Overview**, in this case a short talk about the topic—just enough to frame the students' thinking about the topic and to raise their curiosity. The talk goes like this:

**Teacher:** *Today we will be talking about the problems of protecting endangered species. We will focus on elephants, and consider efforts to save them from dying out. We will also look at the question a different way: We will think about problems that are caused by conservation.*

*Some elephants live in Asia, but the most plentiful and largest elephants live in Africa, mostly in the eastern countries of Kenya, Tanzania, and Uganda. (The teacher points to these countries on a map). Elephants live on grassy plains and in forests.*

*Take a minute and think of some threats to elephants. Then turn to your **face partner**—the person sitting in front of you—and share your answers.*

After a minute, the teacher invites answers from three of the pairs.

**Pair 1:** "We think people shoot them."

**Teacher:** *True, in the past, big-game hunters shot them for sport. Many thousands of elephants have been killed that way over the years. In the 1970s many countries outlawed the hunting of elephants, but illegal hunters, or "poachers," continue to kill elephants for their ivory tusks. Ivory is rare and precious, and . . .*

**Pair 2:** "Maybe people are destroying their habitat?"

**Teacher:** *That is another big threat. Much of their habitat has been taken over for farming.*

*On the whole, the population of elephants in the world is still shrinking, so people have taken steps to protect the elephant populations that are left. Can you think of what some of those steps are? Take a minute and think of some. Then turn to your **elbow partner**—the person next to you—and share your answers.*

After a minute the teacher calls on another pair.

**Pair 3:** "Aren't there parks where elephants and other animals can live and nobody will bother them?"

**Teacher:** *Yes. Governments have also set aside large parks or preserves—some of them are many kilometers across—where elephants can live under the protection of game wardens and where their habitat is preserved. Also, jewelers have been discouraged from selling ivory, and many people refuse to buy it, even when they find it for sale.*

*But here's a question for you to think about. In Africa, elephants live in grasslands and in forests, and many of them live near people's farms. What kinds of problems might that cause? Remember, most people believe elephants should be protected. But people need to eat the food that comes from farms too.*

Now the teacher asks the students to pair up and make a list of points they know about conserving the population of elephants:

*Turn to the person beside you. Think of three or four things you know about the conservation of elephants— things you are fairly sure about. Don't limit yourself to the points we just mentioned.*

The teacher draws the **K–W–L chart** on the chalk board:

### Elephant Conservation

| What do we know? | What do we want to know? | What did we learn? |
| --- | --- | --- |
| | | |

Now the teacher asks pairs of students to tell some of the points they thought of about conserving the elephant population, writing them in the K-W-L chart under **What do we <u>know</u>?**

**Teacher:** *Let's write down the important things we already know about the conservation of elephants and the problems related to it.*

The students mention that elephants are endangered, people destroy their habitat, etc. The teacher records these.

### Elephant Conservation

| What do we know? | What do we want to know? | What did we learn? |
|---|---|---|
| Elephants are endangered.<br>People shoot them. Poachers kill elephants for ivory.<br>People destroy their habitat.<br>There are laws against shooting them.<br>There are game reserves set aside for them.<br>Some elephants live near farms.<br>Elephants might harm farmers' crops. | | |

The teacher now asks the students about the things they are unsure of, and helps them turn their uncertainties into questions, recording them on the K-W-L chart. The teacher begins by reading out loud the points in the What do we know? column.

**Teacher:** *We know a lot about the conservation of elephants. But what more do we need to know?*

The students wonder aloud if elephants ruin crops, how much damage elephants do, etc. The teacher writes the questions on the chart in the column labeled **What do we <u>want to know</u>?**

### Elephant Conservation

| What do we know? | What do we want to know? | What did we learn? |
|---|---|---|
| Elephants are endangered.<br>People shoot them. Poachers kill elephants for ivory.<br>People destroy their habitat.<br>There are laws against shooting them.<br>There are game reserves set aside for them.<br>Some elephants live near farms.<br>Elephants might harm farmers' crops. Poachers kill elephants for ivory.<br>Elephants live in grasslands and forests. | Do elephants ruin crops?<br>How much damage do elephants do?<br><br>How do people who live near elephants feel about them?<br><br>Who should decide whether to protect elephants? | |

 **BUILDING KNOWLEDGE**

The Teacher now prepares the students to read the text. The students will use the method of **Paired Reading/Paired Summarizing** to help them think about the material they are reading. Since this method is new to the students, the teacher takes time to thoroughly introduce it.

**Teacher:** *Now we are going to read a text that tells about the conservation of elephants, and some of the issues it raises. Before we read, let's remember the questions we had, and see if we can find answers to them as we read.*

The teacher rereads the questions from the <u>Want to Know</u> column. *Also, be watching for new ideas for which we did not think of questions.*

Before the students begin reading, the teacher demonstrates how they should perform Paired Reading/Paired Summarizing.

**Teacher:** *I want you to read the text a special way, called "Paired Reading/Paired Summarizing." Watch closely as I demonstrate what you will do. First I am going to read a paragraph, and then summarize it.*

The teacher reads:

### ELEPHANTS AND FARMERS

The elephant population continues to dwindle in many African countries. In others, however, long-standing conservation measures have been so successful that elephants are more numerous than at any time in recorded history.

**Teacher:** *I will demonstrate what you do when you summarize a paragraph. The paragraph said that the number of elephants is mostly going down, but in some African countries there are more elephants than before. That is because efforts to conserve them have worked. Did you see? I told you the important ideas but not all of the details.*

*Reading a paragraph and summarizing it is what one partner will do. The other partner will ask questions about the paragraph. I will demonstrate that too. Here is a question about the passage we just heard: "What might be some of the 'conservation measures' the passage mentioned?"*

The students offer answers.

**Teacher:** *Those sound like good answers. And here is another question: "The article says the elephant population is larger in some places than ever before. Do you think that is a good thing or a bad thing? What is good about it? What is bad about it?"*

The students offer more answers.

**Teacher:** *Now that I have shown you how to summarize and how to ask questions, I want you to pair up. One of you will go first, and read the next paragraph. Then that same person will summarize it, as I have just done. The other student should ask two or three good questions about the paragraph. Both of you should try to answer each question.*

Wildlife experts are calling this a victory, but to the struggling African farmer, it is yet one more example of how the forces of nature threaten her precarious livelihood. Elephants foraging for food that their expanding population has made scarce can destroy an entire plantation in a matter of hours. Profits on the larger farms, already under threat from rocketing seed and fertilizer prices and the effects of globalization, are plummeting. For the subsistence farmer and her family, a single act of trespass by an elephant herd can mean the loss of a season's work, the destruction of house and home, and possible destitution.

The teacher allows time for students to read the passage and summarize it. The teacher walks quietly among the pairs and listens to their summaries.

**Teacher:** *Stop, please. Who can do a nice job of summarizing that paragraph? There is a lot of information there, isn't there? What did it tell us?*

**Student 16:** "The paragraph says that some farms are ruined by the elephants."

**Teacher:** *That's true. But let's try to capture a few more important ideas in the summary. Let's hear someone else.*

**Student 17:** "When there are a lot of elephants, they have to search further and further for food. The elephants come onto big farms and do damage, so the farm doesn't make money. They ruin the small farm and leave that farmer with nothing."

**Teacher:** *That summary captures several important ideas nicely. Does everyone see that a summary should be shorter and simpler than the original paragraph, but it should also contain the most important ideas?*

*Now, let's continue. It's time now for the other partner to ask questions about the paragraph.*

The teacher passes around the room for several minutes and listens to the students' questions. When most students are finished, the teacher says, *Let's hear one of your questions.*

**Student 18:** "Why did the author say 'she' when he was talking about a farmer?"

**Teacher:** *Good question,* says the teacher. *Why don't you ask the class?*

The student does so, and students offer answers.

**Teacher:** *All right, I see you know how to summarize a paragraph, and how to ask questions about it. I won't stop you as you read the next two paragraphs. Remember: the one who asked the questions last time will read the next paragraph and summarize it. The other student will ask two or three questions about it, and both will try to answer the questions. Then you will switch roles when you read the next paragraph. Keep trading roles for each new paragraph as you read the rest of the article.*

The article continues:

It is these facts which have led many farmers to call for a revival of the right to shoot elephants and to trade their meat, hides and ivory. The price of a single tusk can be equivalent to many years' income for an impoverished farmer. In a world where the livelihoods of poor people are more at risk than those of elephants, this is an increasingly persuasive argument. In addition to this, legalization would reduce the need for the expensive, military style policing currently used to control the violent behavior of ivory smugglers.

However, many conservationists have reacted with horror to this proposal. Legalizing the shooting of elephants, even on a controlled basis, will, they argue, lead to a free for all which will drive the elephant back to the brink of extinction. The corruption and exploitation linked to the trade in ivory will return. And to many, the very idea of killing an animal as majestic, noble and intelligent as the elephant is every bit as abhorrent as killing a whale.

The teacher circulates among the pairs as they summarize the paragraphs and ask questions about them. If she finds they understand what they are doing, she lets them continue. If she finds a particular student needs help making a summary or thinking of probing questions, she intervenes and offers help. If she were to find that many students needed such help, she would ask for their attention and remind the whole class how to summarize and how to ask questions.

 **CONSOLIDATION**

The consolidation phase is the part of the lesson where the students think back over what they learned, apply the ideas, and reconsider what they already knew before in light of what they have learned. In this lesson, the consolidation activity consists of the conclusion to the **Know/Want to Know/Learn Activity** and the **Value Line.**

Returning to the K-W-L chart, the teacher now asks the students to reflect on what they have learned. They will begin by recounting answers they found to their questions.

**Teacher:** *Now let's see what we learned from this article. First I wonder if we found answers to our questions. Please pair up, read the questions from the* <u>Want to Know</u> *column, and see if you found answers to them. I'll give you two minutes to do this.*

After two minutes, the teacher asks students to start offering answers.

**Student 21:** "Yes, they ruin crops, and a whole lot more."

**Teacher:** *Then the answer to the first question is "yes.,"* and she writes that in the <u>What Did We Learn</u> column on the chart.

**Student 22:** "The article told us about a lot of damage elephants do."

**Teacher:** *Yes? Show us where in the text you found that information.*

**Student 22:** "Here, for example, the text said, 'For the subsistence farmer and her family, a single act of trespass by an elephant herd can mean the loss of a season's work, the destruction of house and home, and possible destitution.'"

**Teacher:** *Good. By the way, can someone tell us what* <u>destitution</u> *means?*

**Student 21:** "It means being completely without money."

**Teacher:** *Nice job. Let's go on.*

**Student 23:** "Anyway, before that it said, 'Profits on the larger farms, already under threat from rocketing seed and fertilizer prices and the effects of globalization, are plummeting.' In other words the big farms are losing money."

**Teacher:** *Good. Let's write these on the chart.*

The teacher adds these answers to the <u>What Did We Learn</u> column.

The students offer several more answers they encountered in the text, and the teacher records those in the <u>What Did We Learn </u>column.

**Teacher:** *How about the last question:* "Who should decide whether to protect elephants?" *Did you find an answer to that one?*

**Student 26**: "The text didn't say. It said some people were really against killing elephants, but it didn't say who should decide."

**Teacher**: *Then that's a question we may have to answer for ourselves. In the meantime, did we find out anything else from the article, something we didn't already have questions about? Turn to your face partner, and see if you can locate any new ideas you learned.*

The teacher gives them a minute to do this.

The students offer more ideas. At the end of the discussion, the K-W-L chart looks like this:

### Elephant Conservation

| What do we know? | What do we want to know? | What did we learn? |
| --- | --- | --- |
| Elephants are endangered. People shoot them. Poachers kill elephants for ivory. People destroy their habitat. There are laws against shooting them. There are game reserves set aside for them. Some elephants live near farms. Elephants might harm farmers' crops. Poachers kill elephants for ivory. Elephants live in grasslands and forests. | Do elephants ruin crops? How much damage do elephants do?<br><br>How do people who live near elephants feel about them?<br><br>Who should decide whether to protect elephants? | Yes! They destroy farms and houses. They make big farms lose money.<br><br>Farmers fear elephants. They also want to make money from killing them.<br><br>We need to decide who should decide. That is, who should determine if some elephants are to be hunted or not? |

The lesson could end at this point. But because the teacher wishes to pursue the ethical question raised by the text, she adds another activity called a **Value Line**. The Value Line is an activity that requires students to take a position on an issue and to support it with reasons. The teacher begins by posing a polarizing question:

**Teacher:** *One of you raised a good question that the text didn't answer. It was, "'Should farmers be allowed to kill elephants?" I want you to discuss this question. First, please take a piece of paper and write your own answer to it. You can answer 'yes' or 'no,' but you must also explain your reasons for your position. Take two minutes and do that now.*

After two minutes, the teacher explains the next step:

**Teacher:** *You are about to hear two statements of positions that are the opposite of each other.*

Now the teacher walks to one end of the room and makes an extreme statement in answer to the question.

**Teacher:** *Elephants should not be harmed under any circumstances. If elephants want to eat a farmer's crops, they should be allowed. The farmer should just move. Elephants were on the land before people were, and they have a right to live anywhere and any way they want.*

The teacher asks for one student to volunteer and stand at the other end of the room and state the opposite view.

**Student 1:** *"It's people who are important, not animals. Farmers need to make food for people to eat. They shouldn't protect elephants. They should kill them and eat them and sell their tusks for ivory."*

Next, the teacher invites the rest of the class to stand somewhere between the teacher and the other student.

**Teacher:** *Now that you have heard these two extreme views, I want you to stand up and take your position between the two of us. If you agree that elephants should not be killed under any circumstances, come stand close to me. But if you think farmers should be completely free to kill elephants, go stand close to* **student 1**. *However, if you agree mostly but not fully with one position or the other, stand somewhere along a line between the two of us.*

After the students position themselves, the teacher asks them to talk to those around them to see if they have the same opinion—if not, they should move in one direction or the other.

---

These methods promise to free the student's thinking from the dictatorship of the teacher's belief that "I know everything and I want you to know the truth that I have."

(Primary-school teacher, Romania)

---

**Teacher:** *Now that you have taken your position, you need to check and make sure you are standing with people who hold the same position you do. Take a minute now and take turns telling the people around you your position and why you believe it. If it turns out you do not agree with your neighbors after all, you should move to another place in the line. Talk to the people around you in the new place and make sure you agree on your answers.*

While they are talking, the teacher identifies a spokesperson for three or four clusters of students among those standing in the line.

**Teacher:** *Now please come up with a statement that represents the views of the people in each cluster. Those of you who are standing in the same place need to help your spokesperson create a short statement that represents your position.*

The spokesperson for each cluster of students shares the group's position.

**Group 1 (closest to the teacher):** "So what if elephants destroy farms and rip up forests? People do that all the time and call it 'development.' We are pretty sure the elephants were there first, and the farmers invaded their territory. We think the farmers should leave."

**Teacher:** *Okay, that's a pretty strong statement. By the way, for the rest of you, maybe you will hear something said here that will make you change your mind. If you do, it's all right to change your position, to move closer toward someone you agree with or further away from someone your disagree with. Now let's hear from the next group.*

**Group 2:** "We think maybe the farmers shouldn't be there either, but still, the farmers deserve help. People who love elephants should take up a fund and pay the farmers to go set up somewhere else. Then there would be more land for the elephants—but the farmers would be taken care of too."

**Teacher:** *That's considerate of you. Does anyone want to move?* (No one does). *No? Then I will. I'm persuaded by that position because it takes everybody's interests into account.* (The teacher moves to stand beside Group 2). *Let's hear from another group.*

**Group 3:** "We think the farmers should be allowed to shoot the elephants. Not shoot all of them, but only some of them. The article said there are too many elephants. OK, then the government should decide on a number of elephants that could be hunted each year, and farmers could buy licenses to hunt them. Anyone who hunted without a license would be arrested."

The teacher wishes to end the lesson by having students write down their thoughts, so she assigns a **quick-write**, a five-minute essay.

**Teacher:** *All right, you have now heard five positions on the question of whether farmers should be allowed to shoot elephants. Now I want you to go back to your seats and write for five minutes in your notebooks on this question. First say what you think should be done: Should farmers be allowed to shoot elephants? Second, explain why you think as you do.*

The students return to their desks and write. At the end of five minutes the teacher tells them they have one minute more to write. Then she stops them, and invites three students to share their papers.

<u>**the lesson ends here**</u>

REVIEWING THE LESSON

At the beginning of this lesson, you were invited to think about it in two ways: as *a student in the class* and as *the teacher*.

Take a moment and reflect on how it would have felt to be a student participating in this lesson. (It may help to write down your thoughts on a piece of paper).

**How did you feel**—interested, engaged, important, detached, controlled, or bored?

**What kind of thinking did you do**—memorize details, find main ideas, look below the surface at important issues, or make interpretations and support interpretations with reasons?

**What will you carry away from the lesson**—information, important ideas, or thinking skills?

Now think back over this lesson as if you had been the teacher. Recall the steps to this lesson. They were:

**Structured Overview:** A brief lecture to set the stage for the lesson.

**Know/Want to Know/Learn:** A method for reminding students of what they know and drawing out their questions before they seek more understanding about a topic.

**Paired Reading/Paired Summarizing:** A method in which partners help each other read with understanding.

**Value Line:** A method in which students take and defend a position on a debatable issue.

**Quick-write:** A brief reflective essay that has students collect their thoughts and reasons on a topic.

# METHODS

### STRUCTURED OVERVIEW
The **Structured Overview** (Ausubel 1968) is a brief lecture or explanation that is given at the beginning of a lesson to arouse students' curiosity, introduce key concepts, and get them ready to learn from the lesson proper.

**RATIONALE:** Learning theory teaches us that students learn by relating new information to what they already know. But if their prior knowledge about a topic is incomplete or incoherent, it helps to make a short presentation of background knowledge to prepare them to learn new information. The Structured Overview allows the teacher to give students just enough information to learn from the unfolding lesson.

 **GROUP SIZE:** Six to sixty

 **TIME REQUIRED:** The structured overview should be kept brief—usually not more than five minutes.

 **ACTIVITY:**
**Step 1:** Think over the lesson and decide what ideas or issues it contains that will be familiar and interesting to the students. Think of what concepts and what vocabulary students should understand in order to learn from the lesson. Make a list of all these.

**Step 2:** Prepare maps or diagrams or bring in real objects that will spark students' interest.

**Step 3:** Make up a short talk of not more than five minutes that will present the key points.

**Step 4:** Make the talk engaging and interactive: ask questions and encourage comments.

**Step 5:** Close by saying, "We shall see." That is, create a sense of anticipation.

 **REFLECTIONS:** Remember to keep the Structured Overview brief. It is meant to give students enough information that they can participate in an active lesson, but not to replace that active lesson.

 ## KNOW/WANT TO KNOW/LEARN (K-W-L)
The **K-W-L** activity can be used to structure a whole lesson. It asks students to think of what they already know about the topic of the lesson, raise questions about it, and find answers to those questions.

 **RATIONALE:** Learning theory tells us that active learning is better than passive learning. Students learn best when they (1) remember what they already know, (2) ask questions, (3) confirm their new knowledge. This method leads them to do all three.

 **GROUP SIZE:** Six to sixty.

 **TIME REQUIRED:** 45 minutes to multiple periods.

**ACTIVITY:**
**Step 1:** Begin by naming the topic, and asking students to think of what they already know about it. It helps to have students list their ideas, and to share their ideas with a partner before they answer.

**Step 2:** Create a K-W-L chart on the chalk board or on chart paper.

**Step 3:** Ask the students to call out what they know about the topic. Write their ideas in the column marked **What do we Know?** You may organize their thoughts into categories, as you receive them.

**Step 4:** Now ask students to think of questions they have about the topic. They may begin by reviewing what they know, and finding areas where their knowledge is incomplete. Write their questions on the chart in the column marked **What do we Want to Know?** Feel free to add some of your own.

**Step 5:** The students should now read the text (or listen to a lecture, or do some other kind of investigation). They are reminded to look for answers to their questions, and for any new ideas they did not anticipate.

**Step 6:** The students report the things they learned from the text. First they report answers they found to their questions, and then they report any other interesting or important ideas they discovered. The teacher records these on the chart in the column labeled **What did we Learn?**

 **ASSESSMENT:** There are three ways to assess the students' learning in this lesson:

**1. The teacher can observe how well the students participated in the learning activities.** The first thing the teacher needs to know is how well the lesson worked. When new teaching methods are being introduced, it may take some repeated trials for both the students and the teacher to learn to carry them out well. The teacher can ask:

> How well did the class, and each student, carry out the roles in the paired reading and paired summarizing activity?

> How fully and productively did the class, and each student, participate in the value line?

**2. The teacher can assess their learning of the content—their understanding of the ideas in the text.** The teacher also will need to know if the students learned the essential information and concepts from the lesson. Through a paper-and-pencil test or a recitation, students can be asked to demonstrate their understanding of what the text said and what it meant, answering such questions as,

> Why is the question of killing elephants being raised now?

> For what reasons do the farmers want to kill elephants?

> For what reasons do conservationists not want them to?

**3. The teacher can assess the students' thinking—in this case their ability to take a position and support it with evidence.** The students' papers can be assessed according to criteria such as these:

> Did the student clearly state a position?

> Did the student support it with two or more reasons?

Did the student make a clear link between the stated position and the reasons offered to support it?

 **REFLECTIONS:** The K-W-L method is a fine way to structure a lesson that covers an informational topic. It is not recommended for works of fiction. In cases where students do not possess much background knowledge about a topic, the K-W-L can be preceded by an Advance Organizer, as we did in this lesson.

 ## PAIRED READING/PAIRED SUMMARIZING
**Paired Reading/Paired Summarizing** (Vaughn 1986) is a technique for having pairs of students read a text closely for understanding.

 **RATIONALE:** Like all cooperative learning tasks, Paired Reading/Paired Summarizing allows students to take more initiative in their own and each other's learning. The method is intended to encourage different kinds of thinking, all of which encourage comprehension.

 **GROUP SIZE:** Two to two hundred.

 **TIME REQUIRED:** Paired Reading/Paired Summarizing takes three to four times as long as simply reading a text aloud. In order to save time, you may have students do paired reading with the first four to six paragraphs, and then read the rest of the text independently.

 **ACTIVITY:**
**Step 1:** Choose an informative text of reasonable length. It should have short paragraphs (not more than three sentences each), or you should mark it into short sections.

**Step 2:** If the students are new to the procedure, you should demonstrate the procedure first.

a. Read a passage aloud and give a summary of it. Explain that this is one role in the activity. Explain the features of a summary: it is shorter than the original text, but it contains all of the important ideas.

b. Ask two questions about the text for the students to answer. Explain that this is the other role in the activity.

**Step 3:** Ask the students to pair up. Explain that one student will read the first paragraph or marked section of the text and then give a summary of it, as you have demonstrated. Allow time for everyone to do this. Then check for understanding by asking several students to share their summaries. Offer suggestions as necessary.

Now ask the other student to ask questions about the passage. After they have had a chance to do so, check for understanding by asking several students to share their questions. Again, offer suggestions for improvements if needed.

**Step 4:** Once the students understand the procedure, have them proceed on their own to read, summarize, and ask questions about the text, passage by passage. Remind them to switch roles after each passage has been read and discussed.

 **REFLECTIONS**: Paired reading and paired summarizing is a good way to have students carefully read difficult text.

 **VALUE LINE**

The **Value Line** is a cooperative learning activity that is recommended for evoking students' opinions on issues to which there can be varied responses (that is, degrees of agreement and disagreement with a statement).

 **RATIONALE:** Recognizing and respecting differences of opinion is a useful disposition to have. It is useful for students to stand up for their beliefs even when friends disagree. The Value Line is intended to help students pay attention to an issue and decide what they think about it; recognize that there can be varying opinions about the same issue; and take a position on an issue and state their reasons for it.

 **GROUP SIZE:** Six to sixty.

 **TIME REQUIRED:** The Value Line may be done in 15 minutes.

**ACTIVITY:**
**Step 1:** The teacher poses a question to the whole class. It should be one on which opinions can vary from a strong "yes" to a strong "no." Such a question might be, "Which is more important: protecting the environment or meeting people's immediate needs?"

**Step 2:** Each student considers the question alone and may write their answers.

**Step 3:** The teacher and another student stand at opposite ends of the room. Each states an extreme position on the issue, and their two statements are diametrically opposed to each other.

**Step 4:** The students are asked to take their place along an imaginary line between the two extreme positions, according to which pole of the argument they agree with more.

**Step 5:** The teacher reminds the students to discuss with other students in the line their responses to the question, to make sure they are standing among people who share their position. If they do not, they should move one way or another.
**Step 6:** Students may continue to discuss their responses with the students on either side of them.

**Step 7:** The teacher asks one person from each cluster of students to state that small group's posi-tion on the issue. Any student who wants to change positions after hearing a statement is invited to do so.

**REFLECTIONS:**
The Value Line is enjoyable for students because they like moving around in the class and sharing their opinions with others. It is interesting to demonstrate for them physically what is meant by "having a position" and "changing one's position" on an issue.

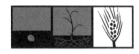

## QUICK-WRITE
**The Quick-write** is a brief written reflection on a topic.

**RATIONALE:**
Quick-writes are informal essays meant to capture thoughts. In a heated discussion many thoughts are aired in a hurry, and good ideas may be lost if they are not recorded. Quick-writes are meant to be informal—the idea is to capture thoughts and not be preoccupied with style.

**GROUP SIZE:** Any size.

**TIME REQUIRED:** The Quick-write can be done in five to ten minutes. It can be used at the beginning, in the middle, or at the end of a lesson.

**ACTIVITY:**
**Step 1:** Tell the students you want them to write very briefly about a topic you will give them. They are to write without stopping during the allotted time.

**Step 2:** State the topic.

**Step 3:** Time the students as they write. (It may help to give them an extra minute.)

**Step 4:** Students may keep the papers in their journals, or you may collect them to use in assessing your lesson.

# VARIATIONS AND RELATED METHODS

## WHAT? SO WHAT? NOW WHAT?
A method for applying ideas from a fictional or informational text.

**RATIONALE:** Educators often complain that knowledge learned in school can stay disconnected from students' real lives. The influential educator Paolo Freire insisted that from every important idea some action should follow. What Freire called *praxis* is the link between a compelling idea and social action. The technique called *What? So What? Now What?* aims at helping students find connections between ideas learned in school and actions in the world. The method teaches students to find the main ideas of the text, think of practical implications of those ideas, and choose and carry out social action based on those ideas.

**GROUP SIZE:** *What? So What? Now What?* is done with the whole class.

**RESOURCES:**
A chalk board or chart paper to write upon; otherwise the resources will vary with the activities that follow from the lesson.

 **TIME REQUIRED:** The planning part of the procedure can be carried out in 15 minutes, but the activities that follow from it may stretch well into the future.

 **ACTIVITY:**
It is assumed that the students will have been introduced to a topic (through reading or lecture or discussion) and will have discussed it to the point where they have a basic understanding of it.

Now the teacher explains that the class will decide what actions they might take, based on the ideas they have just considered.

The teacher produces the following table on the chalk board or on chart paper, large enough for everyone to see:

| What? | So What? | Now What? |
|---|---|---|
|  |  |  |

**What?** Pointing to the *What* column, the teacher asks the students to summarize the most important ideas they have just discussed about the topic. After some discussion, the teacher writes summary ideas in the box under the heading *"What?"*

**So What?** Now the teacher asks the students to consider what is important about the ideas they just listed. Why do they matter? What difference do these facts or ideas make in people's lives? After some discussion, the teacher writes the summary points in the box under the heading *"So What?"*

**Now What?** The teacher now asks the students what they can do about the problem or issue they have been discussing. The teacher may ask the students to **brainstorm** about activities they might do in order to help solve the problem they have been discussing. (*Brainstorming* is described below). The activities might be things that:

*individual students can do*
For example, if the problem is pollution, individual students can sign a contract promising not to throw litter on the ground.

*groups of students can do*
For example, a small group of students can make posters to put around the school and the community, urging others not to throw trash on the ground.

*the whole class can do*
For example, the whole class can spend a Saturday picking up trash in a public park or along a roadside.

**REFLECTIONS:** The teacher should think flexibly of a range of actions that can follow from ideas introduced in lessons. Often a solution will be a decision by individual students to change their behavior in some way. But sometimes, solutions should be group projects, in order to generate more discussion among the class about the ways their actions relate to the problems they identified. It helps to keep the *What? So What? Now What?* chart posted, so the students can be reminded of the connections between the issues they identified and the actions they took.

## BRAINSTORMING

A method for generating many ideas about a topic.

**RATIONALE:**

The rule of brainstorming is to think of many ideas, think of different ideas, and to suspend judgment until students have produced many different ideas. Brainstorming can help "open students' minds" so they can think of ideas that might not normally have occurred to them. Not all of the ideas they arrive at will be equally useful, but in thinking of many different ideas, they may discover some valuable ideas among the less important ones. Students who practice brainstorming often may become more prolific and less rigid thinkers.

**GROUP SIZE:** Brainstorming can be done by individuals, pairs, small groups, or the whole class.

**RESOURCES:** Brainstorming requires only pencil and paper or chalk board and chalk for recording ideas.

**TIME REQUIRED:** A brainstorming activity should be conducted in 10 minutes or less.

**ACTIVITY:**
**Step 1**: Introduce brainstorming to the whole class first.

**Step 2**: Introduce the topic or problem very clearly.

**Step 3**: Give students a time limit to solve the problem.

**Step 4**: Encourage them to share any idea, no matter how odd, that is related to the problem. Remind them not to criticize each other's ideas in any way. Encourage them to build on each other's ideas. Do not stay on any one idea for too long.
**Step 5**: Write down their ideas as they offer them

**Step 6**: Later, have students brainstorm individually or in pairs.

## PAIRED BRAINSTORMING

When doing a variation of brainstorming called **Paired Brainstorming** (De Bono 1973), ask students to individually list ideas about a topic. Then, after a few minutes, ask them to form pairs, share their ideas with each other, and then keep adding to the list. You can later ask the pairs of students to share their ideas with the whole group, as you write them on the chalk board.

 **TIPS:**
Practice brainstorming often in order to help students develop the idea of imaginative and flexible thinking—what is sometimes called *lateral thinking*. You can practice it with meaningless topics first, just to get them used to the idea. You can show the class an object such as a stick and ask them to think of uses for it. For example, the uses for a stick might be:

To write in the sand
For a bean plant to climb on
To beat the dust out of a jacket or a carpet
To beat the bushes to scare away snakes
To help measure the height of a building (sighting across the top of the stick to the top of the building and knowing the angle of the line of sight)
To wrap with cloth to make a doll
To make a bow or an arrow.

 **QUESTION BOARD**
A **Question Board** is simply a site for posting questions that grow from class discussion. It might be a section of the chalk board, or it could be newsprint that students would be free to write on when a question comes to mind. Its purpose is to be available for students to write any questions they have as they:

- participate in class discussions
- do independent or assigned reading
- write
- experiment
- engage in other class activities.

**RATIONALE:** Questions are sparked by many different encounters—materials that are of interest, surprising events, books, illustrations, and conversations. But whatever the source, questions are at the heart of teaching and learning. The Question Board is designed to capture and dignify students' authentic curiosities. The Question Board has many purposes:

- It celebrates and dignifies student questions and it takes the pressure off the teacher to answer all questions.
- It gives students an opportunity to do extra, meaningful work if they choose to help answer a question, and gives the teacher an opportunity to praise especially thoughtful questions or answers.
- It encourages students to put oral questions into written form, and provides good topics for writing assignments.
- It serves as the basis for lesson planning as the teacher develops activities based on student curiosities and interests.

**ACTIVITY:** The Question Board is posted in an easily accessible location (usually on a wall) of the classroom. When the teacher doesn't have the time or the desire to be the "all knowing" source of information, or just plain doesn't know the answer, students can write their question (along with their name) on the Question Board. During free moments of the day, students read each other's questions and add their own. After three to four weeks, the teacher or student volunteers will make the questions available for distribution to the class. Using this list, the class will analyze and discuss the questions. Questions become the spark to ignite inquiry-based activities.

 **TIPS:** What Questions Lead to Inquiry? For our purposes we will categorize questions in two ways:

**Research Questions** are the most commonly asked questions and require secondary resources (encyclopedias, information books, the Internet) to answer them.

Example: How hot is the surface of the sun?

**Testable Questions** enable students to find answers on their own through observation or manipulation of experimental variables. Too often schools privilege research questions over testable questions.

Example: Which evaporates faster—hot water or cold water?

The questions from the Question Board can be analyzed and categorized in various ways, but using this categorization scheme develops in the class a common classroom language and a way of pursuing questions. The next activity will help you develop effective questioning skills.

 ## QUESTION SEARCH
The **Question Search** activity (Pearce 1999, 2003) can be used early in the school year or as an introductory activity:

 **ACTIVITY:**
**Step 1:** Distribute baskets of unusual items on small tables to groups of students. Anything unfamiliar will do—odd-looking shells, electrical components, seeds, interesting rocks, pieces of disassembled appliances, tools—use your imagination.

**Step 2:** Have students write the name of the object or make up a name.

**Step 3:** Create a written description and sketch of the object.

**Step 4:** Below the sketch draw two columns. In one write as many questions about the object as possible. In the second column list ways it might be possible to find answers to the questions.

**Step 5:** Open a class discussion with students displaying their item and sharing their questions and sources. Sources usually suggested include books, computers, teachers, parents, perhaps experts. Be ready for the student who suggests doing something to answer their question—this is now a testable question.

**Step 6:** Now the class can decide which questions are testable. They can extend their understanding by thinking about what kinds of experiments or investigations could be designed to answer those questions.

**Step 7:** Guide students from the "Can I...?" questions ("Can I blow big bubbles?" OR "Can I build a tall tower?") to phrasing more meaningful questions. For example, "How big a bubble?" OR "How tall a tower?" Developing questions that lead to quantifiable answers will lead to more meaningful investigations. Move away from yes-and-no questions to richer questions like, "When comparing bubble solution A to bubble solution B, which will make the biggest bubbles?"

**Step 8:** Develop other testable phrasing for questions. For example, "Is it possible to ... [grow plants in salt water]?" OR "What would happen if ... [we poured oil into a model ocean]?" OR "How can we ... [prevent erosion on our model mountain]?"

**TIPS:** While reading a book aloud, pause and model the ways readers process what they are reading by verbalizing teacher questions. You might even go over to the Question Board and record your own questions while the class watches. For example, Charlie Pearce reads to his class "A Snake-Lover's Diary," by Barbara Brenner, which is a story about a boy who persuades his parents to let him keep a snake he has captured. His little brother thinks the snake is lonely and puts his own pet frog in the new cage to keep the snake company. The frog disappears. As Charlie reads, he wonders aloud about snakes and frogs and what they might eat. "Do snakes eat frogs? If so, how do snakes capture frogs? How fast are frogs? How far can they jump?" The students tell Charlie to write his questions on the board, which he promptly does.

By modeling his own questions and use of the Question Board, this teacher is encouraging his students to read, to think, and to develop and record their questions.

Question Boards can be used in all curricular areas. Here are a few examples taken from a Question Board in a fifth grade class:

**Mathematics**: How many seconds are there in a year?

**Literature**: What would happen if this character...

**Social Studies**: How important was the library in Alexandria to the people at the time of its founding?

**Art**: How do you decide if a painting is good?

**REFLECTIONS:** The Question Board is a strategy that fits well into the K-W-L strategy and also with a thematic unit approach to curriculum planning. In its simplest form, it is a place in the classroom where students or groups of students can place questions about their work on a chart to share with others. If a classroom is divided into cooperative learning groups in which students have roles, such as leader, data collector, materials manager, and reporter, then the reporter would be assigned the task of adding new questions and information to the question board. Teachers may occasionally add a question to the question board, or they may suggest to a student who poses a question in class that it would be a good addition to the question board.

A Question Board can also be topical. For example, if a class has an interest in a crosscutting issue, such as soil erosion, then students may find that questions arise as they read, discuss, work in their cooperative learning groups, search for information on the Internet, and interview community experts. The new questions added to the Question Board will provide motivation for further studies, searching out new sources of information, and sometimes forming new groups.

For <u>older</u> students, questions recorded on Question Boards may reflect important crosscutting issues, such as gender equity, special needs and inclusion, HIV/AIDS, environmental issues, life skills, globalization, civics, and human and children's rights. The questions posed on a Question Board might prompt them to seek out information from multiple sources in addition to their own textbooks.

An important consideration in preparing questions for Question Boards is the nature of the questions themselves. As we have seen above, an open-ended question will provoke more critical thinking and active learning than a closed-ended question. For example, "What are community conditions that promote the spread of HIV/AIDS?" will lead to greater learning than "What causes HIV/AIDS?" Yes/no questions should always be elaborated into open-ended questions. "Is HIV/AIDS dangerous to children?" might be restated as "How is HIV/AIDS dangerous to children?" Students can be encouraged to share their questions with each other before recording them on the question board. The concept of "critical friend" should be encouraged, in which students are able to criticize the ideas of their peers gently and constructively.

# ABC CHART

Let's see how the preceding methods, variations, and related methods fit into the Anticipation/Building Knowledge/Consolidation rubric. This chart will help you use the methods in this guide to make your own lesson plans using the ABC rubric. The chart will grow as we add more methods.

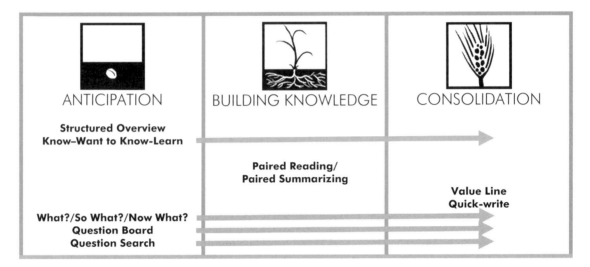

# SECOND CORE LESSON: UNDERSTANDING NARRATIVE TEXT

This lesson shows you ways to help students learn from reading either a narrative or an informational text. The lesson follows the three-part format of **anticipation, building knowledge**, and **consolidation** that was presented in the first section of this guidebook. The lesson will use the **Semantic Map** (Heimlich 1986) and **Predicting from Terms** procedures with **Think-Pair-Share** in the **anticipation** phase. The **Directing Reading Activity (DRA)** procedure (Stauffer 1969; Gunning 2000) will be used in the **building knowledge** activity. The **Character Map** (Gillet 2004) procedure with a continuation of **Think-Pair-Share** will be used as the **consolidation** activity.

The narrative text for this lesson is a short story by Liam O'Flaherty called "A Shilling," but the procedures in the lesson can be used with any narrative text that you have. This lesson is done here with ninth graders, but the procedures can be used with grades below that or up through the secondary level.

## HOW TO READ THIS LESSON

As you read the following demonstration lesson, please bear in mind that its purpose is to demonstrate teaching methods. Think about this lesson in two ways.

> 1. Imagine that you are a *student* who is participating in this lesson. What is your experience? What kind of thinking are you doing? What are you learning?

> 2. Then think yourself into the role of the *teacher* who is leading the lesson. What are you doing? Why are you doing it? How are you handling the three phases of the lesson— anticipation, building knowledge, and consolidation? How are critical thinking, cooperative learning, and active learning incorporated into the lesson?

## LESSON

 **ANTICIPATION**

The **anticipation phase** of a lesson is where students are made ready to learn from the lesson. Here the anticipation phase begins with a strategy called a **Semantic Map** and continues with another strategy called **Prediction from Terms**. The first is used to introduce a vocabulary concept from the story. The second is used to assess the students' background knowledge.

The teacher tells the students that they will read a short story silently. It is about some old men and a yacht. The teacher draws a horizontal oval in the middle of a sheet of chart paper and writes the word *yacht* in the center. Then the teacher asks the students to share knowledge they have about the term *yacht*. The teacher takes about three minutes to gather, organize, and record their ideas into a semantic map. The vocabulary term "yacht" was selected for this activity because it might not be familiar to the students.

**Teacher:** *We're going to read a short story about some old men and a yacht. Who can tell us something about what a yacht looks like? I'm going to write what you tell me on this semantic map.*

**Student:** "It's some kind of boat."

**Teacher:** *Yes, what else do you know?*

**Student:** "It has sails. It goes slow."

**Teacher:** *That's right. Is a yacht big or small?*

**Students:** "Big."

**Teacher:** *What kind of person might own a yacht?*

**Student:** "A rich one."

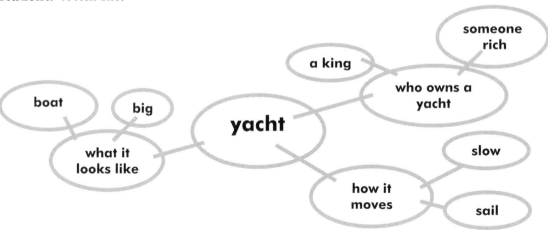

**Student:** "A king."

**Teacher:** *Now I want you to think about these four things: a coin, a yacht, a coiled rope, and a yellow muffler. What story can you imagine that would contain these four things? Think about that for a couple of moments. Think about a scene, characters, and events from a story that has these objects in it.*

After two to three minutes, tell them: *Now form yourselves into pairs and combine your ideas into a story. One member of your pair should be ready to tell your story.*

After about five minutes, ask them: *Who wants to share their story?*

**Student Pair:** "A yacht sank in a big storm. The next day, they found a coin, a coiled rope, and a yellow muffler on the beach."

**Student Pair:** "A rich old man was sailing on his yacht. He slipped on a coin, tripped on a coiled rope, and caught his neck in his yellow muffler. He died. His yacht continued to sail."

 **BUILDING KNOWLEDGE**

In the building knowledge phase of the lesson, the teacher will use the **Directed Reading Activity** (DRA). The teacher directs the students' silent reading with comprehension-level questions. They will read with stops, pausing to discuss every few paragraphs. See Section 1 of the guide for information about making good questions.

**Teacher:** *You will now read a short story called "A Shilling" by Liam O'Flaherty. The story contains the four terms we talked about above You will read silently with stops. I will ask a question before each part of the story, you will read silently to find the answer, and I will tell you where to stop reading. Please read the first two paragraphs of the story to find out: "How did the old men know that the yacht was expensive?" Read silently and look for the answer as you read.*

The students read the first two paragraphs from the story silently.

> Three old men were sitting on the splash wall of Kilmillick Pier with their backs to the sea and their faces to the village and the sun. A light breeze came from the sea behind them, bringing a sweet salt smell of seaweed being kissed by the sun. The village in front was very quiet. Not a movement but the lazy blue smoke curling slantwise from the cabin chimneys. It was early afternoon, Sunday, and all the young men and women were in Kilmurrage at a football match. The three old men were telling stories of big fish they had caught in their youth.
>
> Suddenly there was a swish of canvas and a little white yacht swung around the corner of the pier and came alongside. The three old men immediately got to their feet and advanced through the turf dust to the brink of the pier looking down at the yacht. Patsy Conroy, the most active of the old men, seized the mooring rope and made the yacht fast. Then he came back and joined the other two watching the yachtsmen getting ready to go ashore. "She's a lovely boat," said old Brian Manion, the old fellow with the bandy right leg and the bunion behind his right ear. "Heb," he said, scratching the small of his back, "it must cost a lot of money to keep that boat. Look at those shiny brasses and you can see a carpet laid on the cabin floor through that hatchway. Oh boys! I'd like to have her for a week's fishing," said Mick.

**Teacher:** The teacher repeats: *"How did the old men know that the yacht was expensive?"*

**Student:** "It had shiny brass."

**Student:** "It cost a lot of money."

**Student:** "There is a carpet inside the cabin."

**Teacher:** *Who can read the sentence aloud that proves your answers?*

**Student:** "It must cost a lot of money to keep that boat. Look at those shiny brasses and you can see a carpet laid on the cabin floor through that hatchway."

**Teacher:** *Why was the village so quiet?*

**Student:** "Everyone had gone to a football match."

**Teacher:** *Now we're going to read the next two paragraphs to find out how you feel about Patsy Conroy. How did the author make you feel that way? Be ready to read a sentence aloud that gives evidence for your opinion.*

The students read the next two paragraphs from the story silently.

> Feeney breathed loudly through his long red nose. His big red-rimmed blue eyes seemed to jump in and out. He gripped the top of his stick with his two hands and looked down at the yacht with his short legs wide apart.
>
> Patsy Conroy said nothing. He stood a little apart with his hands stuck in his waist-belt. Although he was seventy-two, he was straight, lithe and active, but his face was yellow and wrinkled like old parchment and his toothless red gums were bared in an old man's chin. His little eyes beneath his bushy white eyebrows roamed around the yacht cunningly as if they were trying to steal something. He wore a yellow muffler wound round and round his neck up to his chin, in spite of the heat of the day.

**Teacher:** *How do you feel about the main character, Patsy Conroy? How did the author make you feel that way?*

**Student:** "I don't like him. The author made him ugly."

**Student:** "I don't trust him. The author said that he had eyes like a thief."

**Teacher:** *Now read to the next stop to find out what happened to catch the old men's attention? What do you predict will happen next?*

> "Where is the nearest public-house?" drawled a red-faced man in a white linen shirt and trousers from the yacht deck.
>
> The old men told him, all together.
>
> "Let's go and have a drink, Totty," said the red-faced man.
>
> "Right-o," said the other man.
>
> When the red-faced man was climbing the iron ladder on to the pier, a shilling fell out of his hip pocket. It fell noiselessly on a little coil of rope that lay on the deck at the foot of the ladder. The red-faced man did not notice it, and he walked up the pier with his friend. The three old men noticed it, but they did not tell the red-faced man. Neither did they tell one another. As soon as the shilling landed on the little coil of rope and lay there glistening, the three of them became so painfully conscious of it that they were bereft of the power of speech or of coherent thought. Each cast a

glance at the shilling, a hurried furtive glance, and then each looked elsewhere, just after the manner of a dog that sees a rabbit in a bush and stops dead with one paw raised, seeing the rabbit although his eyes are fixed elsewhere.

**Teacher:** The teacher repeats the question. *What happened to catch the old men's attention? What do you predict will happen next?*

**Student:** "One of the men dropped a coin."

**Student:** "One of them will climb down to get it."

**Student:** "Patsy will tell the man that he dropped his coin."

**Teacher:** *Read the next long paragraph to find out why Patsy was so quiet as the men sat there.*

> Each old man knew that the other two had seen the shilling, yet each was silent about it in the hope of keeping the discovery his own secret. Each knew that it was impossible for him to go down the iron ladder to the deck, pick up the shilling and ascend with it to the pier without being detected. For there was a man who wore a round white cap doing something in the cabin. Every third moment or so his cap appeared through the hatchway and there was a noise of crockery being washed or something. And the shilling was within two feet of the hatchway. And the old men, except perhaps Patsy Conroy, were too old to descend the ladder and ascend again. And anyway each knew that even if there were nobody in the cabin, and even if they could descend the ladder, the others would prevent either one from getting the shilling, since each preferred that no one should have the shilling if he couldn't have it himself. And yet such was the lure of that glistening shilling that the three of them stared with palpitating hearts and feverishly working brains at objects within two feet of the shilling. They stared in a painful silence that was loud with sound as of a violent and quarrelsome conversation. The noise Mick Feeney made breathing through his nose exposed his whole scheme of thought to the other two men just as plainly as if he explained it slowly and in detail. Brian Manion kept fidgeting with his hands, rubbing the palms together, and the other two heard him and cursed his avarice. Patsy Conroy alone made no sound, but his very silence was loud and stinking to the other two men, for it left them in ignorance of what plans were passing through his crafty head.

**Teacher:** *Why do you think that Patsy was so quiet? Why do you think so?*

**Student:** "He was thinking about how to steal the coin. He was a sneaky man."

**Student:** "He was planning. He didn't want his friends to know what he was thinking about."

**Student:** "He wanted the coin for himself—he didn't want to share it. Patsy was selfish."

**Teacher:** *Let's finish reading the story to find out how Patsy Conroy showed that he was the smartest of the three.*

> And the sun shone warmly. And the salt, healthy smell of the sea inspired thirst. And there was excellent cool frothy porter in Kelly's. So much so that no one of the three old men ever thought of the fact that the shilling belonged to somebody else. So much so indeed that each of them felt indignant with the shameless avarice of the other two.

There was almost a homicidal tendency in the mind of each against the others. Thus three minutes passed. The two owners of the yacht had passed out of sight. Brian Manion and Mick Feeney were trembling and driveling slightly at the mouth.

Then Patsy Conroy stooped and picked up a pebble from the pier. He dropped it on to the deck of the yacht. The other two men made a slight movement to intercept the pebble with their sticks, a foolish unconscious movement. Then they started and let their jaws drop. Patsy Conroy was speaking. "Hey there," he shouted between his cupped hands. A pale-faced gloomy man with a napkin on his hip stepped up to the second step of the hatchway. "What d'ye want?" he said.

"Beg yer pardon, Sir," said Patsy Conroy, "but would ye hand me up that shilling that just dropped out a' me hand?"

The man nodded, picked up the shilling, muttered "Catch," and threw the shilling on to the pier. Patsy touched his cap and dived for it. The other two old men were so dumbfounded that they didn't even scramble for it. They watched Patsy spit on it and put it in his pocket. They watched him walk up the pier, sniffing out loud, his long, lean, grey-backed figure with the yellow muffler around his neck moving as straight and solemn as a policeman.

They looked at each other, their faces contorted with anger. And each, with upraised stick, snarled at the other: "Why didn't ye stop him, you fool?"

**Teacher:** *How did Patsy show that he was the smartest of the three?*

**Student:** "He tricked the man on the yacht."

**Student:** "He tricked his friends, too."

**Student:** "He got the coin without stealing it."

**Student:** "Patsy won't have to share the coin with his friends."

 **CONSOLIDATION**

In the consolidation phase of the lesson, the students will construct a **character map**. They will continue in the same pairs they worked with in the anticipation phase of the lesson.

**Teacher:** *Now we're going to think about the characters in the story. Please get back into the pairs you had at the beginning of the lesson. Now select two characters from the story—one will be Patsy Conroy and the other will be any character you wish. Then complete the character map below. Write the other character's name in the figure at the top right. Then write character traits for each character in the circles with evidence from the story to support each trait in the rectangles below.*

Student pair: Below is the response from one student pair.

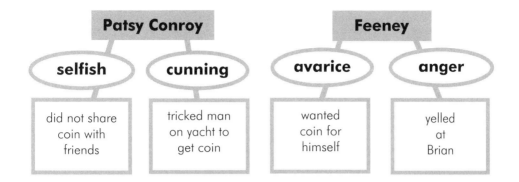

**Teacher:** *Now I would like you to predict what Patsy and the other character would each do in ONE of the following situations:(a) The characters are lost in the forest.(b) They find a valuable lost dog. c) They are caught in the rain with only one umbrella. On a sheet of paper, select one of the situations. Then write your prediction of what Patsy would do and of what the other character in your character map would do.*

**Student:** Here is one student response.
"(b) Patsy and his friend find the lost dog's owner. They return the dog and receive a reward. Patsy keeps the reward, and his friend receives nothing."

<u>**the lesson ends here**</u>

## REVIEWING THE LESSON

At the beginning of this lesson, you were invited to think about it in two ways: as *a student in the class*, and as *the teacher*.

Take a moment and reflect on how it would have felt to be a student participating in this lesson. (It may help to write down your thoughts on a piece of paper).

**How did you feel**—interested, engaged, important, detached, controlled, or bored?

**What kind of thinking did you do**—memorize details, find main ideas, look below the surface at important issues, or make interpretations and support interpretations with reasons?

**What will you carry away from the lesson**—information, important ideas, or thinking skills?

Now think back over this lesson as if you had been the teacher. Recall the steps to this lesson. They were:

**Semantic Map:** An activity that used a graphic organizer to explore students' associations for a key term in the story.

**Prediction from Terms:** A technique for having students try to anticipate the story they are about to read, from a half dozen terms from the story.

**Think-Pair-Share**: A technique for having students think of individual answers to a question posed by the teacher, and then share their answers with a partner. Later, the teacher calls on two or three pairs to share their answers with the whole class.

**Directed Reading Activity** (DRA). A strategy for directing the students' silent reading with comprehension-level questions. The students read with stops, pausing to discuss every few paragraphs.

**Character Map:** An activity that used a graphic organizer to help students reflect on the main characters.

# METHODS

 **DIRECTED READING ACTIVITY (DRA)**
The **DRA** is a reading comprehension/critical thinking activity for the Building Knowledge part of a reading lesson with either narrative or informational text.

 **RATIONALE:** The DRA or DRTA method is designed to support students' reading comprehension by guiding them to key points in the text and providing opportunities to discuss its meaning with their classmates.

 **GROUP SIZE:** This activity can be done with eight to twenty-five students. It is possible to do with more, but their opportunities for participation are diminished.

 **RESOURCES:** The method requires a sufficient number of texts for all students to read. They also need paper and pencils.

**TIME REQUIRED:** This type of lesson can be completed in 30 to 40 minutes (anticipation phase: 5 to 10 minutes; building knowledge phase: 15 to 20 minutes; consolidation phase: 5 to 10 minutes). A lesson can be extended over several days, with perhaps anticipation activities the first day, building knowledge activities over the second and third days, and consolidation activities on a fourth day.

 **ACTIVITY:**
**Step 1:** Begin with one or two anticipation activities designed to motivate students and to activate or install needed background knowledge, including new vocabulary: semantic map to gloss (introduce) the term *yacht* and activate background knowledge, and prediction from terms to apply knowledge of additional vocabulary from the story.

**Step 2:** Before beginning the Directed Reading Activity, the teacher should chunk the text by dividing it into manageable pieces for the students to read silently. Then the teacher should prepare one or two comprehension-level questions for each chunk to be read by the students.

1. Chunk text with stops to support comprehension
2. Directed Reading Activity (DRA) to guide silent reading with higher order questions
3. Discussion of responses to questions, with evidence provided through brief oral reading

**Step 3:** Provide a culminating activity that allows students to review their understandings of the text and to apply them. In many lessons, this may be provided as a home task.

1. Think-Pair-Share activity to share new knowledge about characters
2. Completion of character map to share new knowledge (graphic organizer)
3. Predictions about characters based on character traits

**REFLECTIONS:** Teachers will notice that comprehension improves quickly when students focus on finding answers to comprehension-level questions instead of just reading aloud. They enjoy the discussion of their answers because there is usually more than one correct answer or more than one opinion about the correct answer.

## ABOUT THE QUESTIONS USED IN THE DIRECTED READING ACTIVITY

What kinds of questions should the teacher ask in the Directed Reading Activity to guide the readers' thinking? Research has shown that questions are most helpful when they follow the contours of the **format and genre** of the text. That is, the questions should help readers follow the presentation of information that is particular to the kind of text the students are reading. The Directed Reading Activity presented in this core lesson used a work of fiction, so the following discussion of questions will focus on fictional or narrative texts.

### Narrative Texts
Narrative texts come in subcategories such as realistic fiction, historical fiction, folk stories, fantasies, legends, and works of magical realism or science fiction. It can be useful to remind readers of the category of story they are reading, and what kinds of possible actions they can expect from it. For example, in realistic fiction the events will be drawn from what is possible in real life, but in a work of fantasy or a folk tale magic can happen. In science fiction, impossible actions may occur, so long as they are derived from a logical extension of what is possible.

Narrative texts usually contain a predictable set of elements: the **setting,** the **characters**, the **problem**, **attempts at solutions**, the **consequences of the actions**, and the **theme or message** of the story.

Questions about **settings** may lead students to visualize the setting, to notice how the author created it in her or his imagination, and to reflect on what kinds of actions and issues the author expects from the setting.

Questions about **characters** similarly call attention to how the author helps the reader know the characters, sense the tensions between the characters, and understand the kinds of problems the main character might have, as well the resources with which that character faces the problems.

Questions about the **problem,** the **attempts at solutions,** and the **consequences of the actions** can guide readers to follow the plots of stories. Readers can be asked to note the main character's problem and to predict how she or he will attempt to solve it, given what they know about the character (and what they could predict from the kind of story they are reading). They can also be asked about the consequences of the actions, and how the situation at the end of the story differs from the situation at the beginning.

**Themes or messages** of stories can be asked about in several ways. Students can be asked what the story meant to them. They can also be asked why they would or would not agree with the message the story seems to convey—because many popular stories suggest ways of living to which we shouldn't readily subscribe, that one must be beautiful or very aggressive in order to be successful, for instance.

### Questions about Other Genres
Teachers may ask questions when using the Directed Reading Activity with other genres of text, such as informational and persuasive texts. Questions for these kinds of texts are described in the core lessons that follow in this guidebook.

## VARIATIONS AND RELATED METHODS

### THE DIRECTED READING-THINKING ACTIVITY (DR-TA) AND CHART
The **Directed Reading-Thinking Activity** (Stauffer 1969) is a popular method for engaging students in reading narrative texts for understanding. It is similar to DRA in that students read silently under the direction of the teacher, but the question prompts are less specific and provide less support for comprehension than DRA. It is suitable for students who have had good success with DRA, because it encourages them to make their own predictions.

 **GROUP SIZE:** From four to forty.

 **RESOURCES:** Copies of text to be read; paper and pencils for students.

 **TIME REQUIRED:** The activity can be done in 15 to 30 minutes.

 **ACTIVITY:**
**Step 1:** Prepare the text by marking four or five good stopping points. Plan stopping points to fall at moments of suspense in the story.

**Step 2:** On the chalk board or on chart paper, prepare a chart like the one below. Explain to the students that they will be reading the story, one bit at a time. Remind them that it is important not to read beyond the stopping points. They will be making predictions and reading to confirm those predictions.

**Step 3:** Ask the students to read the title of the story. Talk about the genre. Name the author. Show the cover illustration, and read the title. Then ask for their prediction about what will happen in the story. Write those predictions in the space labeled "What do you think will happen?" after the title. Ask the students why they think so. Then enter their reasons under "Why?"

**Step 4:** Now, ask the students to read to the first stopping point, and when they have reached it, they should go back and consider the prediction they made before, and say what actually happened. You should record their ideas in the space called "What did happen?"

**Step 5:** The teacher reviews the predictions and asks which ones are coming true so far. The teacher asks them to read aloud parts of the text that confirm or disconfirm their predictions.

**Step 6:** Then, the students should predict what they think will happen in the next block of text, and offer new predictions, with the evidence that led to their making those predictions to be entered in the spaces provided. Then they should read on, check their prediction against what did happen, make new predictions, dictate evidence for those predictions, and read the last section.

**Step 7:** Finally, they should check their last predictions against what actually happened in the story, and dictate their findings about what happened, to be recorded in the space on the form.

# DIRECTED READING-THINKING ACTIVITY CHART

| | WHAT DO YOU THINK WILL HAPPEN? | WHY DO YOU THINK SO? | WHAT DID HAPPEN? |
|---|---|---|---|
| AFTER READING THE TITLE | | | |
| AFTER READING THE FIRST PART | | | |
| AFTER READING THE SECOND PART | | | |
| AFTER READING TO THE END | | | |

# ABC CHART

Let's see how the preceding methods, variations, and related methods fit into the Anticipation/Building Knowledge/Consolidation rubric. This chart will help you use the methods in this guide to make your own lesson plans using the ABC rubric.

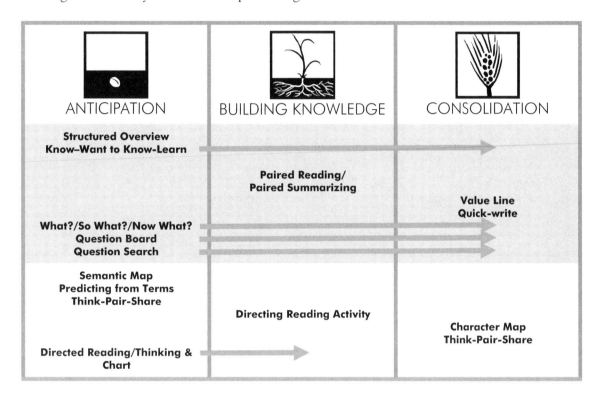

# THIRD CORE LESSON: COOPERATIVE LEARNING

Cooperative learning has been used in schools around the world for several decades. The methods of cooperative learning have proved valuable for several reasons.

**Cooperative learning allows students to learn actively, even in large classes**. Learning experts tell us that in order to learn, students must act and communicate. But in classes of 60 or more, the amount of time any one student can talk is very limited. Cooperative learning techniques allow every student in the class to participate for much of the time, but they organize the activity of many students at once so that the activity will be productive and not chaotic.

**Cooperative learning has academic and social benefits for students.** Cooperative learning is not simply an expedient device to get students in large classes to participate in learning. Cooperative learning also has these benefits:

**1. Higher order thinking**. Students in cooperative learning groups are made to work with ideas and concepts. They are challenged to offer their own interpretations of topics and to solve problems.

**2. Motivation and morale**. Students who take part in cooperative learning feel more attached to the school and to the class. This may lead to better attendance and better retention rates.

**3. Learning interpersonal skills**. Students in cooperative learning groups learn to cooperate with others. Cooperation is increasingly recognized as an important life skill, both for productive work on the job, for happy family life, and for participation in a democratic society.

**4. Promoting inter-personal and inter-group understanding.** Students who work in co-operative groups are more likely to learn to get along with people of different sexes and from different social groups. They are also likely to develop stronger self-concepts.

This lesson follows the three-part format of **anticipation, building knowledge**, and **consolidation** that was presented in the first section of this guidebook. The lesson will use **Mix/Freeze/Pair** (Kagan 1994), **Reading with Text Coding** (Vaughn 1986), and the **Jigsaw** (Slavin 1994).

The text for this lesson is called "Remembering Columbus," but the procedures in the lesson are meant to be used with any informational text that you have. This lesson is done here with eighth graders, but the procedures can be used with grades below that or up through the secondary level.

## HOW TO READ THIS LESSON

As you read the following demonstration lesson, please bear in mind that its purpose is to demonstrate teaching methods (and not to teach you about Christopher Columbus). Think about this lesson in two ways.

> 1. Imagine that you are *a student* who is participating in this lesson. What is your experience? What kind of thinking are you doing? What are you learning?

> 2. Then think yourself into the role of *the teacher* who is leading the lesson. What are you doing? Why are you doing it? How are you handling the three phases of the lesson—anticipation, building knowledge, and consolidation?

# LESSON

 **ANTICIPATION**

The anticipation phase of a lesson is where students are made ready to learn from the lesson. Here the anticipation phase begins with a method called **Mix/Freeze/Pair** (Kagan 1997), and continues with a reading activity that uses a text coding procedure.

The teacher begins the lesson with Mix/Freeze/Pair, mixing the students in the class up and having them discuss a question with new partners.

**Teacher:** *Please get a notebook and a pen, then stand up. When I say "go," you are to move around the room. Mix it up. Go in lots of different directions. When I say, "Freeze," you are to stop, shake hands with the person nearest you, and silently wait for more instructions. "Go."* The teacher plays recorded music for about one minute while the students move around the room.

**Teacher:** *Freeze! Now, shake hands with the person closest to you. Introduce yourselves. Tell your partner one thing that you have done lately that you are proud of.*

After one minute, the teacher gives the **quiet signal:** he raises his hand over his head. The students see him doing this, and they are immediately silent, and raise their hands above their heads too, facing the teacher. A couple of students do not notice and keep talking. Someone close to them taps each one on the shoulder, and they are silent and raise their hands too.

**Teacher:** *Thank you. Now I have another task for you. We will be talking today about Christopher Columbus, and what happened when he came to the New World. I want each pair of you to take a clean sheet of paper and divide it vertically into two columns. Label one column "East to West" and the other column "West to East." Do that now.*

*Thank you. Now, in three minutes, please list everything you can think of that traveled from east to west after 1492 and write them in the right-hand column. Do the same for the things you can think of that traveled west to east. Begin now.* The teacher circulates among the pairs for three minutes and listens to their conversations.

**Teacher:** (Gives the **quiet signal**). *Thank you. What were some things you thought of that traveled east to west?*

**Pair 1:** "Guns and gunpowder."

**Teacher:** *OK. Something else?*

**Pair 2:** "Christianity."

**Pair 3:** "Diseases. The Europeans had diseases that the Indians had no resistance to."

**Teacher:** *Good. And what things traveled the other way?*

**Pair 4:** "Tobacco."

**Pair 5:** "Corn and potatoes."

**Teacher:** *Good. That's a nice beginning. Now please go sit in your* **home groups** *of four. These are the groups you have been working in for the past three weeks.*

 **BUILDING KNOWLEDGE**

The building knowledge phase of a lesson is the phase of inquiry, in which the students discover or construct new knowledge about the topic.

The students will **Read with Text Coding**; they will be given a text to read and will mark certain passages with symbols indicating the theme.

**Teacher:** *You all have copies of the text, "Remembering Columbus." I want you to read it in a special way.*

*Whenever you come across a passage that describes products or goods that moved from east to west or from west to east —that is, from the Old World to the New World or vice versa—pencil this mark in the margin:* **X**

*Whenever you come across a passage that names historically interesting people, pencil this mark in the margin:* ☺

*Whenever you come across a passage that describes cultural or economic changes that came about because of the coming of the Europeans to the New World, pencil this mark in the margin:* **C/E**

*Finally, whenever you come across information that involves geography, pencil this mark in the margin:* **Geo.**

*Now please read and mark the article.*

# REMEMBERING COLUMBUS
Bucksnort Trout

Twenty thousand years ago the land bridge over what is now the Bering Strait sank too low to be passable, and two halves of the world began to grow up separately. Plants and animals, peoples and cultures, gods and diseases, all went their separate ways—until one sunny morning, 500 Octobers ago, when a skiff bearing Christopher Columbus crunched into the sand on San Salvador Island and brought the two parts of the world together again.

It is amazing to think that one person could have engineered that first contact, however unknowingly. When he did, Christopher Columbus was caught in the glare of world scrutiny forever. Columbus was an Italian map-maker and some-time wool salesman from Genoa. Somehow he persuaded Isabella, the Spanish queen of Castilla (but not her husband Ferdinand, the king of the neighboring province of Aragon), into giving him three ships to command on his improbable trip to China. But the queen made him wait until Spanish soldiers pried the last of the Moors, the Muslims from the south, loose from their 800 year occupation of Spain. What a year that was, 1492. The Moors were pushed out of Spain. The Spanish Inquisition was established, and all religions but Christianity were outlawed. And in August, Columbus embarked on his famous journey. For Spain, 1492 was a bizarre combination of fanaticism, intolerance, and discovery.

The powers that flowed through Columbus' point of contact changed the whole world profoundly and rapidly. The plants that the Indians offered to the Europeans—plants that they had bred carefully and improved through many, many generations—potatoes, corn, long-staple cotton—soon reversed the Old World's cycles of famine and led to population explosions—and changed everything from economies to cooking. Who can imagine Italian food without tomatoes? Or Indian food without hot peppers? Or an Irish meal without potatoes? (Or Sherlock Holmes without pipe tobacco?) All came from the New World. Without long-staple cotton, Europe wouldn't have had a textile industry. Without long-staple cotton and the example of the sugar mills of the Caribbean—which were arguably the world's first factories—Europe may not have had an Industrial Revolution.

Going the other way, who can imagine "the Wild West" without cattle, or cowboys and Indians without cows, or horses on which to chase them? The Spanish brought both cows and horses to the New World in 1493, and they quickly adapted, multiplied, and spread. In the 1580s, the Spanish explorer Cabeza de Vaca was blown across the Gulf of Mexico and shipwrecked on the Texas coast. He was the first European to see Texas, but Spanish cattle already had beat him there, and they looked so wild, so much at home, that he assumed they were native to America. The Lakota Sioux, Indians of the American Great Plains, have legends about the coming of wonderful animals that improved their lives. The Elk Dogs were said to have been brought up from a magical land at the bottom of a deep lake. They were horses, of course.

But the diseases Columbus and his followers brought with them wiped out whole civilizations within a few decades. The Taino people who lived on the Caribbean island of Hispaniola (the location of present day Haiti and the Dominican Republic), for example, were reduced from perhaps half a million souls to virtually none within a space of only 50 years. And even though European explorers didn't arrive on the seaboard of North America until many years after Columbus' voyage, the diseases introduced by the Spanish are believed to have spread rapidly northward, so that by the time Captain James Smith reached Jamestown in Virginia in 1607, the indigenous population was already in disarray because at least a fourth of them had died from a plague of smallpox that had originated with the Spanish explorers far to the south, and had been passed northward from tribe to tribe.

Back a century earlier in the Caribbean, when the Taino population began dying off at an alarming rate, the Spanish imported forced workers from Africa, and the troubled heritage of slavery, as well as the multiracial character of the New World, began to take shape.

All of this happened because of a man who didn't know where he was.

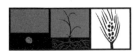 **CONSOLIDATION**

The consolidation phase of the lesson is the part where the students reflect back on what they know, apply it to other problems, and interpret the new knowledge.

When the students have finished reading the article, the teacher moves to the **Jigsaw** activity. The teacher writes four questions on the chalk board:

1. What were some products and goods that were exchanged between the east and the west right after 1492? Which ones where the most important? Why do you say so?

2. What were some cultural and economic consequences of the first contact between the Euro-peans and the people of the New World? Which ones where the most important? Why do you say so?

3. Who were some of the famous people and groups who were involved in the first contact? Who are some other important people whose names we don't know?

4. Trace the geography of the first contact. What do you know that Columbus didn't?

**Teacher:** *We are going to carry out a Jigsaw activity. I have written some questions on the chalk board here. Each one of you should be able to give an intelligent answer to all four of them by the end of the period. You will be responsible for teaching each other—but I repeat, each one of you is responsible for knowing all of the material yourself. Please count off at your tables, 1, 2, 3, 4.*

*If you are number 1, please stand up. Bring a notebook and your text with you and go to this corner of the room* (indicating one corner). *If you are number 2, bring a notebook and your text with you and go to that corner of the room* (indicating another corner). *Number 3? You will go there, and number 4, there.*

The students move to their new seats.

*Now that you are in your groups, I will give you your assignment. Group number 1, you are responsible for question number 1. Group 2, question 2; group 3, question 3; and group 4, question 4. But pay attention: You should first discuss the question among yourselves to make sure you can answer it. And second—this is important—you should prepare to teach your question to the others in your home group. By "teach" I don't mean to explain. I mean to question the others in your group: Hear their answers, debate with each other, and make sure everyone has a thorough understanding.*

*You will have eight minutes to prepare to teach your question. When you return to your home group, each of you will have five minutes to teach your question to your home group. Good luck.*

As the students work in their groups, the teacher moves among the four groups to hear how they are doing and to offer suggestions. After eight minutes, the teacher gives the quiet signal.

**Teacher:** *Thank you. Now in a moment you will return to your home groups. You should deal with the questions in order, one though four. You will have five minutes for each question. Use your whole five minutes: remember to ask others to share their ideas and don't just share yours.*

Now the teacher walks among the groups and listens to their discussions. After 20 minutes, the groups are done. The teacher gives the quiet signal.

**Teacher:** *Let's share your ideas with the whole group. I will call out a number and ask the person with that number to summarize your group's answer to the question. I will ask number 4 to tell us your group's thinking on question 1, number 3 to share question 2, number 2 to share question 3, and number 1 to share question 4. Let's start with the person with number 4. Take a minute now and remember what your group said.*

The teacher waits one minute.

*Good, let's hear from someone in this group over in the corner. Who is number 4, and what was your group's answer to the first question?*

**Student 4:** "A whole host of things were exchanged. But we thought the most important were the diseases, which weakened the Indian populations and made it easier for the Europeans to take the land away from the indigenous peoples. And we also thought potatoes were important because they kept people in Europe from starving."

**Teacher:** *Nicely done. Now let's get person number 3 from this group in the other corner. You have question 2.*

**Student 3:** "We thought all that business about cotton and factories and the Industrial Revolution was fascinating. That showed that coming to the new world—we don't want to use the word 'discovery'—helped advance technology and commerce in Europe. We didn't know that before. Religion was important. But we shudder to think about people bringing Christianity and disease at the same time. That was very strange about the priest who argued for bringing in African slaves. And we wanted to mention that the diseases and food had cultural and economic consequences too, obviously."

**Teacher:** *Again, nicely done. Number 2, you have question 3.*

**Student 2:** "We noted Cabeza de Vaca, and Captain John Smith, and the king and queen of Spain, and of course Columbus. We remembered the Taino people, who died, and the Lakota Sioux Indians, who thought horses were elk dogs But the question made us realize that we don't know the names of the Muslims or the Jews who were expelled from Spain, or of the Indians who died of diseases. We only have the names of the people who got to tell the story."

**Teacher:** *Well put. Finally, Number 1, you have question 4.*

**Student 1:** "There was a lot of geography. The article mentioned the Bering Strait. That's between Alaska and Siberia. The people who became the Indians walked across that strait up until 20,000 years ago. But then it sank, and they couldn't get across. Then we had Genoa in Italy where Columbus came from, and two provinces in Spain. Then across in the New World we had the island of Hispaniola, where Haiti and the Dominican Republic are. We don't know much about what Columbus didn't know about the geography—except that he thought he was in Asia when he was really in North America."

### <u>the lesson ends here</u>

## REVIEWING THE LESSON

At the beginning of this lesson, you were invited to think about it in two ways: as *a student in the class*, and as *the teacher*. Take a moment and reflect on how it would have felt to be a student participating in this lesson. (It may help to write down your thoughts on a piece of paper).

**How did you feel**—interested, engaged, important, detached, controlled, or bored?

**What kind of thinking did you do**—memorize details, find main ideas, look below the surface at important issues, or make interpretations and support interpretations with reasons?

**What will you carry away from the lesson**—information, important ideas, or thinking skills?

Now think back over this lesson as if you had been the teacher. Recall the steps to this lesson. They were:

**Mix/Freeze/Pair:** Here the teacher stirred up the class and had students walk around until they found random partners to talk to.

**Reading with Text Coding**: Students next read a text with certain things to look for and instructions to mark the text with special symbols corresponding to each item they were looking for.

**Jigsaw:** All of the class was given a set of questions to answer, but students went to expert groups to prepare to teach the students in their home group only one of the questions. Then they returned to the home group and led their group in learning their part of the material.

You may want to learn exactly how you would conduct each activity. Here are the steps to each one.

## METHODS

### MIX/FREEZE/PAIR
**Mix/Freeze/Pair** (Kagan, 1994) is a lively means of having students work with new partners to complete a closely defined task.

**RATIONALE:** Having students move around can rekindle their energy and make them more alert. Finding a random partner with whom to solve a problem develops social skills, especially the ability to work cooperatively to solve problems.

 **GROUP SIZE:** Six to sixty.

 **TIME REQUIRED:** Mix/Freeze/Pair should be done quickly, in two to five minutes.

 **ACTIVITY:**
**Step 1:** Think of a question or a series of questions ahead of time.

**Step 2:** Give the directions ahead of time, to avoid chaos! Tell students that when you give the signal, they are to get up and move around the room. When you say "freeze" they should stop and pair up with the person closest to them.

**Step 3:** Give the signal. Allow one minute for them to move. Then say, "Freeze!" and tell them their task.

**Step 4:** Give the students a fixed amount of time to accomplish their task. Then ask them to go back to their seats.

 ## CLOSE READING WITH TEXT CODING
**Close reading with text coding** refers to the act of having students look for certain things in a text, then mark the text when those things are found.

 **RATIONALE:** When students are reading texts as part of a lesson, it helps to use a reading strategy that links their reading closely with their questions and purposes. Close Reading with Text Coding help students set purposes for reading, read to achieve those purposes, and later be able to use information from the text.

 **GROUP SIZE:** Unlimited.

 **TIME REQUIRED:** Close reading with Text Coding might add 25% or more to the amount of time otherwise needed to read a text.

 **ACTIVITY:**
**Step 1:** Ahead of the activity, think of four or five kinds of information you wish students to locate in a text. Come up with a simple symbol for each kind.

**Step 2:** Carefully explain to the students the kinds of information you want them to look for as they read the text. Give examples. Then show them the symbols with which they should mark each one.

**Step 3:** Tell the students to begin reading the assigned text and to mark (in light pencil) each piece of information of each type.

**Step 4: (Optional):** As an optional step, or to occupy those who finish early, ask the students to construct a table like this:

Tell them to put the symbols they used in their close reading between the parentheses. In pairs, have them list several pieces of information they found for each category.

## 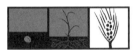 JIGSAW

**Jigsaw** (Slavin 1994) requires students to help each other learn. It can be used when students are reading a text, listening to a presentation, or carrying out a group investigation. Like other cooperative learning activities, the Jigsaw method employs both **home groups** and **expert groups**. The method requires some prior work from the teacher, who must prepare **task sheets** in advance of the lesson.

 **RATIONALE:** The Jigsaw technique helps all of the students to study and learn all of the material. They become "experts" as they teach each other parts of the material. Each student thus has an active role in teaching and learning and experiences deep understanding and higher order thinking.

**GROUP SIZE:** At least nine students, up to ninety. The Jigsaw method can be used in classes of nine to ninety students. **Home groups** are best kept to four members. These groups should continue to work together for three weeks or more, and should be composed of a mix of students: boys and girls, more and less capable students. It is worth taking the time to help students work effectively in groups, especially in their home group. **Expert groups** may also be kept to four or five members. That means when you are doing a Jigsaw you may have more students in each home group than the number of expert groups, you will need to randomly assign the "extra" students to different expert groups so that the sizes of the expert groups may remain balanced. If the number of students in the class requires it, you may have more than one of each expert group.

**TIME REQUIRED:** The Jigsaw strategy can be used in a single class period of 45 minutes, but the time will be limited. Assuming that the meeting of the expert groups requires 8 minutes, and that each "expert" will need 4 minutes to lead her or his part of the discussion, there will be 20 minutes left to divide between starting and ending the class and reading (or otherwise experiencing) the class material. In order to gain more time, the students may read the materials over night, or experience the lecture or class experiment on another day to have more class time to participate in the Jigsaw activity.

**RESOURCES:** The questions that will guide the "experts" discussions must be prepared in advance. They may be written on the chalk board. The students may be given material to read—but they may also be told a story, given a lecture, or engaged in some other stimulating experience.

**ACTIVITY:**

**Step 1:** The teacher prepares expert sheets. The teacher begins by reviewing the materials to be learned, and writing questions about it to guide the students' learning. The teacher should prepare the questions in groups, with as many groups of questions as there will be expert groups—usually four or five. Each group of questions might pertain to its own section of the material. (See **Preparing Questions** for suggestions of ways to write questions).

**Step 2:** The teacher assigns the students to home groups. Students should be assigned to home groups of four or five members. Each group should have a mix of boys and girls and of more capa-ble and less capable students. The home group is important, because the students in it will work to-gether for a period of time and will take responsibility for each other. Thus they should at least be-gin to feel some loyalty to each other. Students should be assigned to the same home group for at least three weeks, and they should carry out many cooperative activities together besides this one Jigsaw lesson.

**Step 3:** The teacher assigns a warm-up or team-building exercise for each home group. In order to make the team members relaxed together, they should be given a warm-up or team-building exercise the first time they meet together and periodically after that. A useful warm-up is to invite each home group to develop its own "team cheer." They may be given three minutes to develop the cheer, and then each group should be asked to demonstrate it to the whole group. (Note that there are many suggestions for warm-ups given in the section below.)

**Step 4:** Students read the materials or otherwise experience the lesson. Each student should now be given a copy of the text to be read. Or, if there is not a text, the teacher may read or tell a story, give a lecture, or lead the students in a learning activity.

**Step 5:** The teacher shares study questions and assigns students to expert groups. Now the teacher may either write the questions on the chalk board or distribute copies of the questions on repro-duced sheets. The questions are listed in groups (see above). The teacher asks the students to "count off" within the groups: "one, two, three, four." The teacher points to different parts of the classroom where each expert group should meet. The teachers asks every student number one to go to seats in one corner of the room, every student number two to go to seats in another corner of the room, and so on until all of the expert groups have an assigned place to meet. The teacher then appoints a discussion leader for each expert group.

Now the teacher explains that group number one is to prepare to teach certain of the questions (The teachers names the questions), group number two is to take certain other questions, and so on until all of the questions are assigned.

**Step 6:** The expert groups prepare to teach their portion of the questions. The teacher allows time for the expert groups to discuss their questions and decide on ways to teach them. The students in each expert group should locate ideas in the text or in the lesson that answer their questions. In the expert groups, the students' task is to *decide how best to lead a discussion of each question once they return to their home groups*. The teacher should make sure everyone understands that their task is not to answer the questions for their groups, but to lead the other members of their group to answer them. Then the students should think of strategies for getting their home groups to discuss them. As the expert groups meet, the teacher should circulate among them to help them stay on task and provide any clarification they need.

**Step 7:** Experts return to their home groups and take turns leading discussions. Once they have prepared to teach their part of the expert questions, the participants leave the study groups and return to their home groups. Experts take turns discussing their assigned questions on their expert sheets with the other members of their home groups. Each participant should take about five minutes to lead his or her part of the discussion. The expert's task is not just to report ideas, but to ask and entertain questions from the group to ensure everyone has thoroughly considered and learned the piece of the text or lesson that the expert has been assigned to cover.

**Step 8:** Evaluate the process. The teacher asks everyone to think about what he or she contributed to the discussion, and ways to improve the activity.

 **ASSESSMENT:** The catchphrase of cooperative learning is "collective responsibility, individual accountability." This expression means that cooperative learning activities require students to be responsible to each other, in order to enable each other to learn. But they are also individually accountable: that is, each student must also learn all the material. All of that means that each student should be tested on her or his mastery of the materials in a written or oral examination. It is possible for the teacher to reward group effort, however, by tracking the average grades of each group over time and awarding points to each member of the group if the average performance of the group impr6oves.

 **TIPS:** So that you can give them directions, such as telling them when it is time to move from one group to another, you will need some way to quickly get the attention of everyone in the workshop when they are working in groups.

Teach the participants a **quiet signal**: For example, raise your hand in the air and make a vee with your fingers. Each student who sees you do that should immediately stop talking, turn around, face you, and wait to hear what you will say. She or he should gently tap the shoulders of others who are talking so they will know to be quiet and listen to you.

Practice using the quiet signal several times at the beginning of a workshop so that everyone learn to do it.

# VARIATIONS AND RELATED METHODS

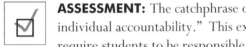 ## ROLES IN COOPERATIVE GROUPS
Cooperative learning groups may work more efficiently if students are assigned certain roles within the groups. The roles may rotate among the group members, though, so each student will have plenty of opportunities to practice each role. Together, the roles outlined below add up to the habits and skills of a talented group member.

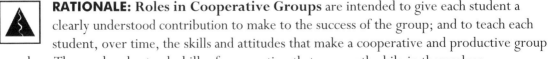 **RATIONALE: Roles in Cooperative Groups** are intended to give each student a clearly understood contribution to make to the success of the group; and to teach each student, over time, the skills and attitudes that make a cooperative and productive group member. These roles also teach skills of cooperation that are worthwhile in themselves.

**GROUP SIZE:** Roles in cooperative groups can be introduced to the whole class and practiced when students are working in home groups and expert groups.

 **RESOURCES:** No special resources are required to introduce roles in cooperative groups.

 **ACTIVITY:**
**Step 1:** Introduce the following roles to the students:

| | |
|---|---|
| **Questioner**. The Questioner presents the task to the group. | **Encourager**. The Encourager encourages the others to answer, congratulates them on their good ideas, and asks them to say more. |
| **Checker**. The Checker makes sure that everyone understands the task at hand, and sticks to it. | **Reporter**. The Reporter shares the small group's findings with the whole group. |
| **Timekeeper**. The timekeeper keeps track of the time allotted for the task and makes sure every group member stays within his or her time limit. | |

**Step 2:** Explain one role at a time. Describe the role. Demonstrate to the students how to perform in that role.

**Step 3:** Ask for several students to provide their own versions of its use and offer correction and clarification as needed.

**Step 4:** After the students understand all of the roles, ask the students in groups to count off, one through four or five. Assign the roles to the students according to their numbers.

**Step 5:** The teacher explains that the role of the reporter will be assigned later, so everyone must listen carefully, in case they turn out to be the one assigned that role.

**REFLECTIONS:** It is important for the teacher to give students a different role each time they work in groups. This may be done by having them keep the same numbers, and matching a different role with each number each time the students participate in groups. After the students have experience working within each role, they will become better rounded group members. Each of these roles stresses a different aspect of what a competent group member does.

 **COMMUNITY AGREEMENTS**
**Community Agreements** are rules of behavior that students agree to abide by when they participate in cooperative learning activities.

**RATIONALE:** Community Agreements are meant to teach students to behave responsibly and cooperatively in a group, to conduct learning groups that get their work done, and to manage their own behavior.

 **GROUP SIZE:** Community Agreements are derived and discussed with the whole class. They are reinforced later, any time the students are participating in group activities.

 **RESOURCES:** The teacher will need a chalk board to record the initial discussion in which the Community Agreements are reached, and chart paper to display the agreements permanently thereafter.

 **ACTIVITY:**

**Step 1:** The teacher begins by asking the class to get into home groups. Ask each home group to think of a group activity they have done that went particularly well. That is, one in which their group was particularly productive, and being a member of that group was particularly enjoyable. Then the teacher asks them to think of rules of behavior they might suggest to others to make a group work as effectively as that one.

**Step 2:** Now the teacher asks a group to name one rule. It is listed on the chalk board. The teacher asks each group to list one new rule that hasn't been mentioned before, and the teacher writes these on the chalk board.

**Step 3:** When all of the groups have contributed ideas the teacher reviews those ideas with the whole group. The teacher explains that the class is now trying to arrive at a set of Community Agreements—guidelines for productive behavior in groups to which all members can voluntarily subscribe. There should be no more than four or five of these, because that is the maximum number that students can easily remember. The teacher tries to combine the ideas that are similar, and to eliminate those that are redundant, so that the class ends up with four or five ideas on the chalk board or flip chart.

 **TIPS:** Typical community agreements often include these:

- *Everybody participates*
- *Nobody dominates*
- *Students stay on-task*
- *There are no "put-downs" (students take pains not to offend or criticize anyone else).*
- *Students practice <u>active listening</u>.*

**Step 4:** Next, the teacher explains that having a list of community agreements is important, but more work needs to be done before students will be guided by them as they work in groups. Write an "M-Chart" on chart paper.

Label the M-Chart with one of the community agreements, like this:

## PRACTICE ACTIVE LISTENING

| What does it look like? | What does it sound like? | What does it feel like? |
|---|---|---|
|  |  |  |

**Step 5:** Ask the group to describe what it <u>looks like</u> when students are actively listening to each other. You may have to demonstrate active listening. (The teacher may say: *Students lean toward the speaker. They look at the speaker. They nod in agreement.*)

**Step 6:** Now ask the students to say what it <u>sounds like</u> when students are practicing active listening. (The students may say: *"Only the speaker is talking." Others may say "Um, hum," or "that's right!"*).

**Step 7:** Now ask what it <u>feels like</u> to be the speaker when others are practicing active listening. (The students may say: *"The speaker feels confident." "The speaker feels important." "The speaker feels smart!"*).

**Step 8:** Finally, make an M-Chart of each of the Community Agreements and post these around the classroom.

**Step 9:** In the future, remind the students to practice the community agreements. For example, when the students are engaged in group work, you should walk around the room and observe the students. From time to time you should point out the examples you have seen of the community agreements in action (active listening, students talking in a friendly way without criticizing each other, etc.). Remind the students what it looked like and what it sounded like.

 **REFLECTIONS:** It is worth the time to elicit community agreements from students and teach them how to follow them. Group learning activities will be much more effective if students know how to behave in groups.

**TIPS:** A problem that groups of students commonly experience is unequal participation of the members. Some students are outgoing by nature and may dominate the group's discussion, while others are quieter by nature and may hold back their valuable contributions. The following two procedures are meant to get students used to participating equally in discussions. Use them occasionally—not all the time—to remind the group of the benefits of equal participation

 ## PENS IN THE MIDDLE
A cooperative learning strategy that helps students share group time equitably.

**RATIONALE:** In cooperative learning groups, one student occasionally dominates the conversation. Other students have difficulty contributing. **Pens in the Middle** method is intended to ensure that all students have the opportunity to participate in a cooperative learning group, and provide the teacher with a stimulus for asking students about their contributions.

**GROUP SIZE:** Pens in the Middle works well in small groups of from three to ten students.

 **RESOURCES:** No special resources are required except that each student should have a pen or pencil.

 **TIME REQUIRED:** The activity is carried on at the same time students are carrying out another cooperative activity.

 **ACTIVITY:**
**Step 1:** When students begin to share ideas in the typical cooperative learning group of three to seven members, each student marks his or her contribution by placing a pen or pencil on the table in the middle of the group.

**Step 2:** That individual may not contribute again until every other student has placed his or her pen in the middle. All members are equal in their ability to contribute, and no one may dominate.

**Step 3:** A student who has not contributed and who has nothing to add at that point can say, "Pass," placing his or her pen in the middle when speaking.

**Step 4:** At any time, the teacher may go to the group, select a pen on the table, and ask what contribution its owner made.

 **TIPS:** When students are discussing an issue in a small group, a useful way to make sure everyone participates is to have them pass an object (a stone, a small ball) from speaker to speaker. Only the speaker holding the object may speak.

 ## WALK AROUND—TALK AROUND
A cooperative learning activity for sharing ideas during the anticipatory phase of a lesson.

 **RATIONALE:** This method is useful for quickly sharing ideas among a large group of students in a very short time. It is highly active, and motivation is high during the activity.

 **GROUP SIZE:** A large group—20-30 or more.

 **RESOURCES:** A large space.

 **ACTIVITY:**
**Step 1:** The teacher asks each student to think briefly about a problem related to the lesson.

**Step 2:** The students then stand up and walk to a clear space in the classroom.

**Step 3:** The students walk around randomly in the space until the teacher claps one time.

**Step 4:** The students stop and talk to the nearest person about the question that the teacher asked.

**Step 5:** After about one minute, the teacher claps two times. Everyone should walk around again.

**Step 6:** The teacher claps once again. The students stop again and talk to the nearest person.

**Step 7:** Repeat this process a third time.

**Step 8:** After they talk with other students three times, the teacher asks them to sit down again.

**Step 9:** The teacher asks a few of them to share their ideas with the large group. The teacher asks them if any questions came up. The teacher writes their ideas and questions on a chart.

**Step 10:** The teacher then tells the students: *"Let's talk about these ideas and then identify two important issues."*

---

We found out how much it means to be listened to by the others, to express your feelings, beliefs, and to hear those of others.

(Secondary-school student, Macedonia)

---

 **ONE STAY/THREE STRAY**
A cooperative learning activity for sharing ideas within a classroom.

 **RATIONALE:** This method is a very useful strategy for quickly sharing ideas within a large class. It has the advantage, shared by many cooperative learning techniques, of putting students in responsible roles in which they function as expert providers of information to others.

 **GROUP SIZE:** The method of One Stay/Three Stray can work well with home groups of four or five. There may be any number of groups within a classroom.

 **RESOURCES:** It helps if the groups have paper and pencils with which to record the group's deliberations, and if individual students also have paper and pencils to record ideas they learn in the other groups.

 **TIME REQUIRED:** As far as time, the moving about can be done in a matter of seconds once students are used to it, and the visit to the new groups should take no more than five or six minutes.

 **ACTIVITY:**
**Step 1:** The students are assigned to **home groups** of four or five.

**Step 2:** Going clockwise around the room, the teacher numbers the tables. The teacher also gets the students sitting at each table to count off, one through four or five.

**Step 3:** The students are assigned a question to discuss, or a task to perform.

**Step 4:** After they have worked on the task for an interval, perhaps 15 minutes, the teacher asks everyone with the number one to stand up, then move one table to the next highest numbered table (from table one to table two, from table two to table three, and so on).

**Step 5:** Once the students with number one have moved, the teacher asks those with number two to stand. They should move from table one to table three, from table two to table four, and so on. Those with number three move three tables: from table one to table four, and so on. **Those with number four or five should stay at their original tables.**

**Step 6:** The teacher asks the students who are visiting each table to interview the remaining member from the original group to find out how that group answered the question. They should take notes and prepare to take them back to their own table. The student who stayed behind explains as clearly as possible his or her group's answers to the question.

**Step 7:** After five to eight minutes, have everyone go back to their original group and report on what they learned from the other tables. Each student should take three minutes to report on what they learned.

 **REFLECTIONS:** One Stay/Three Stray can be fun for the students, because it gets them up and moving around, and exposes them to other faces. Students enjoy being interviewed, and they also enjoy telling their table mates what they learned when they visited the other groups. If the procedure is set up properly, students can learn to move around quickly to their new places. We once observed a class of 80 sixth graders in rural Tanzania get up, move to new groups, and sit down again—all in 10 seconds.

 **ACADEMIC CONTROVERSY**
A cooperative learning activity that leads students to argue different sides of an issue.

**RATIONALE:** Learning to take a position and defend it with reasons is an essential skill in a democratic society. Learning to entertain arguments that are contrary to one's own belief is an important step toward sound consideration of an issue and informed decision making. **Academic Controversy** gives students the support of a group while they practice these skills of critical thinking.

**GROUP SIZE:** The method works best if students work in home groups of four. Groups of five will work if necessary. There may be any number of groups of four in the classroom.

**RESOURCES:** The method requires no particular resources, but it will help if each student has paper and a pencil for recording ideas.

**TIME REQUIRED:** The activity takes about 20 minutes to carry out.

 **ACTIVITY:**
**Step 1:** The teacher assigns the students to groups of four. The teacher gives them a question to discuss. Note that the question should have a "yes" or "no" answer.

**Step 2:** The teacher has the students discuss the question in groups of four, so they reach a common understanding of what the question means and why it matters.

**Step 3:** Then the teacher has the students count off in the group, 1, 2, 3, 4. Tell students with numbers 1 and 2 that they should prepare to argue for the point of view that "Yes, we should." Tell numbers 3 and 4 that they should prepare to argue the point of view, "No, we shouldn't."

**Step 4:** The teacher tells both pairs within each group to go off by themselves and spend five minutes listing reasons to support their position.

**Step 5:** After five minutes, the teacher calls time. The teacher than tells each student with a number 1 or 2 to go find a different student with a number 1 or 2. Those with number 3 or 4 should find a different partner with number 3 or 4. In three minutes, they should hear their partner's reasons, and write down any they had not thought of.

**Step 6:** The teacher calls time again. Now the teacher has the students return to their original partners and pool their ideas. Each pair should now think of the best reasons that support their position, and prepare to debate the other pair within their group of four. In order to debate, they should come up with a sentence stating their position and two or three good reasons for their position.

**Step 7:** After five more minutes, the teacher tells the pairs to join the other pairs in their group and join the debate. In order to debate, one side states its position with the reasons for it, then the other does the same. Then they debate each other's reasons and conclusions.

**Step 8:** The teacher lets the debate go on for six or seven minutes. Then he or she tells each group that they are now free to drop their assigned positions and argue for whatever positions they truly believe. The teacher asks the groups if they can come up with a consensus position: that is, a position with which everyone agrees, and reasons to support it.

**Step 9:** The teacher can now call on a member of each group to give a statement of the group's conclusions from their debate.

 **TRADE A PROBLEM**
**Trade a Problem** is a cooperative activity that requires students to locate an important issue in a topic of study and then formulate a problem about it for another group to answer.

 **RATIONALE:** The method teaches students to identify important issues in course material, formulate problems about those issues, and to interact with others.

**GROUP SIZE:** The method works best if students work in home groups of four. Groups of five will work if necessary. There may be any number of groups of four in the classroom.

 **RESOURCES:** The method requires no particular resources. But it will help if each student has paper and a pencil for recording ideas.

 **TIME REQUIRED:** The activity takes 15 to 40 minutes to carry out.

 **ACTIVITY:**
**Step 1:** Ask each group to write the problem down on a sheet of paper, and hand that piece of paper to another group.

**Step 2:** That group must solve the problem. Once they are handed a problem statement, each group has a fixed amount of time in which to think of a solution to the problem.

**Step 3 (Optional):** Once they have solved the problem, the group may plan a lesson in which they teach the problem and its solution to another group In teaching their lesson, they must

1. **show** and not **tell**
2. engage the students.

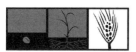 ## SPECIALIZED ROLES IN DISCUSSIONS

**Specialized Roles in Discussions** is a cooperative learning technique for managing discussions in small groups within particular discipline areas. Specialized Roles in Discussions is used after a text has been read or a topic has been presented. The technique has everyone discussing the same topic or text. By playing a different role, each student takes a different perspective on the discussion. Because the roles are chosen to highlight aspects of comprehension, the method enables students to learn those aspects deliberately through active practice. Later, when they study on their own they will combine the different roles into a comprehensive ability to make sense of a topic.

 **RATIONALE:** A literary text can be considered in different ways, and this method allows students to practice those ways. When the method is applied to other disciplines, it highlights different ways of thinking about topics in those disciplines. The method teaches students to play an active role in the discussion, learn all of the material under discussion, accept responsibility for their classmates' learning, and practice one aspect of comprehension of the topic at a time.

 **GROUP SIZE:** Specialized Roles in Discussions is done in groups of four or five students. There may be any number of groups in a classroom.

**RESOURCES:** If a text is to be read, there needs to be a copy to read aloud, or enough copies for the students to read themselves. If the desks can be moved, they can be arranged in clusters for the groups. If the students sit on benches, the students can turn around to work with a cluster of students around a bench top.

**TIME REQUIRED** The activity takes 15 to 40 minutes to carry out.

**ACTIVITY:**

**Step 1:** Before this activity begins, the text will have been read or the material will have been presented. Also, the teacher will choose a number of roles corresponding to the number of students in the home groups. Here are some potential roles for use in a literature class:

**Quotation Finder.** This student's job is to pick a few special sections of the text that the group would like to hear read aloud.

**Investigator.** This student's job is to provide background information on any topic related to the text.

**Connector.** This student's job is to find connections between the text and the world outside.

**Question asker.** This student's job is to write down (in advance of the discussion) questions for the group to talk about--questions he or she would like to discuss with the others.

**Word finder.** This student's job is to find interesting, puzzling, important, or new words to bring to the group's attention and discuss.

**Character interpreter.** This student's job is to think carefully about the characters and to discuss with the other students what the characters are like.

**Illustrator.** This student's job is to draw pictures of important characters, settings, or actions, so that the other students may discuss the pictures.

**Travel Tracer.** When characters move from place to place in a text, this student's job is to keep track of their movements.

**Step 2:** The students are assigned to home groups of four or five members.

**Step 3:** Within each group, the students count off, one through four or five. Each number is given one of the roles from the set chosen by you.

**Step 4:** As you would if you were using the Jigsaw technique, send the students to **expert groups** to plan ways to teach the material from each role. For example, send all the students who will be **quotation finders** together to decide which quotations to share, and how they will have their home groups discuss them. Give them five to eight minutes to work in expert groups.

**Step 5:** Call the students back to their **home groups**. In their home groups, give each student a fixed amount of time—three to five minutes—to lead their own part of the discussion.

**TIPS:** Five suggestions will make the use of these roles more successful:

1. The first is to teach the roles to the whole class, one at a time. You may read or tell a story, then introduce one of the roles—for example, the connector. You may then call attention to a connection between something in the text and something in real life. Then you will invite several students to do likewise. Over several days, many of the roles can be introduced in this way, before students use them in a group discussions.

2. Students should be encouraged to **ask questions** from their roles, rather than to say what they know. For example, the character interpreter might invite the other students to construct a character map or a character web about a character, and only venture his own ideas after the other students have shared their own.

3. Choose only the most useful roles for a particular discussion. Sometimes four or five roles are sufficient.

4. Rotate students through the roles. Each student should play many roles over the course of several discussions; the accumulated experience of playing many of these roles adds dimensions to each student's awareness of literature.

5. Be careful not to stress the roles more than the rich discussion of the literary work. Having students carry out the roles is a means to the end of sharing their insights about a work. Once the conversation is under way, you should feel free to suspend the roles and let the conversation proceed.

## DISCUSSION ROLES FOR OTHER SUBJECTS

Different subjects require different kinds of thinking to understand and apply the material. To adapt the method of assigning roles in discussions to a **geography class**, one teacher came up with these roles:

> **Mapmaker**, the student who drew a map of the area in question;

> **Historian**, the student who gave a bit of historical background to the area in question;

> **Geologist,** the student who described the land forms, soil types, and climate of the area under study;

> **Economist**, the student who talked about the kinds of economic activity students engaged in and related that activity to the land forms;

> **Anthropologist**, the student who talked about the people who live in an area, their traditions, and their culture.

In a **mathematics class**, the roles might be these:

> **Problem interpreter**, the student who restates the problem so that everyone understands the task at hand;

**Term finder**, the student who identifies and labels the relevant numbers in the problem that must be used in solving the problem;

**Calculator**, the student who sets up the problem in mathematical terms and leads the others through solving it;

**Checker**, the student who checks over the work to make sure it has been done correctly;

**Connector**, the student who leads a discussion to find examples of other problems that can be solved the same way.

 **REFLECTIONS:** Specialized Roles in a Discussion is an engaging strategy to use. You must watch the groups carefully, though, to make sure the discussions are carried out deeply and at some length. Otherwise, students may simply say what they know and be done with their role, the activity will go too quickly, the other students will not fully understand, and you will end up with some groups finished well before others. As with the other cooperative learning methods, once the students learn to carry out the activity they will be able to do it efficiently.

## THE REQUEST PROCEDURE

**The ReQuest Procedure** (Manzo 1969) is a useful activity partners can use when they are reading through a text that is difficult for them.

 **RATIONALE:** The ReQuest Procedure is an older and simpler learning technique than Reading and Questioning and Reciprocal Teaching (see below). It is fairly easy to teach students to do, and does not take as much time for reading the text as the other two methods.

 **GROUP SIZE:** The method will work with an unlimited number of pairs.

 **RESOURCES:** Each pair will need at least one text between them.

 **ACTIVITY:**
**Step 1:** Assign the text to be read, and decide on the units of text that will be discussed (Each sentence? Each paragraph? Each page?).

**Step 2:** One of the partners reads the first paragraph out loud.

**Step 3:** The other partner asks questions about what the text said. The partner must try to answer them. Both partners should try to agree on good answers to the questions.

**Step 4:** Switch roles. Now the partner who asked the questions reads the next paragraph aloud. The other partner then asks questions, as explained above.

**TIPS:**
Here is what we mean by a "good question":

Ask about main ideas (*"What is the most important thing the author has said here?"*)

Try to clarify details (*"What do you think the author meant by_____? What does that idea have to do with the main point?"*)

Make inferences (*"Why do you suppose the process works that way?"*)

Relate what was said to what will be coming in the text (*"What do we need to know now? What do you think the author will tell us next?"*)

 **READING AND QUESTIONING**

**Reading and Questioning** (Temple 2003) is a more complicated reading and questioning procedure that is carried out in pairs. It is recommended for studying materials that must be understood and recalled.

 **RATIONALE:** The Reading and Questioning procedure helps students read carefully and study materials with a partner. Working together can be more motivating than working alone.

 **GROUP SIZE:** Like the ReQuest Procedure, Reading and Questioning will work with an unlimited number of pairs.

 **RESOURCES:** Each pair will need at least one text between them.

 **TIME REQUIRED:** A Reading and Questioning activity may take half an hour to complete. Often it is done by students independently, outside of class time.

 **ACTIVITY:**
**Step 1:** The students take turns reading an assigned text in sections. The first student reads a section aloud, from one heading to the next heading.

**Step 2:** The two students decide on key terms to write in the margin of the text.

**Step 3:** When student 1 has finished reading the section, student 2 makes up questions about the text, using the terms from the margins. The questions should resemble test questions the students think might appear on an examination covering the material. The student writes each of these questions on a small piece of paper small slips of paper (8 cm by 12 cm) or an index card.

**Step 4:** Student 1 says aloud the answer to each question. If student 2 agrees with the answer, they write the answer to the question on the other side of the index card.

**Step 5:** Trade roles. Student 2 now reads a section. Both students decide on key terms to write in the margin of the text. Student 1 comes up with questions for the terms, which student 2 answers out loud. If they agree on the answer, they write it on the other side of the index card or piece of paper. They continue to trade roles until the assigned text is read.

**Step 6:** Using the cards or slips of paper with the questions and answers on them, the students continue to quiz each other on the assigned material in the days after the activity.

 **TIPS:**
The first time you do the Reading and Questioning procedure stop the class after the students have finished reading and questioning the first section of the text. Review their terms, questions, and answers, and suggest corrections as necessary. Thereafter, you should circulate among the students and listen to their questions and answers. Also, before the students study from their questions and answers, it is a good idea for you to review the questions and answers to make sure they are adequate, and accurate.

 ## RECIPROCAL TEACHING
**Reciprocal Teaching** (Palincsar 1984) was developed by learning theorists for the purposes of having students read carefully for understanding.

 **RATIONALE:** As all teachers know, the best way to learn about something is to teach it to others. In Reciprocal Teaching, students not only teach materials to their peers, but they also practice important comprehension skills while doing so. Reading and Questioning teaches students to read for understanding: find main ideas, locate details, and make connections among ideas in a text.

 **GROUP SIZE:** Reciprocal Teaching is best done in groups of four. It will work with an unlimited number of foursomes.

 **RESOURCES:** Each foursome will need at least one text among them.

 **TIME REQUIRED:** Reciprocal Teaching is time consuming, but the pay-off in comprehension is usually worth it.

 **ACTIVITY:**
**Step 1:** Assign the participants to groups of four or five. Explain that they will be doing a cooperative learning activity called "Reciprocal Teaching." They will take turns being the teacher within their group. The person playing the role of teacher will carry out these five tasks:

1.  Read a paragraph aloud. Read slowly, in a clear voice, with emphasis.

2.  Summarize what it said. Say aloud the main points of the text in a sentence or two.

3.  Ask questions about it. Formulate and ask questions about—

    •   *the main ideas* ("What two kinds of soil erosion are there?")

- *explanations behind those ideas* ("Why does wind erode the soil on some land more than others?")

- *the implications of those ideas* ("According to what we have read, is the land around here prone to soil erosion?")

4.  Clarify the hard parts. Try to make the more obscure parts clear—

- *vocabulary* ("When the text says 'wind break,' it means 'trees planted to prevent wind erosion.'")

- *background knowledge* ("Topsoil is the layer of fertile soil that lies on top of the subsoil. It has the organic matter in it that nourishes plants.")

5.  Predict what will come next. Try to predict where the author's presentation is going. Say what we need to know next. Point to words in the text that preview coming ideas, such as "as we shall see...."

**Step 2:** Read a paragraph aloud yourself. Then **summarize it** carefully. Explain to the participants how you have brought out the main ideas in your summary. Then **ask two questions** about it. Call attention to the kinds of questions you asked (main idea, explanation, implication). Then **clarify the hard parts** and point out that you stressed vocabulary or background knowledge. Finally, **predict** what is coming next, and say what you based your prediction on.

**Step 3:** At each step, you may ask participants to try the step themselves and comment on what they say. Once you have explained the procedure, ask the participants, in groups of four or five, to practice Reciprocal Teaching with the text on soil erosion.

**Step 4:** After they have all had time to do the first step, "summarizing," ask for the group's attention, then ask volunteers to give you examples of the summaries. Point out what is good about the summaries, or suggest improvements. Then have them go on to the next step, and again, call for people to share their questions, and critique those.

**Step 5:** Now let the groups go ahead independently. After they have read at least four paragraphs, you may let them read the rest of the text independently, if time is short.

 **TIP:** Before asking the participants to try out Reciprocal Teaching, it is important to explain and demonstrate each step very carefully.

 ## FOCUS ON: WARM-UP ACTIVITIES

In order to learn, students must be emotionally ready to take risks. Educational psychologists remind us that learning happens most easily in psychologically "safe" environments (Marzano, 1992). That means they will feel free to venture answers to questions, ask new questions, and state original opinions without fearing that they will "look stupid." It also means that they should be willing to work together and support each other in learning tasks.

It is a good idea to begin the school year with a series of warm-up activities to help "break the ice" between students who do not yet know each other well. The teacher should repeat the warm-ups periodically throughout the school year. When students are working in cooperative learning groups, they should use warm-ups often—twice a week at least—especially when new groups are getting to know each other.

The following warm-up activities are recommended as a starter set. See if you can add to them by asking other educators what works for them.

These activities will work best in groups of 20 or less. Since most classrooms have more students than that, the activities can be practiced in small groups functioning at the same time. You may explain the activity to the whole class at once, and then have them practice it in smaller groups. If the weather permits, many of these activities can be done outside, where the groups have room to spread out.

## SCAVENGER HUNT
**Step 1:** On a flip chart write:

> Find a person who—
> 1. Is a middle child
> 2. Has an interesting hobby
> 3. Knows a good joke (and have them tell it!)
> 4. Is left-handed
> 5. Speaks more than two languages
> 6. Has recently learned a new skill

**Step 2:** Ask the participants to take a piece of paper and make a grid with six numbered boxes. Give them seven minutes in which to go around and collect two signatures of people who fit each criterion.

## SECRET TALENTS
**Step 1:** Distribute pieces of paper and have students write one thing they like to do that the other students probably don't know about.

**Step 2:** Collect the papers, mix them up, and distribute them to the students, making sure no one gets his or her own.

**Step 3:** The students go around and try to find the student who has the secret talent.

## TWO TRUTHS AND A LIE
**Step 1:** Have each student write down three things about herself—a favorite pastime, a chore they perform at home, etc. Two of these three statements must be true and one must be a lie. The lie should be plausible, though, and the true statements can be surprising.

**Step 2:** The rest of the class (or small group) must guess which statement is the lie.

**SPIDER WEB**

This builds inclusion and a sense of community through the practice of attentive listening.

**Step 1:** Ask the group to sit in one large circle.

**Step 2:** Explain that during this activity each student will have an opportunity to share his or her name and something special about himself or herself. Give the students a minute to think of something special.

**Step 3:** Have one student begin the activity by stating his or her name and something about himself or herself. (Example: "My name is Ana, and I am wonderful at remembering things.") Then, have the student hold onto the end of the yarn and roll the ball to someone across from him or her in the circle. Have the students continue this process until everyone has either shared or passed and a "spider web" pattern has been created.

**I LOVE YOU, DEAR** (For any size group)

**Step 1:** Have the students stand in a large circle.

**Step 2:** Choose one student to stand in the middle. He must walk up to one person in the circle and say, "I love you, dear." That person must respond, "I love you too, but I'm not supposed to smile," without smiling. It can be said twice to the same person in the same way.

**Step 3:** If the person smiles—and most will—the smiler may then trade places with the person in the center. As an alternative, the student who smiled may join the student in the center in tempting others to smile. The second may be easier for shy students, and it makes the activity proceed faster.

**TALK TO ME** (For groups of 10 up to 30)

This warm-up is very entertaining. It also provides practice in reading comprehension.

**Step 1:** Count the number of participants you have. Make a small sheet of paper for each participant. Write an instruction on each one. Here are some sample instructions:

> Lie to me.
> Talk to me in an angry way.
> Look at my shoes.
> Close your eyes often.
> When you talk to me, touch your nose.
> Ignore me.
> Look at the ceiling.
> Give me compliments.
> Change partners.

You can write many more similar instructions. Some can be used twice.

**Step 2:** Do not let the participants see the papers. Tape one sheet of paper with an instruction on the back of each participant.

**Step 3:** Tell the participants to walk around the meeting room. They should read the instruction on another participant's back.

**Step 4:** Tell them to talk to that participant and follow the instruction. For example, if the instruction says, "Close your eyes often," talk to the participant and close your eyes often. After a few minutes, move on to another participant. Of course, other people will be reading that participant's paper on his or her back. Everyone will be reading everyone else's note and following the directions.

**Step 5:** At the end of the activity, each participant should try to guess what his or her note says.

## LOOK UP, MON!

This warm-up is a good way to choose random pairs to work together when the group numbers 10 to 30 students. Each two who say, "Mon" to each other make a pair. Continue until everyone is paired up.

**Step 1:** Ask the students to stand in a circle. Tell everyone to look at the floor.

**Step 2:** The teacher calls out, "Look up, mon!" Everyone should look at the face of another person in the circle.

**Step 3:** Almost everyone will be looking at someone who is looking at someone else. But a few will be looking at each other. Those who are looking at each other must say, "Mon." They are out and must leave the circle.

# ABC CHART

Let's see how the preceding methods, variations, and related methods fit into the Anticipation/Building Knowledge/Consolidation rubric. This chart will help you use the methods in this guide to make your own lesson plans using the ABC rubric.

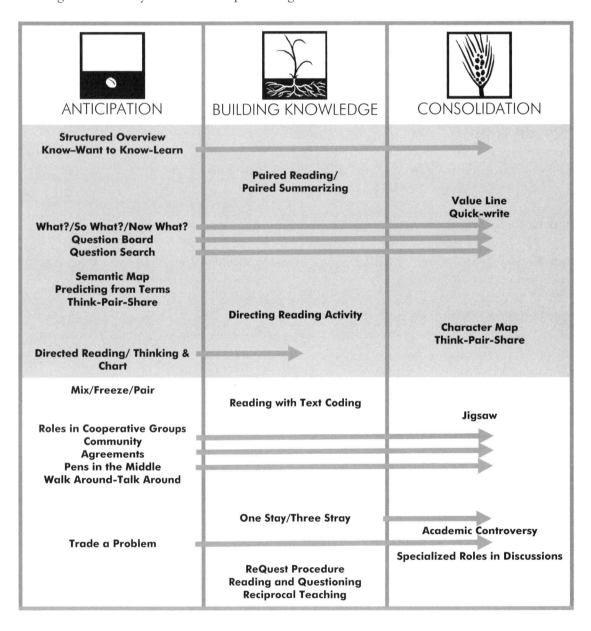

| ANTICIPATION | BUILDING KNOWLEDGE | CONSOLIDATION |
|---|---|---|
| Structured Overview Know–Want to Know–Learn | | |
| | Paired Reading/ Paired Summarizing | Value Line Quick-write |
| What?/So What?/Now What? Question Board Question Search | | |
| Semantic Map Predicting from Terms Think-Pair-Share | | |
| | Directing Reading Activity | Character Map Think-Pair-Share |
| Directed Reading/ Thinking & Chart | | |
| Mix/Freeze/Pair | Reading with Text Coding | Jigsaw |
| Roles in Cooperative Groups Community Agreements Pens in the Middle Walk Around-Talk Around | | |
| | One Stay/Three Stray | Academic Controversy |
| Trade a Problem | | Specialized Roles in Discussions |
| | ReQuest Procedure Reading and Questioning Reciprocal Teaching | |

# FOURTH CORE LESSON: CONDUCTING A DISCUSSION

Previous lessons have presented ways to get students to inquire into the meaning of a text or a lesson. This lesson presents more methods for conducting discussions with groups of students. Discussions strategies, along with the kinds of questions teachers ask, are very important in teaching, because they orchestrate the kind of *thinking* that students do. Interesting questions inspire interesting answers. Of course, getting 40, 50, or 60 students participating in discussions requires not only good questions but good management frameworks and teaching strategies. This core lesson and the methods that follow present all of these areas.

This core lesson will highlight the **Shared Inquiry Method** and the **Discussion Web**, and will also employ the **Predicting from Terms** technique and the **Directed Listening-Thinking Activity.**

## HOW TO READ THIS LESSON

As you read the following demonstration lesson, please bear in mind that its purpose is to demonstrate teaching methods (and not to teach you about Scotland or seals!). Think about this lesson in two ways:

> 1. Imagine that you are *a student* who is participating in this lesson. What is your experience? What kind of thinking are you doing? What are you learning?

> 2. Then think yourself into the role of *the teacher* who is leading the lesson. What are you doing? Why are you doing it? How are you handling the three phases of the lesson—anticipation, building knowledge, and consolidation?

## LESSON

 **ANTICIPATION**

The anticipation phase is the part of the lesson that arouses students' curiosity and sets purposes for learning. Here we use the **Predicting from Terms** technique.

The teacher lists several terms from the story the students are about to hear, and invites student to use them to invent their own story.

**Teacher**: *Today you are going to hear a story from Scotland. It will be a folktale. That means it will tell about someone who wants something and strives to get it. Maybe the actions are right or maybe they're wrong—either way, the actions are sure to have consequences. Maybe the story will suggest something about how we should live our lives. Strange things will happen in the story—maybe it will have magic in it, maybe not. Anyway, that much makes it a folktale. Also, I can tell you this: the people who originally told this story—they were fisher folk from the north coast of Scotland—believed that it was true.*

*I am going to write five terms on the chalk board. These terms will appear in the story I will tell you. The terms are:*

- seal skin,
- marriage,
- locked trunk,

- sea coast,
- a transformation (that is, a mysterious change).

*I want you to turn to your face partner. The pair of you should try to imagine your own folktale that will have those five elements in it. That is, let those terms suggest a story to you. Let your imaginations go, and make up a story. You have three minutes to do so.*

After three minutes pass, the teacher invites three pairs to share their imagined stories.

**Pair 1:** "We said there is a man who wants to marry a woman, but she doesn't want to marry *him*. But one day he is walking on the shore feeling bad about the woman and he finds a locked trunk washed up on the beach. He breaks it open and finds a seal skin. He gives it to the woman. She is so happy she has a transformation and decides to marry him."

**Student 1:** "But where's the magic?"

**Pair 1:** "OK, so after a while, the seal skin magically disappears, but the woman doesn't mind because by now they're happily married."

**Teacher:** *Hmmm. OK. Thanks for that. Who else?*

**Pair 2:** "Ours is sort of a mermaid story. One day a man and woman are walking on the beach. They say they want to get married. But secretly the woman is very curious, and she's not quite able to settle down to the idea of getting married. While they're walking on the shore, they find a locked trunk. They find a key beside it and open it up and find a seal skin inside. The woman holds it up. It's just her size, so she puts it on. Suddenly she is transformed into a seal. What can she do? She can't marry him now. Anyway, he's terrified at the change in her and stands staring in amazement. She goes into the sea. The end."

**Student 2:** "But every year at that time…"

**Pair 2:** "Yes, that's right. Every summer at just that time she comes back, looking for her husband that might have been."

**Teacher:** *That one certainly sounds like a folktale.*

**Pair 3:** "Here is ours. It's a little bit like the one we just heard. Except in ours there are creatures who sometimes live in the sea as seals, and sometimes live on land as people. Somehow one of their skins got into a locked trunk that was stored away for years and years in these people's attic. A boy is exploring in the attic and finds the trunk. He opens it and pulls out the skin. Suddenly a beautiful young woman is standing in front of him...."

**Student 4:** "Wearing a fur coat!"

**Pair 3:** "Sure. Why not?"

**Student 5:** "What about the sea coast?"

**Pair 3:** "We didn't get that far."

**Teacher:** *Well, now we have heard three stories. In one, a man finds the seal skin on the shore, and gives it to his beloved to coax her into marrying him. In another, a restless woman finds the skin, puts it on, and is transformed into a seal. And in the third, a young man finds a long-forgotten skin, and it turns into a young woman—presumably his mate. Listen to the story I am about to tell, and see how it compares to your own story. I will be stopping from time to time to ask for predictions.*

 **BUILDING KNOWLEDGE**

The building knowledge phase is the one in which students are encouraged to explore and make meaning. In this lesson the **Directed Listening-Thinking Activity** will be used.

**Teacher:** *I will begin reading now. Listen and picture the scenes in your minds as I read to you.*

### IVAN AND THE SEAL SKIN
Retold by Bucksnort Trout

Along the north coast of Scotland, the winter wind howls through dark nights and gray days, and towering seas smash against black rocks. But in summer, the sea calms, and the days grow long, until the daylight lasts through twenty-four hours. Then the few fishermen who live on that remote coast row their nets out into the sea, to catch their livelihood. Even in summer, a sudden storm may overtake them; or a silent fog may creep upon them and make them lose their way. Then their loved ones go down to the shore, and gaze for some sign at the mute waves, perhaps to see a seal stare back with big sad eyes. The people see the seals, and they wonder...

On a little cove by the sea lived a fisherman and his wife, and their one son, Ivan Ivanson. It was the longest day of the year: Midsummer's Eve. Close to midnight, with the sky still a radiant orange, young Ivan, barely seven years old, was exploring the rocks by the shore, searching for shells and bits of net and whatever else the waves might have washed up.

Suddenly a strange sound drifted to him on the wind. It was like the singing of unearthly voices, blended in beautiful harmony. No, perhaps it was the song of shore birds. No, it was voices. He looked up. Away down the shore to his right he could see a tendril of smoke rising from a hole at the base of the rocks, near the point. Was it mist from the breaking waves, perhaps? No, it was smoke.

## First stop

**Teacher**: *Can you picture the scene? What do you think is going to happen now? What do you think this story will be about? Think for a minute. Then tell us.*

**Student 6:** "I think he's going to go down the shore."

**Teacher:** *Do you think so? Then what will happen if he does?*

**Student 7**: "I think he will go down the shore and find mermaids singing around a campfire."

**Student 8**: "I think he might go eventually, but I don't think he will go yet. The story has to build up more suspense first."

**Teacher:** *Does anyone agree? How many of you think he will go down the shore now? Raise your hands.* (Most of the hands are raised.). *How many think he will not go now?* (A few hands are raised.) *Those of you who think he will go, what do you think he will find if he does?*

**Student 9:** "Mermaids."

**Student 10:** "Seal hunters. They have captured a seal who will turn into a woman. She's really a mermaid."

**Student 11**: "An old sailor sitting on a locked trunk, by a campfire."

**Teacher:** *Come on, press yourself. What do you think is in the trunk?*

**Student 10:** "A seal skin. And the sailor has a fascinating story to tell, but I haven't thought what it is yet."

**Teacher:** *Very well. You have heard many good predictions. Choose one that you think is most likely to happen—it can be your own prediction or someone else's. Go ahead and choose that prediction now. And listen and see if it comes true. I will continue reading.*

Ivan would have explored, but his short legs wouldn't carry him over the large boulders, so when his mother called, he returned to the family cottage without investigating further.

Seven years went by. Ivan, now fourteen, found himself once again down on the shore, right at midnight, on Midsummer's Eve. Once again he thought he heard strange singing, and again he saw smoke rising from a hole at the base of the rocks, down by the point. I don't know why he didn't go to the source this time. Perhaps some emergency called him back to his parents' cottage. His father's health, like as not. For both his parents were growing old.

## Second stop

**Student 8:** "See? I was right!"

**Teacher:** *You were right. Were any other of our predictions borne out yet?*

**Student 10:** "No. We don't know what's making the sounds or the smoke. It could be mermaids. We don't know."

**Student 11:** "We're hearing a lot about the singing. I think it's mermaids."

**Student 12:** "It's got to be something like that. It couldn't be people, really, because Ivan would know about them. It's a mystery."

**Student 13:** "I think it's a teenager with a very loud CD player."

**Student 14:** "Come on! We're talking about a folktale!"

**Student 15:** "Somebody said something about a woman who turned into a seal. I've heard legends about that. I think it might be seals that come out of the ocean on Midsummer night and turn into people."

**Student 16:** "It's true that Ivan only heard them on Midsummer's night. And every seven years. It's got to be something like that."

**Teacher:** *Go on with your prediction then. What do you see happening in this story?*

**Student 15:** "I think Ivan is going to go down there and meet them."

**Student 17:** "Maybe he'll join up with them."

**Student 18:** "Maybe he'll marry one of them. We know there is going to be a marriage in this story."

**Student 16:** "No, he's not old enough to get married yet."

**Student 19:** "I don't think anything's going to happen yet."

**Teacher:** *What do you mean?*

**Student 19:** "Because he's not old enough to get married yet, but eventually he will. And do you know how things in folktales happen in threes? I don't think he will go yet."

**Teacher:** *Who thinks he won't go explore yet?* (Half the hands go up.) *And who thinks he will go now?* (The other half go up, though some look tentative.) *OK. We have a lot of predictions to listen for. It might be a person with a CD player.* (Students laugh.) *No, keep an open mind. It could turn out to be mermaids. Or it could turn out to be seals who have come ashore and become people. It's been predicted that Ivan will join them. That he will marry one. Or that he won't go yet. Choose a prediction that you think is most likely to happen. Listen and see if it comes true. I will continue reading.*

Seven more years went by. His father had worn out from fishing the cold brine, so his parents had retired to town, leaving their cottage to Ivan. Ivan lived all alone, with only the cries of the shore birds for company. He fished long days, and warmed himself at night by the little peat fire. I imagine he was lonely.

When Midsummer's Eve came again, Ivan remembered the singing, and the smoke. At the dimmest part of the day, which was really midnight, he walked down to the shore. The same strange singing reached his ears, woven into unearthly and beautiful harmonies.

## Third stop

**Teacher:** *Now what?*

**Student 18:** "We were right. He didn't go. But this time he will."

**Teacher:** *And if he does, do you have the same predictions as before?*

**Students:** "Yes. Please keep reading. We want to hear what happens."

**Teacher:** *OK. Here goes:*

This time, no boulders would stop him, and there was no one to call him back. Ivan made his way down the shore toward the point. As he drew closer, he could hear the crackle of a fire, and could see its reflection against the rocks. Beautiful singing came from inside the cave. And there at the cave's mouth lay a pile of sleek and beautiful gray furs: seal skins.

Ivan chose the one he thought the most beautiful one and slowly, carefully, he pulled it from the pile. He rolled the seal skin into a ball and made straight off for home with it. Once there, he locked the seal skin in a wooden trunk, slipped the key onto a leather thong tied around his neck, and went to bed.

In the morning he took the blanket from his bed and returned to the cave. There he found...

## Fourth stop

**Teacher:** *Yes?*

**Student 9:** "A woman. A beautiful woman."

**Teacher:** *Does anyone think differently?*

**Student 10:** "It will be a woman. Please read."

**Teacher:** *OK, I'll continue.*

There he found a sad and beautiful young woman, huddled and shivering, covering her nakedness with her arms and long hair. Without a word, Ivan wrapped the young woman in his blanket and led her home to his cottage.

Ivan treated the woman kindly, and in time they fell in love. They had one son, then another. Ivan was happy enough, and the woman was a good mother. But often Ivan saw his wife staring off at the sea with big, sad eyes. He never told her what was in the wooden box, and he forbade her to open it.

**Fifth stop**

**Teacher:** *We need to stop and see where we are. Have any predictions come true so far?*

**Student 21:** "That's amazing. It turned out to be seal people after all."

**Teacher:** *Are you sure?*

**Student 22:** "That's the only explanation. They were seals who came ashore every seven years on Midsummer's night and became people. Then they had some kind of ritual."

**Student 23**: "And we predicted that he would hold off going until he was old enough to marry. And then he would find a seal woman and marry her."

**Teacher:** *Those are amazing predictions. But let's talk about the story now. What are you noticing in the story? What are you thinking will turn out to be important?*

**Student 24:** "I don't understand why he doesn't tell her about the seal skin."

**Student 25:** "Yes, that's mean. And the story says Ivan is happy, but the woman is not. I have a bad feeling about what is going to happen."

**Teacher:** *And what is that?*

**Student 25:** "Well, it can't come to a good end if she isn't happy. And besides, she's cut off from her own people."

**Student 18:** "But she's with her own people. She has a family now. A human family."

**Student 26:** "But that's the trouble. She's divided between two families, between two worlds. I agree: something has to change. This has to be resolved.

**Teacher:** *It's time for predictions, then. What do you think will happen?*

**Student 27:** "I think she'll leave."

**Teacher:** *For good?*

**Student 27:** "No, I think she'll come back, but only every seven years."

**Teacher:** *Why do you think so?*

**Student 27:** "Because the seal people came every seven years at Midsummer's night.

**Teacher:** *Anyone else?*

**Student 28:** "I think she'll leave for good."

**Student 29:** "I think the husband will show her the seal skin, and she'll make up her mind then to stay."

**Teacher:** *Why do you think so?*

**Student 29:** "Because that's what I want to happen!"

**Student 30:** "Or she'll go away part of the time and come back part of the time."

**Teacher:** *OK, choose predictions. I'll read on.*

> More years passed. One Christmas Eve Ivan readied his family to go to church. The wife said she was feeling poorly, though, and asked Ivan and the boys to go on alone.

> Perhaps Ivan was angry at this. In his haste to dress, Ivan left the thong with the key hanging on his bed stead, and went off to church without it.

> Ivan and the boys returned from church after midnight. They saw the open door before they reached the cottage. They found the wooden box lying open, and the key still in the lock. The wife was gone.

## Sixth stop

**Teacher:** *Quickly, now. We're almost at the end. How do you think the story will turn out?*

**Student 5:** "She'll come back."

**Student 13:** "She'll come back every seven years."

**Student 28:** "No, she's gone for good."

**Teacher:** *Choose a prediction. I'll finish the story now.*

> They say that sometimes when the boys picked their way along the shore, a beautiful seal with large sad eyes would follow along close by in the cold, dark water. And they say sometimes when Ivan was fishing, the same sad and beautiful seal would come and chase the herring fish into his nets. Perhaps the seal was Ivan's wife. No one knows. All we know is that Ivan never saw his wife on this earth again.

**Student 28:** "Aw, I knew she wouldn't come back."

**Student 13:** "But why didn't she? She left her family behind after all."

**Student 29:** "Yes, but don't you see? He was never honest with her, so he never knew what she wanted. It serves him right for not showing her the seal skin."

**Student 30:** "But he was good to her. She had no right to leave her family like that."

**Student 29:** "If you want to talk about rights, he didn't respect her rights, either."

**Teacher:** *Nice job, everybody. You made some really good predictions. But do you remember the stories you made up in the beginning? Did any of them come close to the story I just read you?*

**Student 1:** "There were two stories about humans turning into seals."

**Teacher:** *That's true. Where did those ideas come from?*

**Student from pair 2:** "I don't know. I've read other stories about people turning into animals. I read a Japanese story about a woman who turned into a crane. And the way you introduced us to the story—when you talked about magic and mystery—gave me that thought of something really mysterious happening."

**Student from pair 3**: "And we saw a movie once about people who turned into seals."

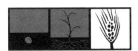 **CONSOLIDATION**

Now that the students have a basic understanding of the story, it is time to see what they can do with the meaning. What are the implications of the ideas they have just constructed? How do these ideas play out in their lives? This is the consolidation phase of the lesson, and here the teacher will first use the **Shared Inquiry Approach** and then the **Discussion Web.**

**Teacher:** *One of you said that the story seemed mysterious. I'd like to probe some of those mysteries now. I've got a question to ask you. I'll write it on the chalk board, and each of you will have two minutes to write your own answer to it. Then we'll discuss what you think.*

The teacher writes: Why did the author have Ivan hear the sounds and see the smoke on two earlier occasions, but only go to the cave when he was 21?

After two minutes, the teach invites a student to respond.

**Student 1:** "I think it was because things in folktales always come in threes."

**Teacher:** *Thanks. Let me write that down.* [The teacher writes the student's name on a chart, and briefly notes her comment underneath.] *OK, but why is that? What is the effect of having the two times he didn't go before the one time that he did?*

**Student 1:** "Well, once he didn't go the first time, and then he didn't go the second time, you *knew* he would go the third time…"

**Student 2:** "… and you were prepared for something really important. The pattern of three built up the suspense, and made you expect something really significant."

**Teacher:** *Thanks.* [The teacher writes down the new response on the seating chart.] *We'll come back to that. Did anyone think about the question a different way?*

**Student 3:** "Yes. He wasn't ready the first time. He was too young. He was too young the second time too."

**Student 4:** "Right. Suppose he *had* gone on those earlier occasions. He might have come running home to his parents to tell them what he had seen. Or they might have taken him away with them back to the sea. But we wouldn't have had this story about the marriage.

**Teacher:** *That's interesting* [Writes down the student's response on the seating chart.] *OK, we have two different ideas on the table. Some people say it took three times, because in folktales, events come in patterns of threes. Others of you think he had to be ready for the real story, and he had to grow up first.* [Indicates student 4.] *Which idea do you agree with, or do you have a different idea?*

**Student 4:** "My idea combines the two other ideas. I think the author had him not go those two times to build suspense, and to make it clear that he had waited all his life for this. The seal woman was somehow his destiny, and when the time was right, he would find her."

**Student 5:** "But how can that be? If she was the woman he was destined to marry, why did he basically kidnap her?"

**Teacher:** *What do you mean, 'kidnap her'?"*

**Student 5:** "Well, he kept her seal skin away from her, and basically kept her imprisoned in human form."

**Teacher**: [Writing down these comments, then reading back.] *Let's follow that question, but first let's review what we've said. Some said he went three times because folktales use patterns of threes. Others said he had to grow up first. Someone else said the pattern of three showed that marrying the seal woman had always been his destiny. Now it's just been said that marrying the seal woman may have seemed to Ivan to have been his destiny, but from the woman's point of view it amounted to kidnapping. Good discussion so far. Let's stay with this question of 'fisherman's destiny' versus 'woman's imprisonment.' Are we talking about good events here, or bad ones?*

**Teacher:** *Several of you have already expressed some disquiet over the way this story turned out. I want to ask you now to debate a question about this story: Should this never have happened? <u>Would it have been better if Ivan had never taken the seal skin?</u>*

*Each pair of you should draw a full page chart that looks like this*

DISCUSSION WEB:

**Ivan should never have taken the seal skin.**

**I agree!**
(It would have been better if he hadn't.)

**I disagree!**
(On balance, it's still better that he did.)

_____

_____

_____

      _____

      _____

      _____

**Conclusion:**

**Teacher:** *First, I want pairs to discuss this question, as follows: pairs, think of two or three reasons why you could agree with the statement, "Ivan should never have taken the seal skin," and two or three reasons why you could disagree. I'll give you five minutes to do that. Please start now.*

After five minutes, the teacher says, *Now let's hear a couple of your reasons why you would agree with that statement.*

**Pair 1:** "He shouldn't have taken it because it didn't belong to him. The skin didn't belong to him, so the woman's loyalty didn't belong to him either."

**Pair 2:** "And by taking it, he made a real mess. Now the children don't have a mother, he doesn't have a wife, and the woman is separated from her human family."

**Teacher:** *Those are powerful reasons. Now let's hear some reasons why you would disagree with the statement. That is, you're saying that when everything is considered, it was still better that he took the seal skin.*

**Pair 3:** "Because look: Ivan was lonely. That was his problem. He took the seal skin, and he had a wife. And now he has children. He solved his problem."

**Pair 2:** "But that's a selfish way of looking at it. What about the woman's feelings?"

**Teacher:** *Hold off on the debate for a minute. I just want to hear your reasons now. Who has another reason why it was better that he took the skin, than not taking it at all?*

**Pair 4:** "We said that at least those two children were brought into the world. It's possible to think of your parents getting together for reasons that weren't so great, but you're still happy to be alive, right?" (Other students laugh.)

**Teacher:** *All right. It sounds like you have reasons on both sides of the argument. Now let's move to the next part of the activity. Now pairs should join other pairs and make groups of four. Then do this. First, share your* *lists of reasons with each other. Second, debate the issue. Each person should argue for one position or another. Third, reach a conclusion to which everyone can agree. Write that conclusion—both what you believe and your reasons for believing it—on the bottom of your sheets of paper where it says "Conclusion." You have eight minutes in which to do this.*

The teacher walks around from group to group as they debate the issue. At the end of seven minutes, the teacher warns the groups that they have one minute left. After eight minutes, the teacher invites students to share their conclusions.

**Group 1:** "We decided that he should have taken the seal skin after all. It was his destiny. He had wondered about the singing and the smoke all his life. He was meant to investigate, to take the blanket, to marry the woman, and to have that family."

**Group 2:** "That's not the way we saw it at all. The seal-woman was minding her own business when this man came and trapped her in her human form and wouldn't let her go. From her point of view, she was as good as kidnapped. He should never have taken the skin. And once he had taken it, he should not have kept it hidden from her."

**Group 3:** "We also took the position that it was better on balance that he took the seal skin, because he made a family. He still has the two children, and he had years of joy with the wife. He may be sad now, but he was happy for years. That was worth something. And you can't say the seal-woman completely hated her life as a human being. Remember, she still followed the children, and she helped Ivan catch fish."

**Group 4:** "The test of whether the woman was happy as a human being was what she did when she finally had the chance to choose. She chose to go back to being a seal. And not to become a human again. (We figure she could have done that if she wanted two, because the story says the seals became people every seven years.) Since she didn't want to live as a woman on earth, it was wrong for Ivan to keep in that state against her will."

**Group 3:** "But that wasn't the question. Sure, maybe Ivan was wrong to take the seal skin. Taking things that don't belong to you is wrong. But because he did take it, he had a marriage, and years of happiness, and those children were born. Like somebody said before: 'We don't get to choose our parents, but we're still happy we were born.'"

**Group 2:** "You said he had years of happy marriage. But what kind of marriage can that be, based on a lie? He was never honest with the woman he lived with—never honest about something that was really important to her. How can that be a happy marriage?"

**Group 1:** "Why are we making such a big deal about happiness? (Students laugh.) Really. Happiness isn't the only thing in life. For instance, maybe you move to a new town. At first you are unhappy. Of course you are—everything is strange and you miss your old friends. But in time you come to appreciate the new place. Maybe it has more to offer than the old place did. Maybe it has a lyceum, and the old place only had a primary school. It would have been short-sighted not to try out the new place, just because you wanted to be happy all the time."

**Teacher:** *We have to stop soon. But first, let's see if we can summarize what has been said. Some groups consider that it would have been better if he hadn't taken the skin. You said that is because he trapped the woman in human form against her will, and was never honest with her. She wasn't really happy—the evidence for that is that she turned back into a seal when she had the choice.*

*Other groups said that, on balance, it was better that he did take the seal skin. A family was created, children were brought into the world, and Ivan and the woman had years of companionship—whether or not you could say they were really happy. And besides, as we just heard, happiness may not be the only factor in deciding if something was a good decision or not.*

*We might say that those of you who took the first view put most of your emphasis on the woman's rights. The woman was treated unfairly, not just in the beginning, but the whole time she and Ivan lived together, and nothing could justify that. And those of you who took the second view focused on the consequences of the action. Stealing the blanket, even if it mean treating the woman unfairly, led to the creation of that family and those children, and that benefit outweighed the harm that was done to the woman.*

**Student 1:** "But who is right?"

**Teacher:** *Who do <u>you</u> think is right*

**Student 1:** "I think in a way, both sides are. At least until we argue this a lot further, we can't say that one position is really better than the other."

**<u>the lesson ends here</u>**

## REVIEWING THE LESSON

At the beginning of this lesson, you were invited to think about it in two ways: as *a student in the class*, and as *the teacher.*

Take a moment and reflect on how it would have felt to be a student participating in this lesson. (It may help to write down your thoughts on a piece of paper.)

**How did you feel**—interested, engaged, important, detached, controlled, or bored?

**What kind of thinking did you do**—memorize details, find main ideas, look below the surface at important issues, or make interpretations and support interpretations with reasons?

**What will you carry away from the lesson**—information, important ideas, or thinking skills?

Now think back over this lesson as if you had been the teacher. Recall the steps to this lesson. They were:

**Predicting from Terms:** A technique for having students try to anticipate the story they are about to read from a half dozen terms from the story.

**Directed Listening-Thinking Activity:** A method of telling or reading a story to the whole class, stopping to ask for predictions, and later for confirmations of those predictions.

**Shared Inquiry Method**: A method of discussion guided by the teacher, in which the teacher puts a series of open-ended questions to the class, asks students to write their individual responses, and encourages discussion among the students.

**Discussion Web:** An activity that employed a graphic organizer, in which pairs working with other pairs first listed reasons for and against a proposition, then joined a discussion with another pair and reached a conclusion.

Here follows a review of the methods that were used in this lesson.

# METHODS

 ## PREDICTING FROM TERMS
The **Predicting from Terms** procedure is used in the anticipation phase of a lesson to encourage the students to think along the lines of a text they are about to hear or read.

 **RATIONALE:** Predicting what a text will contain from knowing terms from the text raises students' curiosity and readiness to learn. It may also reduce some of the distance students feel from written works. For example, they are about to hear a story by a professional author, but the students have demonstrated that they are capable of producing stories too. Predicting from Terms teaches students to listen or read actively, consider important vocabulary, use their awareness of the genre of a text to know what to expect from it, and to collaborate with others to solve a problem.

 **GROUP SIZE:** Predicting from Terms is carried out in pairs. There can be an unlimited number of pairs within a classroom.

 **RESOURCES:** Predicting from Terms requires a chalk board on which to write the terms.

 **TIME REQUIRED:** It should be done quickly: five or six minutes at the most.

 **ACTIVITY:**
**Step 1:** Before the class begins, the teacher chooses five or six terms from the text that point to key concepts, important events, or main characters.

**Step 2:** The teacher writes the terms on the chalk board and tells the students these terms will appear in the story or the text. The teacher names the genre or style of writing they are about to hear, and may explain how the genre will constrain the kind of events or information they should expect.

**Step 3:** The teacher asks pairs of students to try to imagine—as the case may be—a story, an explanation, an argumentative essay that will have all of those terms in it. They have four minutes to do so.

**Step 4:** After three or four minutes, the teacher invites just a few pairs to share their imagined stories or other texts. The teacher accepts these with encouragement, but doesn't say if they are similar or dissimilar to what they are about to hear.

**Step 5:** The students are told to listen carefully to what the teacher is about to tell or read, and see how it compares with what they imagined.

**Step 6:** After they have heard or read the text, students are asked to compare the version they imagined with the actual version. What led them to be more or less successful?

 **TIPS:** Remember that this is an anticipation activity, and there is much more to do in the lesson. So keep it brief. Try to finish up in five minutes. That means usually only two pairs will have time to share what they imagined. Explain to the others that their turn to share will come another time.

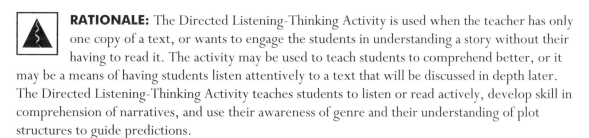 **DIRECTED LISTENING-THINKING ACTIVITY**

The **Directed Listening-Thinking Activity** is used in the building knowledge phase of a lesson, the part of a lesson in which students are inquiring to make meaning. In this activity, students listen to a story that is told or read to them and make predictions about what will come next. They are asked to confirm their predictions from time to time with information from the text, and to make new predictions.

**RATIONALE:** The Directed Listening-Thinking Activity is used when the teacher has only one copy of a text, or wants to engage the students in understanding a story without their having to read it. The activity may be used to teach students to comprehend better, or it may be a means of having students listen attentively to a text that will be discussed in depth later. The Directed Listening-Thinking Activity teaches students to listen or read actively, develop skill in comprehension of narratives, and use their awareness of genre and their understanding of plot structures to guide predictions.

 **GROUP SIZE:** The Directed Listening Thinking Activity may be done with groups ranging from about six students to thirty. More than that excessively limits their participation.

 **RESOURCES:** The Directed Listening Thinking Activity requires only that the teacher know a good story to tell or have a written version to read. Those stories work best that are predictable: where there is a problem and a sequence of actions toward a conclusion.

**TIME REQUIRED:** The time needed for the activity depends on the length of the story and how closely the teacher decides to have students consider it. It should not be longer than about 30 minutes.

**ACTIVITY:**

**Step 1:** The teacher chooses a predicable story for sharing with the class.

**Step 2:** The teacher chooses stopping points—places where something is about to happen or a question is about to be answered. There should be around five of these—more will break up the flow of the story, and momentum (and interest) will be reduced.

**Step 3:** The teacher may share just the title, and explain the genre of the story (folktale, realistic fiction, fable, myth, etc.) and ask students what things they think might happen in it. The teacher presses the students to make the most specific predictions they can. After the predictions have been made, the teacher challenges students to decide which predictions they think will come through (even if someone else made them), and then listen carefully to see what will happen.

**Step 4:** The teacher reads or tells the next section of the story up to the next stopping place, asks which predictions are coming true, and what makes students think so. Then students are asked to make more predictions, and the prediction and confirmation cycle continues until the story is finished.

**Step 5:** After the story is finished, students are asked to reflect on their predictions. Which predictions turned out to be accurate? How were they able to make them? How did their awareness of the genre, plot, or theme of the story help them predict what would come next? What advice would they give other students for making accurate predictions?

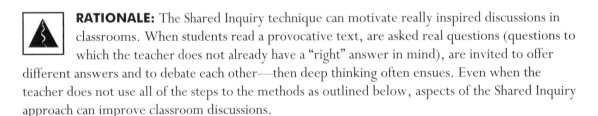

## SHARED INQUIRY APPROACH

The **Shared Inquiry Approach** is one way for a teacher to lead a deep discussion into a work of literature. It is best done with a group of eight to ten students, to maximize participation, but allow for a diversity of ideas.

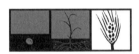

**RATIONALE:** The Shared Inquiry technique can motivate really inspired discussions in classrooms. When students read a provocative text, are asked real questions (questions to which the teacher does not already have a "right" answer in mind), are invited to offer different answers and to debate each other—then deep thinking often ensues. Even when the teacher does not use all of the steps to the methods as outlined below, aspects of the Shared Inquiry approach can improve classroom discussions.

**GROUP SIZE:** The Shared Inquiry Approach works very well with groups of students from six up to twenty. Groups of fewer students may not offer the best variety of ideas, and larger groups may not afford sufficient opportunities for participation. If there are more than 20 students in the classroom, the other students can be given another task to carry out while the first group carries on a Shared Inquiry discussion.

**RESOURCES:** Every student will need access to the text that will be discussed. The text may be read aloud or told to them, or they may be given copies to read.

**TIME REQUIRED:** A Shared Inquiry discussion should take at least 25 minutes. It can run for up to 45 minutes without the students losing interest.

**ACTIVITY:**

**Step 1:** Choose a work that encourages discussion. Before the discussion takes place, the teacher has chosen a work or part of a work that encourages discussion. Such a work should lend itself to more than one interpretation (not all works do this well) and raise interesting issues. Folk stories often meet these criteria surprisingly well.

**Step 2:** Have the students read the material. The teacher makes sure that all of the students have read the material carefully. It is preferable if the students read the material twice before discussing it—or that they read it using the Directed Reading Activity of Directed Reading-Thinking Activity described ealier.

**Step 3:** Prepare questions for discussion. The teacher prepares four or five discussion questions. These should be what Great Books calls **Interpretive Questions**, and they have three criteria:

1. They are real questions: the sort of question one might ask a friend, as you walk together, about a provocative movie.

2. They have more than one defensible answer. (This criterion invites debate. If it is not met, the discussion won't be a discussion, but a read-my-mind exercise).

3. They must lead the discussion into the text. A question like, "Why was the giant's wife kinder to Jack than his own mother was?" leads the students to talk about what is in the text first, even though they may then comment on what they know from experience. A question like, "Have you ever done anything as brave as Jack?" leads the discussion away from the text and out into twenty-five different directions.

**Step 4:** Share a Question. The teacher writes the first question on the chalk board for all of the students to answer.

**Step 5:** The students consider the question and write down their answers. The teacher asks the students to think about the question, and then briefly write down their answers. (If the students are so young that writing answers is laborious, the teacher can say he will count to 60 before he calls on anyone, so they should be thinking about their answers for all of that time).

**Step 6:** The teacher elicits answers from the students. As the teacher invites students to answer she may encourage reluctant speakers to read what they wrote. She provokes debate between students, pointing out differences in what they say and asking those and other students to expand on the differences. She may press students to support their ideas with references to the text or to restate ideas more clearly. She does not, however, correct a student or in any way suggest that any one answer is right or wrong. Finally, the teacher does not offer her own answer to the question.

**Step 7:** The teacher keeps a *seating chart.* A seating chart is a list of the students' names with a brief version of each student's answer. The teacher uses the seating chart to convey respect for the students' thoughts, to slow down the conversation, to keep a record of what has been said, to make note of who has participated and who has not.

**Step 8:** The teacher summarizes the discussion. When discussion of a question seems to have run its course, the teacher reads aloud her summaries of the students' comments. Then the teacher or one of the students makes a summary of the discussion of that question.

**Step 9:** The teacher asks more questions. The teacher may write another question on the chalk board and proceed as before. But at the teacher's option, once the discussion gets going, she follows the students' lead and continues to discuss the issues and questions they raise.

---

I have gained optimism and self-assurance, but the main thing—I am ready to listen and to accept different viewpoints, even though they radically differ from my opinion.

(Teacher from Latvia)

---

 **ASSESSMENT:** It is a challenge to assess students' performance in a Shared Inquiry discussion, because the students are not expected to reach a correct answer. Nonetheless, the teacher can observe each student as she or he participates, and assess the quality of her participation by means of a **rubric**. The teacher may wish to know:

- How willing is each student to participate?
- Does the student reach an insightful answer?
- Can the student support her answer with evidence from the text?

**TIPS:** Even when they don't use the whole approach, many teachers use aspects of the Shared Inquiry Approach in conducting book discussions. For example, they may ask students to write down ideas to bring to a discussion, or they may take notes during the discussion, or they are careful to draw out the students' ideas and not dominate the discussion themselves.

The teacher can construct a rubric for assessing the students' participation in the activity that may look like the following:

| RUBRIC TO ASSESS PARTICIPATION IN DISCUSSION | TO A SMALL EXTENT | TO A MODERATE EXTENT | TO A GREAT EXTENT |
|---|---|---|---|
| How willing is each student to participate? | | | |
| Does the student reach an insightful answer? | | | |
| Can the student support her answer with evidence from the text? | | | |

Another way to assess the students' performance is to ask them to write an essay following the discussion, in which they set out an interpretation and support it with reasons from the text. The essay can be evaluated using the last two criteria in the above rubric, plus others specific to writing:

| RUBRIC TO EVALUATE A WRITTEN ESSAY | TO A SMALL EXTENT | TO A MODERATE EXTENT | TO A GREAT EXTENT |
|---|---|---|---|
| Does the student reach an insightful answer? | | | |
| Can the student support her answer with evidence from the text? | | | |
| Is the paper of adequate length? | | | |
| Is the paper well organized? | | | |
| Does the paper make its points clearly, and stick to the topic at hand? | | | |
| Does the writer use words precisely and clearly? | | | |

For more information about rubrics, please see the discussion on assessment in Section 3.

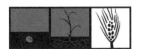

## DISCUSSION WEB

The **Discussion Web** combines the dynamics of a good discussion with cooperative learning techniques. Because the interaction in the activity takes place in pairs and within groups of four students, the activity can be successfully done in classes of any size. For older students, the Discussion Web can serve as a sound preparation for writing an argumentative essay. The Discussion Web is used in the consolidation phase of the lesson, the part in which students reflect back on what they have learned, and think further about the implication of the meaning they have made.

**RATIONALE:** Taking a position on a controversial issue and supporting it with reasons is an aspect of critical thinking. It is useful preparation for participation in an open society. The Discussion Web teaches students to play an active role in the discussion, take a position on a debatable or controversial issue, support their position with reasons, and collaborate with others to promote a point of view.

**GROUP SIZE:** The Discussion Web is done with at least eight students in groups of four, and there can be any number of these groups.

**RESOURCES:** The Discussion Web requires that each pair of students have a piece of paper on which to write the Discussion Web graphic organizer (see next page). Students will need pencils or pens for recording their ideas.

**TIME REQUIRED:** The activity can be conducted in 20 to 30 minutes.

**ACTIVITY:**

**Step 1:** The teacher prepares a thoughtful *binary* question. A binary question is one that has two possible answers. It might be answered "yes" or "no" with support. For example, if discussing the story "Ivan and the Seal Skin," a binary discussion question might be, "Was Ivan right to steal the seal skin?"

**Step 2:** The teacher asks pairs of students to prepare a Discussion Web chart. The chart looks like the one on the next page. Each of those pairs of students take four or five minutes to think up and list three reasons that support **both** sides of the argument. They list those argument on one Discussion Web sheet.

**Step 3:** Each pair of students joins another pair. They review the answers they had on both sides of the issue, and add to each other's list.

**Step 4:** The four students argue the issue through until they reach a conclusion. That is, the four students reach a position they agree upon, with a list of reasons that support it. They enter their position in the box labeled **conclusion** on the Discussion Web sheet.

**Step 5:** The teacher calls on several groups of four to give brief reports of their position and the reasons that support it. The teacher can invite the groups to debate each other, if they took different sides of the argument.

**TIPS:** It is a good idea for the teacher to decide in advance how much "closure," or agreement, you want the students to reach on a question. Those we call "higher order" questions (see below) often have more than one answer that can be justified with good reasons. It would be a mistake to try to force the students to reach one answer to such questions. For example, in the discussion of "Ivan and the Seal Skin," the question of whether it would have been better if Ivan had not taken the skin has no final answer. As teachers, we want to see students take a position on this question and justify it with reasons. On the other hand, where certainty is possible, we should not shrink from it. Suppose, for example, the question were this: "Would it have been better if Ivan had been honest with his wife, given her back her skin, and let her decide whether to stay or go?" Then it would be reasonable for students to agree that, yes, that would have been better.

## VARIATIONS AND RELATED METHODS

 **DEBATES**
With students in third grade and up, it is often useful to follow the Discussion Web activity with a **Debate**. The purpose of the debate is not to declare winners and losers, but to help the students practice making claims and defending them with reasons, even when others defend different claims. Working with claims, reasons, and arguments; debating ideas without attacking people—these are key elements in critical thinking.

 **RATIONALE:** Learning to debate issues often requires thorough comprehension of the topic. The Debate method also teaches students to take a position on a debatable or controversial issue, support their position with reasons, defend a position against counter-arguments, and focus on ideas without attacking people.

 **GROUP SIZE:** Debates are done with the whole class.

 **RESOURCES:** The debate requires no resources.

 **TIME REQUIRED:** The activity can be conducted in 20 to 30 minutes.

This is more dynamic activity, based on constructive contradiction. The student is forced to find arguments on both sides, which means they will think critically and reach a conclusion that they will have to support. This means they will have to confront their own beliefs and entertain arguments against them.

(Middle-school teacher, Romania)

**ACTIVITY:**

**Step 1:** Prepare a binary question. To have a Debate, you need a *binary question*—that is, a question that has a yes/no answer. (Since the Discussion Web we saw above also uses binary questions, we often follow the Discussion Web with a Debate.) The teacher thinks of a question that will truly divide the students' opinions, and puts the question on the chalk board for all to see. (If you are not sure the question will divide the students roughly equally, ask for a show of hands on each side of the issue before proceeding with the debate.)

**Step 2:** The students think about the question and discuss it freely. They may first jot down their response on a piece of paper, and after two minutes share their answer with a partner in order to stimulate more ideas.

**Step 3:** The teacher asks students to divide up. Those who believe one answer to the question is right should go stand along the wall on one side of the room; those who think the other is right should stand along the wall on the other side. Those who are truly undecided (that is, after thinking about it, they believe both sides are partially right or neither side is right) should stand along the middle wall.

**Step 4:** The teacher explains the two ground rules:

   a. Students must not be rude to each other. (The teacher may have to explain and demonstrate what this means.)

   b. If students hear an argument that makes them want to change their minds, they should walk to the other side (or to the middle).

**Step 5:** The students on each side have three or four minutes to decide *why* they are on that side. Then the teacher asks them with a sentence that states their position. The teacher asks the students on each side to appoint someone to say that sentence.

**Step 6:** One person from each side (including the undecided group) states that group's position.

**Step 7:** Now anyone on any team may say things (counter-arguments or rebuttals) in response to what the other team has said, or more reasons in support of their own side.

**Step 8:** The teacher monitors the activity to make sure the tone stays away from negative attacks. The teacher asks for clarification. He offers an idea or two as necessary from the devil's advocate position. He changes sides. He encourages the students to change sides if they are persuaded to.

**Step 9:** When the debate has proceeded 10 or 15 minutes, the teacher asks each side to summarize what they have said.

**Step 10:** The teacher "debriefs" the debate by reviewing the ideas and arguments that came to light. Or she may ask each student to write an argumentative essay, writing down what she believes about the issue and why.

**TIPS:** As the debate proceeds, you can model the behavior of changing sides with a pantomime: by looking thoughtful for a moment after someone offers a good argument, and moving to the other side.

 **REFLECTIONS:** Debates can be a useful and energizing way of exploring ideas. But the teacher must be careful to see that competitive spirits don't take over the activity and push past nuanced ideas.

 ## SAVE THE LAST WORD FOR ME
**Save the Last Word for Me** provides a framework for class discussion of a text, either narrative or expository. This strategy is particularly helpful in getting the quieter and more reluctant students to participate in class discussions

 **RATIONALE:** Teachers are usually the ones who have "the last word" on a topic during a class discussion. Giving students the opportunity to have "the last word" on a topic can be motivating and can give their ideas a sense of read importance. The Save the Last Word for Me method teaches students to identify issues of interest to themselves in a text they read and to take responsibility for a whole-class discussion

 **GROUP SIZE:** Save the Last Word for Me is done with the whole class.

 **RESOURCES:** "Save the last word for me" requires small slips of paper for students to write their comments on. It also requires a text to read or a topic to consider.

 **TIME REQUIRED:** The activity can be conducted in 20 to 40 minutes.

 **ACTIVITY:**
**Step 1:** The teacher tells the students before they read a text to find passages that intrigue them, perplex them, excite them, or enrage them.

**Step 2:** The students write those passages on one side of a small piece of paper. They should be sure to note the number of the page it came from.

**Step 3:** The students should write a comment on the other side of the piece of paper. That is, they should say what it was that intrigued them, perplexed them, excited them, or enraged them.

**Step 4:** During the next class period, the teacher calls upon one student at a time to read her quotation (but not her comment). Then that student has control of the class, as he invites other students to comment on that quotation. The teacher may comment too, but should do so only after several other students have had their say, and while more comments are forthcoming.

**Step 5:** When the class has had their chance to comment, the student who chose the quotation turns over her piece of paper and reads her comment. That is the last word. No other student and not even the teacher should comment on the quotation after that.

**Step 6:** The teacher calls on other students to share their quotations and lead the class discussion. The teacher may also take a turn. It is not necessary to call on every student to share a quotation. Half a dozen may suffice for a single class session.

 **REFLECTIONS:** If a teacher is used to lecturing, she or he may be surprised to see how many points students raise in the course of the Save the Last Word for Me activity that would have been in the lecture notes!

# ABC CHART

Let's see how the preceding methods, variations, and related methods fit into the Anticipation/Building Knowledge/Consolidation rubric. This chart will help you use the methods in this guide to make your own lesson plans using the ABC rubric.

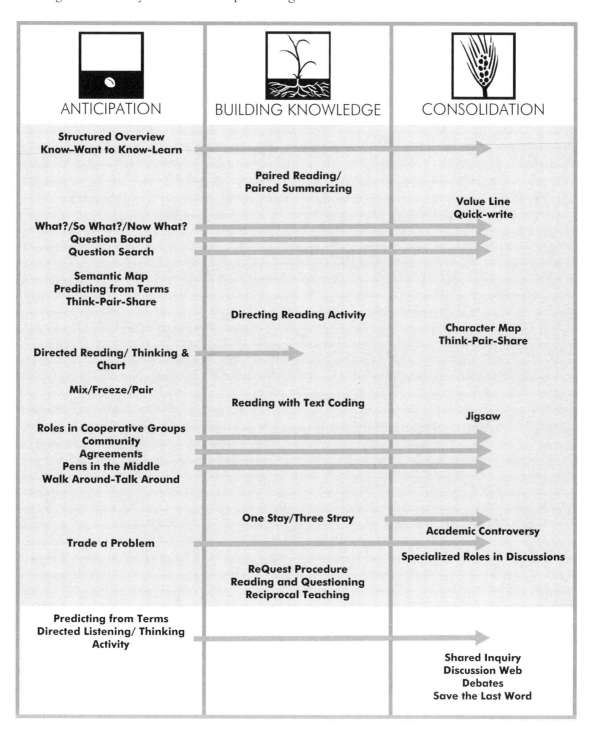

# FIFTH CORE LESSON: WRITING AND INQUIRY

The core lesson in this section creates an opportunity for students to become creators of knowledge themselves, using an inquiry technique called the **I-Search Procedure**. Later in this section is a procedure for guiding students in social action, using an approach called **Service Learning**.

The I-Search Procedure allows students to go beyond the information in their books and classrooms and generate new information through interviews, observations, and other sorts of inquiries outside their classrooms and schools. Given the nature of the procedure, the project will likely take place over several days with parts of the work occurring during the school day and other parts after school or on the weekends. The I-Search addresses several elements of the inquiry process and allows the students to:

- Ask interesting questions that reflect their personal interests and the theme of a recent lesson,
- Develop plans for conducting their searches,
- Carry out their plans, collect, organize, and consolidate the results, and
- Share their work with their peers and others by presenting a final report on the I-Search question and their own experiences while conducting the I-Search.

The I-Search Procedure (Macrorie 1988) can be organized around the **anticipation, building, and consolidation** structure as are other lessons presented in this guidebook and is often used to extend students' learning beyond a recently presented lesson. The teacher and students of an eigth grade class have completed a unit on government and the legislative process in their province.

## HOW TO READ THIS LESSON

As you read the following demonstration lesson, please bear in mind that its purpose is to demonstrate teaching methods. Think about this lesson in two ways.

1. Imagine that you are *a student* who is participating in this lesson. What is your experience? What kind of thinking are you doing? What are you learning?

2. Then think yourself into the role of *the teacher* who is leading the lesson. What are you doing? Why are you doing it? How are you handling the three phases of the lesson—anticipation, building knowledge, and consolidation?

# LESSON

## ANTICIPATION

The first phase of the **I-Search** begins much like the K-W-L in that the teacher orients the students to what they already **know** about a topic and helps them develop questions about what they might **want** to know about some issue of importance to the students. In this case, the teacher reminded the students of the process of decision making in the government, and presented a situation that would be reasonable for the students to investigate.

The teacher reminded the students that a local non-governmental agency (NGO) had committed funds to develop a children's park in our village and the decision about where to build it and what type of park to build was not yet decided, but would be made by the village council.

To begin the I-Search Procedure, the students decide on their questions.

**Teacher:** *In the unit we completed last week, we discussed how the government in our province makes decisions. As you have heard, a local NGO has offered to build a people's park in our village. The village council has not yet decided where this park should be located and how it should be designed. They are gathering information with which to make those decisions. If you were in the village council, what sorts of information might you need as you planned the park? Let's Brainstorm some questions we might ask. I'll write them on the board as you ask them.*

**Student 1:** "I'd want to know where we might build it. Should it be near our river or should it be near the bazaar?"

**Student 2:** "I think the important question is whether or not it would have some places to buy soft drinks or other treats."

**Student 3:** "I don't think it is important to know whether people will sell things in the park."

**Teacher:** *Remember, in brainstorming, we just give our input; we will discuss the merits of the ideas later.*

**Student 4:** "What about the kinds of things we will have in the park? Will we have a carousel or a football field? I think that is important to know."

**Teacher:** *We have some interesting questions. Now, I'd like you to turn to a neighbor and think of other important questions that you would ask if you were on the village council and deciding about the park. Remember, that we are interested in thoughtful questions that provide not only answers, but some reasons for the answers. Take about three or four minutes to discuss some questions and then each pair should decide on one question to ask.*

The teacher walks among the pairs listening to the discussions, prompting when necessary.

**Teacher:** *I want each pair to select one person to read the pair's question. If your question has already been asked there is no need to repeat it.*

Pairs read their questions and the teacher writes them on the board.

**Teacher:** *As you think about your question, are there questions other pairs have suggested that might fit with the theme of yours?*

The students discuss the questions further, until they have agreed on this list of questions:

1. What should be the purposes of the park?
2. Who should the park be for? What will each group of users want to do there?
3. What activities should be supported? What activities should not be allowed?
4. What different areas should be arranged? With what features in each?
5. How will the park be kept safe?
6. How will the park be kept clean and in good repair?
7. Where should the park be located?
8. How much money or effort will it cost to maintain the park? And where will it come from?

Each group chooses its question.

**Teacher:** *The next step is to figure out how we might answer these questions. So, each group or pair now should think about who you might approach to find the answers. Take a few minutes and think about the people who might help you answer your question.*

Students begin discussing who they might approach and how they might approach them to answer their questions. The teacher circulates among the pairs encouraging them and assisting them by asking leading questions to help them identify potential resources.

**Student** [raising her hand to ask the teacher for assistance]: *So, if we want to know where they should build the park, we need to ask some people on the village council, right?*

**Teacher** [walks to the pair working on the "location" question]: *They will make the final decision, so you would likely need to ask them some questions. Who else might be interested in where they put the park?*

**Student** [from "location" pair]: *You know the owners of the shops in the square don't like it when we play soccer in front of their businesses; I think they would want the park away from the center of the village.*

**Student** [from "location" pair]: *I think that our families would want the park to be near the places where the most people live.*

**Teacher:** *It sounds like you two have some interesting questions and ideas. Why don't you think of questions to ask the different people? Remember, when we discussed different types of questions, we found that questions that lead to the best information usually get at how or why something happens or how or why someone thinks a certain way. So, as you construct your questions, remember to think about that.*

Students in the "location" pair continue to work on questions.

The teacher continues to move from group to group helping with their focus and questions.

**Teacher:** *When you have your questions ready, raise your hands and I'll help you edit them.*

**Student 1** ["location" pair raise their hands to signal the teacher]: "We have some questions we think we'd like to ask:

1. How will the village council decide where to put the park?
2. I wonder if they will ask us young people where we want the park.
3. What about older people? Where do you think they want to have the park?

I'll bet the shopkeepers would like the park in the next province."

**Teacher:** *You said you were interested in knowing about what others want. How do you know the shopkeepers do not want the park nearby?*

**Student 1:** "Well, I guess we could ask them. I just thought that since they yelled at us for playing soccer, they did not like us around. Okay, we should ask them too."

**Teacher:** *Again, remember questions like "what" and "where" might get an answer, but you still will not know about the reasons for their answers. Try to rewrite some questions so that you can find out why others think the way they do about the park's location. Be sure to include the people you will interview for each question.*

The teacher continues to circulate about the class helping students refine their I-Search interviews.

**Teacher** [to the whole class]: *I want each pair to finish up on your questions and put them on the paper taped to the wall for others to see. Be sure to write your big question at the top of the page.*

**Students** ["location" pair write their final questions on the paper]:

### The "Big" Question: Where might we place the park?

1. How will the village council decide where to build the park?
2. Where do parents think the park should be built and why do they think it?
3. Where do young people think the park should be built and why do they think it?
4. Where do the shopkeepers think the park should be built and why do they think it?

Now begins the second step in the I-Search—developing a plan.

**Teacher:** *We have many very good questions on a variety of topics. For a home task, each of you is to think of a way you might answer the questions. Tomorrow during social studies, we will make a plan for answering your questions. As you plan for your information gathering, I want you to think about the following questions* [The teacher has written these questions on the board or on a sheet of paper taped to the board.]:

1. How will we identify the individuals we might interview to answer our questions?
2. How will we contact them and arrange for a time to ask them our questions?
3. How will we make sure their answers are recorded accurately?
4. How will we make our interviews polite and respectful to those we interview?

The next day during social studies class the teacher revisits the I-Search.

**Teacher:** *I want you to find your I-Search partner and discuss for a few minutes how you answered the questions you had as a home task. Your job is to list your ideas for each question. When you complete this task, raise your hand and I will discuss your ideas.*

**Students** ["location" pair raise their hands]: "Okay, we can answer the questions for parents, kids, and shopkeepers. We both know our friends' parents, so we could interview them when we visit our friends. We could also interview our friends here at school. Even the shopkeepers will not be difficult to interview, since I have an uncle who owns a small food store in the center of the village. I go there often and he has many friends who are shopkeepers."

**Teacher:** *So, it seems that you have answered your first question for parents, kids, and shopkeepers. What about the village council?*

**Student:** "We don't know. We have never spoken with a government official. Why would they want to talk with us? We are just students."

**Teacher:** *Well, our village council members are also parents and shopkeepers. When one is selected for the village council, one does not give up other things. So, let's talk about how we might find a council member to interview. What are some things you might do to find someone on the village council to interview?*

**Student 1:** "I suppose I could ask my father if he knows someone."

**Student 2** [to the teacher]: "Do you know anyone who is on the village council?"

**Teacher:** *Yes, the brother of the director of our school is on the council.*

**Student 1:** "Do you think we could ask our director to see if we could meet with his brother?"

**Teacher:** *I think when you have your plan made, that would be a good idea. So, what questions have you answered?*

**Student 2:** "Well, we have decided who we will interview."

**Student 1:** "And it looks like that if the director will help us talk to his brother, we have answered the second question."

**Teacher:** *I think so too. Now, what about the third question. How will you record the answers people give you? Take a few more minutes and see what you can do about that?*

After circulating among the student pairs, the teacher discovers that many are having a difficult time figuring out how to record their answers as they interview. So the teacher decides to do a "just-in-time" mini-lesson on this topic.

**Teacher:** *Class, it seems that many of you are having some difficulty deciding how to record the answers to your interview questions. It is a challenge. You have to keep the interest of the person you are interviewing, ask* *the questions in a way that gets the information you need, and record the answers faithfully to the way the person answers. It is a challenge. One advantage you have is that you are working in pairs. On some interviews one member of the pair might ask the questions and the other record. For the other interviews, you might switch roles so both members get practice in both roles. Now, what sorts of information, outside the answers, do you think we need to have?*

**Student 1:** "Well, we need to be able to know who we interviewed after the interview is over."

**Teacher** [writes students' responses on the board as they answer]: *Good, what else?*

**Student 2:** "Maybe we need to know who did the interview and who wrote the answers."

**Teacher:** *Why do you think that is important?*

**Student 2:** "Well, if we are going to take turns doing the interviews, it would be important to keep track of who does what."

**Teacher:** *I think you have a point. Now, we know we need to have the name of the person who is interviewed and the name of the interviewer. What else will we need to write during the interview?*

**Student 4:** "I think the day we do the interview."

**Teacher:** *Yes, I think it is a good idea to write the date and the time also. This just helps you keep good records. Some people who do research this way think when people are interviewed is an important thing to know. What else?*

The students are quiet. They look at each other and the teacher. They seem to be stuck.

**Teacher:** *Okay. I think you are thinking about details. What is the most important thing to record when we ask someone a question?*

**Student 5:** "Oh, yes, the answer!"

**Teacher:** *Yes, that is why you are there. Now, how can we do this? In large research projects, where they have many resources, sometimes they use tape recorders or video recorders. However, we do not have those in our village. So, how do you think we can record what the person said?*

**Student 3:** "Well, you said that one of us would ask the questions and the other would take notes. Isn't that what we will do? Take notes?"

**Teacher:** *Yes, that is the idea. Now, how will we remember to include all the information we just identified—the name of the person being interviewed, the name of the interviewer, and the day and time of the interview?*

**Student 6:** "We will just write it on our journal pages."

**Teacher:** *Yes, but how will you remember to do all that?*

**Student 6:** "We just will!"

**Teacher:** *How do you think your father or mother remembers what to buy at the food store?*

**Student 7:** "They make a list?"

**Teacher:** *Yes, why do they do that?*

**Student 7:** "So they don't forget."

**Teacher:** *Yes, so we might need to make a sort of list of things to remember. Sometimes people who do this type of work use a form that has room for all the information. Let's make a form by drawing one on the board.*

Teacher draws an outline for the form on the board:

| Name of person interviewed | Name of interviewer | Date and time of interview |
|---|---|---|
|  |  |  |

**Question: (Write the question here.)**

**How did I feel about the interview?**

**Teacher:** *What do you see on the form that we have not discussed yet?*

**Student 7:** "You put a question about how we feel about the interview."

**Teacher:** *That's right. Sometimes when researchers do this work, they want to record how they felt the inter-view went. This helps them see how they might do things differently next time, or when they feel an interview went exceptionally well, what they want to do the same next time. This is an important part of the I-Search. So, after you leave the interview, you might take a moment and do a Quick-write on this item. Or, you might choose to discuss the interview with your partner and write something more detailed. Or you might want to do both.*

*So, now we have a form to use in our interviews. This is the way some people record and organize the information they collect from interviews. Another good thing about using this sort of record keeping is that the interviewer is able to read the notes taken by the recorder and add new ideas about the interview. So if the recorder was writing while the person being interviewed said something important, the interviewer might add those ideas after the interview. Be sure to record that the information was added and who added it. Now, what is the last question we have on our list?*

**Student 8:** "It is the question about being polite and respectful of the people we interview."

**Teacher:** *Yes, why is that important?*

**Student 6:** "Well, I guess we want to be nice so they will think we have a good class."

**Student 9:** "Yes, but my father says that we should just be nice to everyone."

**Teacher:** *These are both excellent answers. When you are working on a class project, you are representing our class and our school, so we want to be good representatives. But we also should remember that all people deserve to be treated well. So, for both reasons.*

*So, what are some ways we could be polite and show respect?*

**Student 3:** "We should thank them for helping us."

**Student 7:** "I think we should use the proper titles when we speak with the adults."

**Student 5:** "They need to know what we are doing, not just ask them the question."

**Teacher:** *These are all very good ways to be polite and show respect. One thing you suggested is to tell the people what we are doing and why we are asking these questions. Who can tell me what they would say to someone to let them know why we are doing the interviews?*

**Student 3:** "We could tell them we are doing it for a class project about the park the NGO is going to build."

**Teacher:** *Yes, that is a good thing to let them know. As a matter of fact, I will write a letter of introduction with our school logo on it for each of you so you can show it to the people you are going to interview. This will show them that it is official. Since some of you will be conducting interviews outside of school, I will also send a letter home to your parents telling them about the project just to make sure they know what we are doing and can give their approval.*

*So, we know who we are going to interview, how we will contact them, how we will record the information, and ways to be polite and respectful of those we interview. So, what shall we do next?*

**Student 4:** "Are we ready to do our interviews?"

**Student 7:** "I think I am. I'm ready!"

**Teacher:** *I think we are quite close. Tomorrow during social studies period, we will practice with each other. We will have an opportunity to try out our questions and practice recording our information. I will now hand out the letters for your parents so they will know what we are doing. If they agree, please bring the letter to school tomorrow. If they have questions, they are free to ask me.*

The following day during social studies, the teacher circulates a copy of the form developed the previous day.

**Teacher:** *Okay. Today we will practice our interviewing skills. I want each pair to turn to the pair next to you. Now, one of you in each pair is going to be the interviewer and the other the recorder. Now, each pair will interview the other asking one question from your list.*

The teacher circulates around the class observing the students as they practice their interviewing.

**Teacher:** *Now, it seems that you have completed the interview with your questions. I'd like to hear from you about how the interview went. First, lets hear from the recorders. How did it go for you? What answers did you get? What problems did you have?*

**Student 3:** "I could not write as fast as my friend talked and I am not sure I spelled all the words right."

**Teacher:** *Did any others have that problem?*

**Students** [several speak up at once]: "Yes, it was too fast. I had a hard time writing all the words."

**Teacher:** *Okay, recorders, when you think you missed something, you might simply say: "Excuse me, I missed what you said and I think it was important. Could you repeat it?" That is an excellent way to get the information and to show the person you are interviewing that you really care about what is said. Now, for this, don't worry about spelling all the words correctly. Remember, it is about getting the information accurately, not necessarily about spelling the words correctly. So, do you think you'd like to try this with those outside the class?*

The students all agree that they are ready.

**Teacher:** *Okay, here are your letters of introduction. For the group who is working on the question about the location of the park, remember, you are to meet the village council member at the café near the square after school today. I know it will require several days of interviewing outside of school for you to complete your work. So for the next couple of days, if you have questions or problems, just ask for some help. Otherwise we will continue with our regular lessons. On Friday, we will begin discussion about how to finish by writing a report based on our interviews.*

### the lesson ends here

REVIEWING THE LESSON

At the beginning of this lesson, you were invited to think about it in two ways: as *a student in the class*, and as *the teacher*.

Take a moment and reflect on how it would have felt to be a student participating in this lesson. (It may help to write down your thoughts on a piece of paper).

**How did you feel**—interested, engaged, important, detached, controlled, or bored?

**What kind of thinking did you do**—memorize details, find main ideas, look below the surface at important issues, or make interpretations and support interpretations with reasons?

**What will you carry away from the lesson**—information, important ideas, or thinking skills?

Now think back over this lesson as if you had been the teacher. Recall the steps to this lesson. They were:

**I-Search Procedure**: A somewhat informal approach to writing a research paper, in which students are asked to write in the first person as they explore their topic and their relation to it and later reflect on the process of conducting research.

**Research Plan:** A graphic organizer used to frame the students' research. The students list their research questions and the sources they will use to find answers to those questions.

# METHODS

 **I-SEARCH PROCEDURE**

 **RATIONALE:** The I-Search Procedure is an excellent way to engage students in doing research that matters to them personally. The I-Search Procedures helps students find out information that makes the school curriculum relevant, or even to create their own curriculum material.

 **GROUP SIZE:** The I-Search Procedure is done with the whole class.

 **RESOURCES:** The I-Search Procedure makes no particular demands on resources.

 **TIME REQUIRED:** It may take several days to several weeks to carry out.

 **ACTIVITY:**
**Step 1:** The students formulate questions about a topic. After they have been immersed in a topic, the students are helped to search their knowledge and curiosity and formulate a researchable question. Here you must be careful to make a distinction between a *topic* and a *question*. A topic is usually something you look up because it is assigned in school. A question is something you ask because you really want to find out. For example, "Gender and Education" is a topic; "Do the girls in this school feel that they are treated fairly?" is a question.

**Step 2:** The students make a **Research Plan**. The plan might incorporate several kinds of sources, including not only books and magazines, but interviews, surveys, and Internet-based searches. It can help make a search plan if students make an Inquiry Chart:

MAIN QUESTION:
## DO THE GIRLS IN THIS SCHOOL FEEL THAT THEY ARE TREATED FAIRLY?

|  | WHAT A SAMPLE OF GIRLS SAYS | WHAT A SAMPLE OF BOYS SAYS | WHAT THE SCHOOL DIRECTOR SAYS | WHAT A SAMPLE OF TEACHERS SAYS | WHAT A SAMPLE OF PARENTS SAYS |
|---|---|---|---|---|---|
| DO GIRLS GET CALLED ON AS OFTEN IN CLASS? |  |  |  |  |  |
| DO GIRLS DO AS WELL AS BOYS IN MATH AND SCIENCE AND LANGUAGE? |  |  |  |  |  |
| DO GIRLS GET TO PLAY SPORTS AS OFTEN AS BOYS? |  |  |  |  |  |
| DO GIRLS FEEL SAFE USING THE TOILETS? |  |  |  |  |  |
| DO GIRLS FEEL SAFE GOING TO AND FROM SCHOOL? |  |  |  |  |  |

**Step 3:** The students gather and record information. Students should be given instructions in all of the ways they may do the research. These will depend on the kinds of resources available. If they will mostly be interviewing people to find out about their topic, they will need procedures for arranging and conducting interviews.

They will need to know how to think of good questions to ask, how to treat their informants respectfully, and how to summarize the large amount of information they are likely to get. If they are using the Internet, they will need to know how to tell the difference between credible and unreliable sources—or the teacher may need to recommend some valuable and responsible sources.

If they are using the library, they will need to know how to locate information. They should also be taught note taking and outlining skills, as necessary. They may be taught to use graphic organizers (see the Inquiry Chart, above) as a way of visualizing their information before writing it up. They should also be taught how to make proper citations for the information they get from live interviews, from magazines and books, or from the Internet.

**Step 4:** The students write their paper. The paper should be formatted according to the outline given below.

**Step 5:** The students present their papers. The students submit the written papers to the teacher, and they may also give oral presentations or poster sessions on the papers for the whole class or the whole grade.

**Step 6:** The Paper is evaluated. The evaluation of the paper is conducted according to criteria in that are tied to the process and form of the paper, and that are communicated in advance. One good way to evaluate a paper is for the teacher to prepare a rubric (see Appendix 2). A rubric is a set of criteria with descriptions of good, fair, and poor performance on each standard. A rubric for an I-Search paper might look like the following:

| RUBRIC FOR AN I-SEARCH PAPER | NEEDS WORK 1 | ADEQUATE 2 | SUPERIOR 3 |
|---|---|---|---|
| DID YOU CHOOSE AND NARROW DOWN A GOOD RESEARCH QUESTION? | there is a topic, but it's not stated in terms of a question that can be easily answered | there is a question that can be answered, but the question doesn't promise to lead to an interesting research project | there is a question that is stated so that it invites an answer. It is a real question, we will be interested in seeing it answered |
| DID YOU SET OUT A WELL-STRUCTURED RESEARCH PLAN? | the plan is not clearly described | the plan is described clearly, but the plan is not as ambitious as it might be | the plan is ambitious and interesting and it is clearly described |
| DID YOU DESCRIBE THE PROCESS OF DISCOVERY? | little is said about your discovery process | you described what you did, but not what it meant to you—not what you learned | you described what you did, and what you learned |
| DID YOU PRESENT AND DISCUSS YOUR FINDINGS? | the findings were not clearly or fully presented | many of the findings were presented but not in a complete and interesting way | all of the important findings were presented, and in a complete and interesting way |
| DID YOU DESCRIBE WHAT YOU LEARNED ABOUT INQUIRY AND RESEARCH? | this section is only sketchily developed | this section is developed, but presented in a bland and uninteresting way | your self-analysis is rich and insightful. Others can learn about the process of inquiry from reading your account |
| DID YOU TREAT YOUR REFERENCES CAREFULLY? | the references were incompletely or incorrectly cited | most of the references are correctly or nearly correctly cited | all of the references are correctly or nearly correctly cited |

## A FORMAT FOR THE I-SEARCH INVESTIGATIVE PAPER

### Questions
In this section students will describe what they already knew about their topic when they began their search, and why they cared about or were interested in the topic. They will state a question to which they really wanted to find an answer.

### The Search Process
In this section, students describe the steps they carried out in the search. For example, students will describe what sources they began with, and how these led to further sources. Students will describe problems or breakthroughs in their search-tell when they really got interesting. Students can also tell how their questions changed or expanded as a result of the search process, and they should acknowledge the help they received from others in obtaining valuable sources.

### What Was Learned
Here students name three or four major findings or conclusions and support them with examples, stories, or arguments that will help the reader understand how they arrived at those conclusions. They will try to connect their findings with their original questions. They might also suggest further questions to explore in the future. Students should include any analyses they did: cause and effect, pro/con, compare and contrast, or sequencing.

### Lessons for the Writer
This section will give students a chance to describe how they have developed as a researcher. They will answer the question, "What do you now know about searching for information that you didn't know before?" To answer this question, students will describe those findings that meant the most to them. They might also discuss how their newly found knowledge will affect the way they act or think in the future. Finally, they might want to talk about the skills they have developed as a researcher and writer.

### References
In this section students list their references. These may include the people they interviewed, as well as the web sites they may have consulted, or the magazines or books.


## FURTHER METHODS FOR TEACHING WRITING

### The Writing Process
The **writing process approach** (Calkins 2000; Graves 1982; Murray 2003; Temple, Nathan, and Burris 1982) is a popular and highly successful approach to teaching the skills of effective composition to students of all ages. It requires a lot of pre-planning and organization in the beginning, but the work tapers off remarkably later on, once students begin to use one another as peer reviewers. And the payback in terms of improved student work is enormous. The method is based on research into the writing processes used by skilled adult writers; the steps these writers take to produce satisfying works have been identified and distilled into strategies for composing that can be taught to writers of all ages, including children in the primary grades.

The method actually describes the writing process; how a writer begins with an idea and gradually shapes that idea on the page to the point that it is successfully communicated to the readers. Reflection focuses on how the writers build connections between themselves and their readers around the theme developed by the writer from the original idea. Although the process is not quite step by step, the phases an author uses and returns to are easily taught and revisited. By working with and through these stages, students become credible authors, and writing becomes a vehicle for clarifying and expressing ideas.

Most descriptions of the writing process contain five phases: **rehearsing, drafting, revising, editing,** and **publishing.** The phases need not be followed in a sequence—writing is often recursive: that is, a writer may loop back through previous phases one or more times. The writing process described here may be used in all subject areas.

**Rehearsing:** Rehearsing is the act of finding a topic, gathering information, and collecting one's thoughts about the topic. Writers survey and ponder their ideas, trying to find a "center of gravity" that can become a topic (Elbow 1998). In this way, they begin to plan a way to write about their topic. Survey and pondering take time.

**Drafting:** Drafting is the act of setting ideas on paper in their initial form. The process is tentative and experimental. Writers display their ideas on paper or on a computer screen so they can see what they know and have to say about their topic. Once they have written them out, they can go on to the phase of revising. Although many young writers (indeed, most writers) do not have the habit of writing more than one version of a paper, proficient writers do. "Writing is rewriting," they say. Skilled teachers encourage writers to write freely in draft form, without being self-critical. Elegance and correctness will come later.

**Revising:** Revising is making the written work better. It is not correcting grammar and spelling, but rather the phase in which writers move ideas around, expand upon them, cut out nonessential parts, and otherwise make their ideas clearer, even elegant. Revising usually requires that writers distance themselves from their work. They often do this by holding **conferences** with other writers, or with a teacher. In the process of revising, authors may return to the work laid out in the rehearsal or drafting stages.

 **TIPS**—Student writers often learn a lot by hearing someone else read their work aloud. You can pair up students for conferences. Ask one student to read the paper of the other student aloud to that student. The student who wrote the paper should close his or her eyes and listen carefully as the first student reads EXACTLY what is in the work. Students will often hear errors or problems—missing words, redundancies, lack of coherence, etc.—that they missed when they reviewed their own papers. The student who wrote the paper will then need a few minutes to make changes and corrections. Of course, the two students then change roles and repeat the process.

**Editing:** Editing is the process of making a composition presentable before it is made public. During the editing phase paragraphs or pages may sometimes be cut or added, and the composition may have to be re-edited to ensure coherence. Usually, the editing habit must be taught. It consists of three points:

1. the discipline to ensure that the paper be correct
2. the ability to find errors
3. the knowledge to correct errors

**Publishing:** Publishing, or sharing a work with an audience, does not happen with every piece of writing. Sometimes writers record their thoughts for themselves only or for a single reader, and sometimes a work doesn't have sufficient merit to warrant sharing widely. But many times works that even young authors write can interest and delight others. Then the act of sharing them can be a source of great pride for the author, and fire the whole enterprise of writing with intense motivation. The prospect of sharing with an audience can make students write, rewrite, smooth, and refine—especially if they have seen other students' work received with appreciation. Publishing thus serves another purpose: it enables students to see what others are doing, and becomes a means of informal teaching about composition among peers.

Here are some ways in which students can publish (share) their work:

- Prepare a clean written copy to be posted on a bulletin board or taken home for sharing with the family.
- If a computer and printer are available, input the work into the computer and print it out, again for posting or sharing at home.
- Provide a copy to a classroom or school newspaper or newsletter.
- Share the work orally by reading it from the classroom Author's Chair, a very special chair in the classroom that is used only when an author, whether student or teacher, is sharing her or his original work.
- Ask the teacher to respond to it (not to correct it, but to respond to its content).
- Send it to a friend, perhaps by mail or electronic mail.
- Publish it as a book for the classroom or school library.
- Organize individual student work on a theme or topic into a class anthology.
- Publish it in a multimedia mode with illustrations, music.
- Publish it in a local newspaper, especially if the topic is of community interest.
- Participate in peer reading, in which pairs of students read their completed work to each other.
- Publish the work in the student's portfolio.

**Mini-lessons.** One activity that distinguishes the writing process approach from the traditional composition lesson is the mini-lesson: a "just-in-time" piece of instruction that is given to a whole class or a smaller group of students. A mini-lesson has a limited focus, and it shows writers a skill that they can apply right away. The teacher may introduce a brief lesson about a way of writing strong descriptions, interesting beginnings, or structured arguments. Most mini-lessons have the following format:

1. The teacher identifies a problem or issue common to most students' writing. The problem should be one that the students are capable of understanding and that is immediately relevant. For instance, a lesson on beginnings is most useful when students are working on the drafting or revision stages. There are also developmental concerns. For example, second grade is not the place to teach character development, but it may be a good place for students to learn that like ideas can be "clumped" together in a paragraph.

2. The teacher finds, creates, or helps students to find writing samples that demonstrate a point that is being taught. The example may be a negative one, or it may be a positive one, such as a piece of good professional writing that students can emulate. Alternatively, students may look at the beginnings of pieces that work well and talk about why they seem effective.

3. The teacher has the students apply the lesson immediately to their own writing. To continue the example of introductions, as a next step, we ask the students to pair up, locate papers they are working on, and examine their introductions. Are they as strong as they can be? If not, this is the opportunity to re-write and make them stronger.

4. Add points or features to a list of things students should look for during revision or proofreading conferences. Guidelines for students' conferences and proofreading checklists can be developed to remind students of the points that have been taught in the minilessons.

---

This is a different method of transmitting knowledge that brings you closer to your students and makes you feel forever young, forever capable of learning new things.

(Middle-school teacher, Romania)

---

## VARIATIONS AND RELATED METHODS

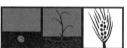 **SERVICE-LEARNING: SOCIAL ACTION AND REFLECTION** Service-Learning (Campus Compact 2003) is comprehensive activity that sends students out into the community to perform some useful service that is related to a course of study.

 **RATIONALE:** Teachers since the time of Comenius have understood the need to connect school learning to the world. Several versions of what is called **experiential learning** have developed to respond to that goal. A more recent development, **Service Learning**, might be described as "experience + commitment." In courses that use service learning activities, students are asked to work some time each week in a local agency that contributes to the public welfare. To the usual goals of adding flesh and blood to the content of the course and outlets for practicing their tools of inquiry, etc., Service Learning adds an emphasis on democratic participation and engaged citizenship.

 **GROUP SIZE:** Service Learning projects usually involve the whole class. Students may be assigned to carry out their service activities in small groups. If the number of students is large, you may have different portions of the class carry out their service activities at different times of the year.

**TIME REQUIRED:** Service Learning activities should be scheduled for periods of four weeks up to most of a year.

**ACTIVITY:**

**Step 1:** The teacher decides on service activities that students can carry out in connection to a course that he or she is teaching. Service assignments require students to provide some useful service outside of school to people or organizations that need it. The service activities may be performed every week for a period of months, or it may be carried out over a few weekends. Here are some examples:

| Subject area | Service activity |
|---|---|
| Biology | Working in a health clinic. |
| Language | Working in a newspaper office, book store, or library |
| Environmental studies | Planting trees and stopping up ravines with old tires and rocks to prevent soil erosion. |
| Social studies | Visiting old people who are confined to their homes, and talking to them about their memories of the past |
| Mathematics | Working for the town government, conducting surveys, and tabulating the results. |

Service placements should meet these criteria:

      a. They involve some work that the service client wants done;

      b. They do not replace a paid worker;

      c. The students have enough preparation to perform the work well;

      d. The work is interesting to the students and not onerous or dangerous.

**Step 2:** The teacher prepares the students to carry out some regular reflection on the service experience, and how that experience relates to the course. There are several ways students can be led to do this reflection:

Dual-Entry Diary: For this journal, students use a spiral notebook. On the left side of the journal, students describe their service experiences, personal thoughts, and reactions to their service activities. On the right side of the journal, they discuss how the first set of entries relates to key concepts, class presentations, and readings. Students may be asked to draw arrows indicating the relationships between their personal experience and the formal course content.

Critical Incident Journal: Students focus on a specific event that occurred at the service site. Students are then asked questions that explore their own reactions, and that lead them to relate their experiences to the course material. They may be asked:

*Describe an incident or situation that created a dilemma for you because you did not know how to act or what to say.*

    *Why was it such a confusing event?*
    *How did you, or others around the event, feel about it?*
    *What did you do, or what was the first thing that you considered doing?*
    *List three actions that you might have taken, and evaluate each one.*

*How does the course material relate to this issue, help you analyze the choices, and suggest a course of action that might be advisable?*

<u>Three Part Journal</u>: The teacher asks students to answer three general questions each time they make a journal entry:

a. **Describe** what happened in the service experience, including what you did, instances that puzzled or confused you, conversations you had, decisions you made, and plans you developed.

b. **Analyze** how what we are studying in the course helps you understand the service experience.

c. **Apply** the course materials and the service experience to your personal life. How are your own values and beliefs changing because of it?. (Campus Compact 2003; Bringle and Hatcher 1999).

<u>Directed Writings</u>: Students are asked to consider how a particular aspect of course content from the readings or class presentations, including theories, concepts, quotes, statistics, and research findings relate to their service experiences. Students write a journal entry based on key issues encountered at the service site.

**Step 3:** The teacher takes time to encourage students to think about what they are learning through the service experience, and how these learnings related to the subject of the class. For instance, the teacher may set aside time for students to give oral reports, have them make and present posters of their work, or have them keep journals in which they make entries on their work in their service placements.

**Step 4:** The teacher sets up a system for assessing the students' learning from their service experiences. Faithful participation at the service activity is expected, and service recipients may be asked to assess the students' service efforts. But for grading purposes, the main evaluation should focus on what the students are learning from the placement. For example, the students can be evaluated on the number and quality of their journal entries and on their care in relating their service experiences to the course material.

# ABC CHART

Let's see how the preceding methods, variations, and related methods fit into the Anticipation/Building Knowledge/Consolidation rubric. The chart on the following page will help you use the methods in this guide to make your own lesson plans using the ABC rubric.

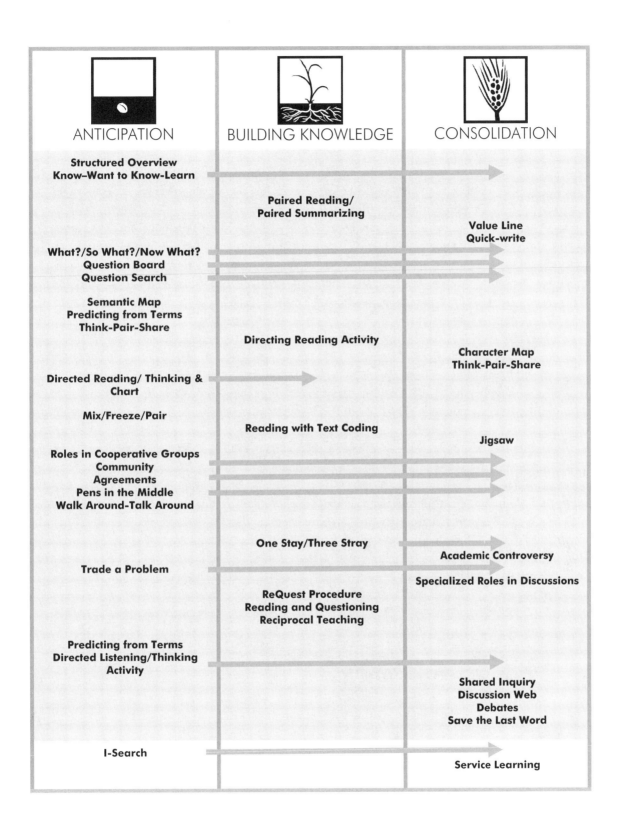

| ANTICIPATION | BUILDING KNOWLEDGE | CONSOLIDATION |
|---|---|---|
| **Structured Overview**<br>**Know–Want to Know-Learn** | | |
| | **Paired Reading/**<br>**Paired Summarizing** | |
| | | **Value Line**<br>**Quick-write** |
| **What?/So What?/Now What?**<br>**Question Board**<br>**Question Search** | | |
| **Semantic Map**<br>**Predicting from Terms**<br>**Think-Pair-Share** | | |
| | **Directing Reading Activity** | |
| | | **Character Map**<br>**Think-Pair-Share** |
| **Directed Reading/ Thinking &**<br>**Chart** | | |
| **Mix/Freeze/Pair** | | |
| | **Reading with Text Coding** | |
| | | **Jigsaw** |
| **Roles in Cooperative Groups**<br>**Community**<br>**Agreements**<br>**Pens in the Middle**<br>**Walk Around-Talk Around** | | |
| | **One Stay/Three Stray** | |
| | | **Academic Controversy** |
| **Trade a Problem** | | |
| | | **Specialized Roles in Discussions** |
| | **ReQuest Procedure**<br>**Reading and Questioning**<br>**Reciprocal Teaching** | |
| **Predicting from Terms**<br>**Directed Listening/Thinking**<br>**Activity** | | |
| | | **Shared Inquiry**<br>**Discussion Web**<br>**Debates**<br>**Save the Last Word** |
| **I-Search** | | |
| | | **Service Learning** |

# SIXTH CORE LESSON: WRITING TO PERSUADE

This lesson shows you ways to help students learn by reading and writing persuasive text. After introducing the topic of persuasive writing, the lesson begins by having students examine two pieces of persuasive writing in order to become familiar them with this type of communication. Then they discuss the strategies and forms of persuasive writing. Finally, they produce a piece of persuasive writing themselves, and evaluate it according to a set of detailed criteria. In the course of the lesson we use several strategies: **brainstorming, coding, building a specification sheet, using a T-Chart** for note taking, and utilizing the **rubric** as an aid in **peer evaluation**.

## HOW TO READ THIS LESSON

As you read the following demonstration lesson, please bear in mind that its purpose is to demonstrate teaching methods. Think about this lesson in two ways.

> 1. Imagine that you are *a student* who is participating in this lesson. What is your experience? What kind of thinking are you doing? What are you learning?

> 2. Then think yourself into the role of *the teacher* who is leading the lesson. What are you doing? Why are you doing it? How are you handling the three phases of the lesson—anticipation, building knowledge, and consolidation?

## LESSON

 **ANTICIPATION**

The teacher introduces the topic of writing to persuade this way:

**Teacher:** *Today's activity involves a skill that will be of use to you throughout your life. Often we see situations that we do not like and the question arises: What can we do to change this situation? It is not enough simply to complain to one another. A more effective approach might be to talk to the person in charge, someone who has a bit of power and is able to change the situation. If we talk convincingly, perhaps we will have some effect. But one of the most powerful tools we have is our ability to write. A persuasive letter not only enables us to refine and think through our arguments, but it also remains as proof that we have, in fact, complained. If you wish to carry your complaint further, you have this letter as evidence.*

*We will begin our work today by looking at two letters that were written to persuade. I want you to work in pairs. Please read these letters and see if you can* **brainstorm** *a list of what makes these letters effective. (I say effective in this case because both had the effect that the students who wrote them wanted.)*

**Brainstorming** *is a strategy we have used at other times. Think of a storm—wind, swirling dust, pelting rain. We want your ideas to come in just this way. Take notes on your ideas as they come—use lists, sentences, whatever suits you—but see if you can figure out what made these letters effective.*

(The teacher passes out copies of letters to students working in groups of 2 or 3. The teacher gives students about 5 or 6 minutes to work on this task.)

**Letter I:**

Dear Ms. Hernandez,

I am writing to you because I think that we should not have to wear school uniforms. I know that there are good reasons for requiring uniforms. Some people believe that they reduce competition among students since no one will have better clothes than anyone else. Also, people believe that when students wear uniforms they think less about their clothes and more about what they are here to learn.

The people who make these arguments, however, are adults and they do not know what students are really thinking. It is true, students compare themselves to one another. We know that some people have better hair or a nicer smile or a better singing voice. These are their gifts. But if we are allowed to wear clothes that express our individual taste, we can showcase our originality and perhaps avoid comparisons that have to do only with things we cannot change.

Everyday when I am getting ready for school I feel a little like a robot putting on my uniform. This is a school that supposedly values our differences and our ability to express ourselves. Why should we not have the ability to express ourselves in our clothes? Also, some students look good in their uniforms, but others have features they would prefer to hide. Shouldn't we have the right to do that?

I do hope that you will take this letter seriously. I know that I am speaking for most of the students in my class when I say that we would appreciate the opportunity to at least try not wearing uniforms. You might set up a committee to evaluate the experiment and see if wearing our own clothes really changes the school atmosphere in negative ways.

Sincerely

XXX

**Letter II:**

Dear Mr. Mfume,

As you know, our class has been studying about the environment and what we might do to make the resources available on this planet last longer. One of the things we believe that we might do is get the children in our school to compost the food that they are throwing away at lunch time. Composting would teach the younger students about this valuable way of recycling and getting added benefit from what we eat and it will provide nutrients for the garden that our class is planting.

Everyday children finish their lunches and simply throw into the garbage the pits or skin from fruit. Others do not finish the food they have brought and add that to the trash. This food sits there, along with paper and other garbage that takes much longer to degrade, and finally get dumped in a place with other non-degradable trash. Wouldn't it be better to see this garbage become something helpful rather than a smelly nuisance?

We are sure that you are wondering how we might go about collecting and composting this garbage. We have a plan. We are proposing to get several large cans with lids (because the organic garbage might become a bit smelly) and paint these cans green so that everyone will be able to identify that they are part of our effort to further green the world. Then the green team, a group of students from our class, will spend a short time after lunch is finished and gather the cans and dump them into the compost pile outside. This group will then wash the cans and they will be ready for use the next day. Students on the green team will rotate, so that no one will miss much school work.

We do hope that you will consider this plan and get back to us if there are things we did not think of that might make you less than accepting of our idea.

We look forward to hearing from you and hope that you are as excited about this plan as we are.

Sincerely,

XXX

Students talk and jot down notes. After five minutes the teacher gives the students a one minute warning and after the time is up calls the class back to order.

**Teacher:** *So, class. What did you find?*

Students offer their suggestion and the teacher simply records their ideas on the board. Students noticed that the letters were:
- Well organized
- Logical
- Had no spelling or grammar errors etc.
- Convincing
- Had supporting details
- Sounded like they knew what they wanted and had good reasons

 **BUILDING KNOWLEDGE**

**Teacher:** *Now let's go back to those letters you just looked at. This time, let's look at the letters more carefully. Where is the purpose of the letter stated? Read me the statement.*

**Student:** "I am writing to you because I think that we should not have to wear school uniforms."

**Student:** "One of the things we believe that we might do is get the students in our school to compost the food that they are throwing away at lunch time."

**Teacher:** *Yes, the first one is a bit more explicit in saying what she wants, but the statement is also there in the second letter. Please note where this statement appears. It is right in the beginning of the letter. Why?*

**Student:** "Because it lets the reader know the purpose of the letter."

**Student:** "Because it doesn't waste time."

**Student:** "Because it makes the author sound more competent and direct."

**Teacher:** *Yes, for all of those reasons. Now, let's look at the endings of these letters. What happens there?*

**Student:** "The author sums up his point."

**Student:** "And calls for a specific action."

**Teacher:** *Now I am going to ask you to look through the letter coding for two different things. One thing you will code for are the **arguments**. An argument is usually a statement of some point the author wants to make. The second thing you will code is the **supporting evidence** presented in defense of the argument. Think about the following statement: "Since we have demonstrated that composting our food waste will allow us to have better soil and reduce the amount of garbage sent to our city dump, we suggest that the school begin the composting process on Monday next." What is the main point in the sentence?*

**Student:** "…we suggest that we begin the composting process on Monday next."

**Teacher:** *Yes, that is the argument the writer is trying to make. Now what evidence does the writer use to convince the reader that the argument is valid?*

**Student:** "I think it is the part about having better soil and less garbage."

**Teacher:** *Yes, those points provide evidence that the argument for composting is on target. Of course, the idea that composting will provide the garden with better soil and the idea of reducing the amount of garbage are both arguments themselves that would need to have supporting evidence. But for this sentence, they are evidence. Now, look at the text and code it for arguments and supporting evidence:*

> when you see an argument or claim the author makes, circle it.
> when you see supporting evidence, or an example, please underline it.

The teacher then discusses their results.

 **CONSOLIDATION**

**Teacher:** *OK, so let's summarize what we have learned.*

**Student:** "That we need to make our point clear and put it first or close to the beginning.."

**Student:** "That we need to make clear arguments and support them."

**Student:** "That we sum up our arguments near the end and ask for the action we want. "

**Teacher:** *People who are quality control experts often use a **specification sheet** (I call it a spec sheet). If you were to become a quality control expert for persuasive letters, what might you look for?*

**Students:** "The author tells the goal in the beginning and grabs the reader's attention."
"The author provides strong reasons and supports them with examples."
"The letter is well organized"
"The author notes objections and answers them."
"The *voice* is confident."
"The author sums up her point at the end and calls for a specific action."

**Teacher:** *Now, let's now look at a real example. In a city not too far from here a child was badly hurt when a car hit her as she tried to cross the street. This happened at a very busy corner and it was not the first time someone was hurt by a vehicle that didn't slow down. There is a similarly dangerous situation on the corner near our school. What might we do about it?*

**Student:** "We could write to the police?"

**Student 2:** "Or the mayor?"

**Student 3:** "Perhaps we should have a crossing guard since so many children cross that street to get to school."

**Teacher:** *I want you to again work in pairs. Think first of what you would like to see done about our corner and then decide who is the person who might be able to make what you want to have happen, really happen.*

Students talk briefly and fill in the following on a sheet of paper:

> 1. What is the problem?
> 2. What is your proposed solution?
> 3. Who could make this solution happen?

**Teacher:** *Today we will use a T-Chart to help you organize your thoughts in preparation for writing. A T-Chart looks like a capital T. On one side of the chart, you will again brainstorm ideas about why someone might not want to take the action you are proposing, and on the other side, what you might say to them in response.*

The teacher demonstrates.

**Teacher:** *Let's look for instance, at our sample letters. In letter 1, what objections does the author anticipate?*

**Student 1:** That students will become too competitive"

Teacher writes on the left side of the T "fosters competition."

**Student 2:** "That students should be thinking of their work, not their clothes."

**Teacher:** *And now on the right, we would jot down answers to those concerns. So what we might we write next to "fosters competition?" Students are already competitive—uniforms don't help. Now let's look at our own problem. Please begin filling in your T-Chart by stating possible objections on the left and your responses to those objections on the right. For homework, please write your letter. Remember, tomorrow we will use our spec sheet to evaluate our work. Here is a copy of the spec sheet we will use:*

1. Was your goal in writing clearly stated? Did you grab the reader's attention?
2. Are strong reasons for your request provided ?
3. Are your ideas clearly ordered and arranged?
4. Are facts and examples used to support your request?
5. Do you answer the objections that might arise?
6. Is the "voice" of the letter confident and persuasive?
7. Does you conclusion sum up your point and call for particular action(s)?

**<u>the lesson ends here</u>**

## REVIEWING THE LESSON

At the beginning of this lesson, you were invited to think about it in two ways: as *a student in the class*, and as *the teacher*.

Take a moment and reflect on how it would have felt to be a student participating in this lesson. (It may help to write down your thoughts on a piece of paper.)

**How did you feel**—interested, engaged, important, detached, controlled, or bored?

**What kind of thinking did you do**—memorize details, find main ideas, look below the surface at important issues, or make interpretations and support interpretations with reasons?

**What will you carry away from the lesson**—information, important ideas, or thinking skills?

Now think back over this lesson as if you had been the teacher. Recall the steps to this lesson. They were:

**Brainstorming**: Students are asked to list everything that comes to mind without being critical of their ideas.

**T-Chart**: A graphic organizer for recording two kinds of information. In this case we used it to record arguments and counter-arguments.

**Coding**: Students read through a text (in this case, letters) looking for particular features. They "code" the letters by writing an identifying symbol in the margin beside each feature that they locate.

**Specification sheet:** Before writing a letter, the students prepare a list of ideas it should contain. The list is the specification sheet. The specification sheet was to be used later in this lesson as a **rubric**, or a set of quality criteria, by the students as they practiced **peer evaluation** of each other's papers.

# METHODS

## PERSUASIVE WRITING

Persuasive writing is not a single method or strategy. In this lesson, several activities were combined to help students write persuasively.

**RATIONALE:** As we saw earlier in this book, taking a position on a controversial issue and supporting it with reasons are aspects of critical thinking. It is useful preparation for participation in an open society. Writing to persuade is an important tool for critical thinkers. The activity below follows naturally from the discussion and debate strategies that have been presented in this book.

**GROUP SIZE:** Writing to persuade can be done with any size group.

**RESOURCES:** Writing to persuade requires that each student have paper and pencils or pens for recording their ideas.

**TIME REQUIRED:** The activity might be conducted in a single class period. Or parts of the activity may be spread across several class periods.

**ACTIVITY:**
**Step 1:** The teacher introduces the topic of persuasive writing by reminding the students of times they have needed to persuade someone of something.

**Step 2:** The teacher shows the students two letters he or she has prepared in advance. In pairs, the students brainstorm a list of features that make the letters effective. This step takes five or six minutes.

**Step 3:** The students share their list of persuasive qualities for the teacher. The teacher writes them on the chalk board for all students to see.

**Step 4:** The teacher asks the students to look at the letters a second time. This time she identifies certain features of the letters. First they find the *purpose* of the letter.

**Step 5:** Now the students go through the letters and "code" or mark two features in them: (1) the **arguments**, that is, the point the author wants to make, and (2) the **supporting evidence**, that is, the reasons offered to convince the reader to agree with the author's points.

**Step 6:** The teacher summarizes the key points the class has learned so far about writing to persuade.

**Step 7:** The teacher now gives the students an example of a real issue that they are to write about. The students first think of the audience; then they are given a set of questions to guide them as they plan their letters:

> What is the problem?
> What is your proposed solution?
> Who could make this solution happen?

**Step 8:** The students use a T-Chart to organize their ideas. A T-Chart looks like a large letter T. On the left side of the vertical line the students list the reasons people might have not to take the action they wish to persuade them to take—and on the right side they list the reasons why the audience should take that action anyway.

**Step 9:** The students write their letters at home after school.

**Step 10:** Before they begin writing their letters, the students are given a set of rubrics or a specification sheet they will use in evaluating their writing. They evaluate their writing the next day in class.

# VARIATIONS AND RELATED METHODS

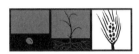 **WRITING TO LEARN: RAFT (ROLE, AUDIENCE, FORMAT, TOPIC)**

 **RATIONALE: RAFT** is a writing activity that is usually used in the consolidation phase of a lesson. It changes the focus of artificial writing assignments to authentic assignments in which students have a purpose for writing (other than writing for the teacher and a grade) and an audience in mind.

| ROLE (who is writing?) | AUDIENCE (who receives it?) | FORMAT (what form?) | TOPIC (what is it about?) |
|---|---|---|---|
| **Examples:** | | | |
| Village women in Tanzania | Village elder | Proclamation | We need a well in the village. |
| Endangered dolphin | Fishermen | Song | Be careful with nets when fishing! |
| Equilateral triangle | Right triangle | E-mail message | My shape is more attractive than yours. |
| Story character | Another character | Poem | I like you because… |
| Voter | Politician | Graffiti | I am angry with you because… |
| Stomach | Mouth | Chant | Things to eat for good health are… |

**GROUP SIZE:** This strategy can be used with classroom groups of any size. Within classroom groups, students can write individually, in pairs, or in small groups.

 **RESOURCES:** Students need pencils or pens and paper. RAFT is most often used as a consolidation activity.

 **TIME REQUIRED:** Students will need from 10 to 30 minutes to write.

 **ACTIVITY:**

**Step 1:** The teacher assigns a RAFT activity, usually as a consolidation activity. Sometimes, the students are given a role that emerges from the lesson, but this varies. The students might write as individuals, as pairs, or as small cooperative learning groups. When students identify and develop their roles, they should consider: personality (who am I and what am I like); attitude (my feelings, beliefs, concerns); and information (what I need to know about myself in the new role).

**Step 2:** The students select an audience for their message.

**Step 3:** Then the students select a format appropriate for their role, audience, and topic.

**Step 4:** The students should have the opportunity to "publish" their messages. This could be an oral reading, a proclamation, sharing in small groups, posting on a bulletin board, publishing in a class newspaper or magazine, sending a letter, reading from the author's chair, etc.

 **ASSESSMENT:** Teachers should consider the:

- Appropriateness of role and audience for topic
- Appropriateness of format for topic; possible formats include: letter, note, graffiti, telegram, proclamation, e-mail, wall newspaper, advertisement, petition, poem, poster, warning, news story, diary, brochure, essay, report, summary, and many others
- Coherence of message
- Mechanics of writing
- Appropriate use of content information (facts to support the topic)
- Inclusion of RAFT and other writing samples in student portfolio to document the developmental nature of writing over time

# FOCUS ON: OTHER WRITING METHODS

## QUICK-WRITE

A quick-write is an opportunity to write on a topic, or to respond to a question, for just a minute or two—not more than five minutes. The prompt can often be an open-ended statement for students to complete. Students should write quickly and without lifting the pencil from the paper, in a sense, "thinking out loud." The focus should be on what they are writing, not on how they are writing it. The teacher can invite a few students to share what they have written. The quick-write strategy is often used as an anticipation activity or a consolidation activity. A quick-write can be used in any discipline, including science and mathematics.

## FREE WRITE

A free write is similar to a quick-write, but more time is provided. The teacher might ask students to write as much as they can about a topic for about five to ten minutes. Then the teacher might give them one more minute to finish the last thought they are writing. As in the quick-write, they should not worry about mechanics and spelling, only their ideas. It can be used in any discipline. Opportunities for sharing their ideas should be provided. A free write is most often a consolidation activity, but it could also be an anticipation activity.

## DUAL-ENTRY DIARY

A dual-entry diary is a strategy that permits students to read for comprehension and then to interact with ideas they encounter. The dual-entry diary is simple to make. Students make a vertical line down the middle of a blank sheet of paper. On the left side, they write a part of the text that affected them strongly. On the right side, they write a comment about the entry on the left side.

### DUAL-ENTRY DIARY—DEMOCRACY TEXT

| Entry from text | Reflection |
| --- | --- |
| Citizens elect their leaders. | Why don't we do that in my country? |
| Everyone has the same rights. | What about women? What about poor people? It seems like they have no rights at all. This makes me angry. |
| Education is available to all. | Even poor people can go to the university. Maybe I could go. |

After students read and record their thoughts, ask them to share some of their ideas. Ask why certain ideas seemed important enough to write down. How did it make them feel? How did the author let them know how he or she felt about the issue? What additional information would they like about this topic? Why?

Teachers should also share ideas that they wrote down from the text and why they were important. This modeling shows the student how their teacher is thinking.

## LEARNING LOG

A learning log is similar in structure to a dual-entry diary. A major difference is that while the students are reflecting on new information gained from reading, listening, or experiencing in the dual-entry diary, they are reflecting on the learning process itself in the learning log. Teachers can raise students' consciousness of their own learning by using learning logs. They are journals in which students set goals, take notes about their study time, describe the problems they are experiencing, and note successes. Writing in learning logs has three benefits:

- Students take personal responsibility for learning as they become conscious of how they study and what is effective.
- Students think about what they are learning and how they are learning it.
- Student learning logs show patterns of progress, strengths, and needs in their study habits.

## LEARNING LOG

Week beginning:_____

| Fill out at beginning of week | Fill out at end of week | Comment on your work. |
|---|---|---|
| What pages will you study this week? | What pages did you study this week? | What parts did you understand best? |
| How many hours will you study? When? | How many hours did you study? When? | What parts caused problems for you? |
| With whom will you study? | With whom did you study? | What parts of the group study worked best? |
| What study strategies do you plan to use? | What study strategies did you use? | What study strategies worked best? |

Learning logs provide a vehicle for continuing self-reflection by students on their learning. Students should be encouraged to review what they have learned each week, the questions they have, and how they have contributed to the group success. They can record key concepts and new vocabulary.

## ABC CHART

Let's see how the preceding methods, variations, and related methods fit into the Anticipation/Building Knowledge/Consolidation rubric. The chart on the following page will help you use the methods in this guide to make your own lesson plans using the ABC rubric.

| ANTICIPATION | BUILDING KNOWLEDGE | CONSOLIDATION |
|---|---|---|
| **Structured Overview**<br>**Know–Want to Know-Learn** | | |
| | **Paired Reading/**<br>**Paired Summarizing** | |
| | | **Value Line**<br>**Quick-write** |
| **What?/So What?/Now What?**<br>**Question Board**<br>**Question Search** | | |
| **Semantic Map**<br>**Predicting from Terms**<br>**Think-Pair-Share** | | |
| | **Directing Reading Activity** | |
| | | **Character Map**<br>**Think-Pair-Share** |
| **Directed Reading/Thinking &**<br>**Chart** | | |
| **Mix/Freeze/Pair** | **Reading with Text Coding** | |
| | | **Jigsaw** |
| **Roles in Cooperative Groups**<br>**Community**<br>**Agreements**<br>**Pens in the Middle**<br>**Walk Around-Talk Around** | | |
| | **One Stay/Three Stray** | |
| | | **Academic Controversy** |
| **Trade a Problem** | | |
| | | **Specialized Roles in Discussions** |
| | **ReQuest Procedure**<br>**Reading and Questioning**<br>**Reciprocal Teaching** | |
| **Predicting from Terms**<br>**Directed Listening/ Thinking**<br>**Activity** | | |
| | | **Shared Inquiry**<br>**Discussion Web**<br>**Debates**<br>**Save the Last Word** |
| **I-Search** | | |
| | | **Service-Learning** |
| **Persuasive Writing** | | |
| | | **RAFT: Role, Audience, Format,**<br>**Topic** |

# SEVENTH CORE LESSON: UNDERSTANDING ARGUMENTS

This lesson shows you ways to help students follow an argument in a written text or a speech. The strategies presented here will enable students to analyze the argument, test it for soundness, and construct counter-arguments. For anticipation the lesson will use an **M-Chart** to focus on vocabulary, in combination with a strategy that was introduced earlier in this guidebook: a **Think/Pair/Share**. For the second phase, building knowledge, the lesson will use **Text Coding for Arguments.** In the third phase, consolidation, the lesson will subject the text to questions from the **Critical Literacy** tradition.

The text for this lesson is called "Let's Hear It for Smokers!" but you can use the procedures in the lesson with any persuasive text that you have—any informative text. This lesson is done here with eighth graders, but you can use the procedures with several grades below or up through the secondary level.

## HOW TO READ THIS LESSON

As you read the following demonstration lesson, please bear in mind that its purpose is to demonstrate teaching methods. Think about this lesson in two ways.

> 1. Imagine that you are *a student* who is participating in this lesson. What is your experience? What kind of thinking are you doing? What are you learning?

> 2. Then think yourself into the role of *the teacher* who is leading the lesson. What are you doing? Why are you doing it? How are you handling the three phases of the lesson—anticipation, building knowledge, and consolidation?

## LESSON

 **ANTICIPATION**

**Text Preview, Think/Pair/Share, and M-Chart** The teacher begins the lesson by reading a short section from the text and calling attention to a key word in it. The talk goes like this:

**Teacher**: *Today we are going to read a piece of writing about cigarette smoking. Let's begin with your own thoughts on the subject. Do you think cigarette smoking should be banned? Take a minute to think about that* *question. Write down your thoughts if you wish to.* [The teacher pauses for one minute while the students think and write.]

**Teacher**: *Now turn to your elbow partner and share your ideas. I'll call on some volunteers to share with the whole class in just a moment.* [The teacher pauses another minute for the students to share their ideas with partners.] *Now let's hear from three pairs. Tell us what you think, and why.*

**Student 1**: "Yes, they should ban cigarettes. They're bad for people. They cause sickness. It makes no sense to allow people to use something that we know will make them sick."

**Teacher**: *Thank you. Does anyone think differently?*

**Student 2**: "It's hard to just ban cigarettes because many people smoke and can't quit. Millions of people, probably. How can you ban something that so many people want to do?"

**Teacher**: *OK, that will do for now. We'll pursue this question further in a few minutes. Now let me read you a short quote from the end of an essay about cigarette smoking. See if you can tell what position the writer is arguing on the question of smoking.*

The teacher reads: '*Those zealots—those fanatics, those moral tyrants who would take away the joys of [tobacco farmers], and invade the privacy of smokers ...ought to be ashamed of themselves. So what is the writer's position?*'

**Student 3**: "This person is in favor of smoking..."

**Student 4**: "Or at least you can say he or she is against people who are trying to ban smoking."

**Teacher**: *Yes. You can say the author is trying to protect the rights of people to grow tobacco and to smoke cigarettes. But let's focus now on the terms the writer uses. Look at these terms: "zealots," "fanatics," and "moral tyrants." Are these the terms that someone in favor of such people would use?*

**Student 5**: "No, no. Those terms are negative and disapproving."

**Teacher**: *Then what would be a positive term for people who want to ban smoking? That is, what might those people call themselves?*

**Student 6**: "Campaigners for clean air."

**Student 7**: "Health guardians."

**Teacher**: *Good. We have negative terms like "fanatic" and "moral tyrant." And we have positive terms like "campaigners for clean air" and "health guardians." Let's get some of these terms on the board.* [The teacher draws an M-Chart on the chalk board]. *And what would be neutral terms for the people we are talking about?*

| Positive | Neutral | Negative |
| --- | --- | --- |
| | | |

**Student 8**: "How about 'anti-smoking activists'?"

**Teacher:** *Yes, that will work.* [The teacher writes the terms on the M-Chart.]

| Positive | Neutral | Negative |
| --- | --- | --- |
| Campaigners for clean air; Health guardians. | Anti-smoking activists | Zealots, fanatics, moral tyrants |

**Teacher**: *Interesting isn't it? Just by the choice of words, a writer can convey positive or negative attitudes toward the subject. Now let's look at some other, more formal ways a writer argues for a position. I'm going to teach a focused lesson to introduce you to some elements we can look for when we read written arguments. Then we will try to find those elements in the full text about cigarette smoking.*

 **BUILDING KNOWLEDGE**

The teacher now instructs the students about elements of argumentation.

The teacher writes these questions on the chalk board:

> *What is the main question posed by this piece?*
> *What answer does it offer?*
> *What reasons are offered in support of that answer?*
> *What evidence is offered in support of each reason?*
> *What reasons or facts are left out—things that might have supported a different answer to the question?*
> *What "facts" are we expected to accept on faith?*
> *What loaded words are used—what words carry value judgments?*
> *Given all we have considered, do the reasons justify the conclusion?*

**Teacher:** *Let's see what these mean. The* **question** *is the idea or problem that the writing is about. It's the matter that the writer is going to argue about.*

**Student 9**: "You mean it's like naming the topic, without saying how you feel about it yet?"

**Teacher:** *Exactly. Now let's look at the* **answer**. *We can also call this the* **claim.** *This is the position that the writer takes on the question.*

**Student 10:** "The writer is telling us how she or he feels?"

**Teacher:** *That's true, but it should be more than feelings. The writer should give you **reasons** for the answer or claim she or he is defending. A **reason** is a statement or a group of statements that support an answer or a claim.*

**Student 11:** "What do you mean 'support' it?"

**Teacher:** *To give us something to make us believe something or do something. I'll give you an example. Suppose your little brother is in another part of the house. Suddenly he shouts, "Come here!" You're busy and don't want to go. So you say, "Why?" He says, "Because I want you to." That's not good enough, so you say, "Give me one good reason." And he says, "Because I have my head stuck in the window." Then you go!*

**Student 12:** "But suppose he doesn't have his head stuck in the window? It would be just like my little brother to say that when it wasn't true!"

**Teacher:** *Right. So sometimes we ask for **evidence** that supports a reason.*

**Student 12:** "I might say, 'If your head is stuck in a window, how come I can hear you?'"

**Teacher:** *Yes, that's a good example. And just like your little brother who sometimes might play tricks on you, some writers make arguments that we shouldn't believe, even though they sound convincing at first. Let's look at three ways they do this. One way is to offer so-called facts, which turn out to be no more than opinions. For example, an article might say "Leading doctors agree that you should use our medicine." But unless the article names the actual doctors, or cites respectable research, we cannot consider that statement as evidence. Another device is to leave important things out of their argument. Here's an example: "A study has shown that the more little old ladies there are in a town, the more crimes are committed. Therefore we should arrest all little old ladies." What is wrong with that argument?*

**Student 13:** "That can't be right!"

**Teacher:** *Of course it's not right. But why isn't it? What is missing from the argument?*

**Student 14:** "I know! If there are more little old ladies in a city, there are more people! If there are more people, there is more crime! Little old ladies don't cause the crime. There is more crime because there are more people, and some of those people are bound to be criminals."

**Teacher:** *Thank you! So you see? Something was missing from the argument. That's another way writers can deceive us. We considered yet another way a little while ago. Suppose a writer is talking about smoking, and he uses terms like "zealot" and "fanatic" to name everyone who is concerned enough to want to limit smoking?*

**Student 15:** "That's not fair."

**Teacher:** *You're right. It's not fair. If a writer uses **loaded words** that convey attitudes without having justified those attitudes, she or he is trying to win the effects of arguing without really arguing. So we will be on the lookout for loaded terms like those. And finally [the teacher points to the last item on the list], we should decide if, when all is said and done, the writer has made a convincing argument.*

*Now, I want pairs of you to read an article called "Let's Hear It for Smoking!" Mark the article with these symbols in the margin:*

| Q | What is the **question**? |
|---|---|
| A | What is the **answer** that is offered? |
| R | What **reasons** are offered? |
| E | What **evidence** is given? |
| "F" | What "facts" are we expected to accept on faith? |
| M | What information or arguments are **missing**? (Write a number in the margin and write out the missing idea) |
| LW | What **loaded words** are used? |

The students then read the following article.

## LET'S HEAR IT FOR SMOKERS!
### Stallmore Dodge

In more and more places in the world there are campaigns against cigarette smoking. Few and far between are the places of work or leisure where smoking is still allowed. In some places cigarette manufacturers are even being sued to pay the medical expenses of people who become ill from smoking. Well, it's time someone stood up for the rights of people who make cigarettes and those who smoke them, and that's what we intend to do here. Let me be clear: many good people are involved in the production of tobacco, and many more good people enjoy their products. Their rights must be respected. Leave them alone!

Picture, if you will, a family farm with a small plot of tobacco, sometimes only two hundred meters on a side. Every day the family walks the rows between the growing plants to tend them, one by one. Even the children can carefully pick off the tassels, so the leaves will grow to their fullest. They harvest the tobacco by hand, and the whole community gathers to pile the broad tobacco leaves carefully on a mule-drawn wagon, and later to hoist racks of leaves up into the barn where they will hang until they are dry. When the tobacco is sold in town at auction, the family makes a tidy profit to spend on its needs. Tell me—would you take that money away from them?

Now picture the smoker. This one is a young woman who's risen before dawn to catch a commuter train to work. In the fifteen minutes she has between arriving at the station and signing in at the office, she can have a cup of coffee—and a cigarette. And in that short space of time, she is truly in charge of her world and fully at peace. The rest of her day may belong to someone else, but for now she is alone with herself, her coffee, and her cigarette. Would you take that joy from her, too?

Those zealots, those fanatics, those moral tyrants who would take away the virtues of family farming, and invade the privacy of smokers like this hard-working young woman—they ought to be ashamed of themselves.

After the students have read and marked the article, the teacher asks the students to call out the parts they had marked.

**Teacher:** *Who found the* **question***?*

**Student 15:** "We marked the whole first paragraph. The author didn't quite come out and say it, but he raised the question of whether we should make it hard for people to smoke."

**Student 16:** "And also whether we should punish people who make cigarettes."

**Teacher:** *Good. And what was the author's answer to that question?*

**Student 17:** "That we should leave them alone."

**Teacher:** *Leave them alone? Does the author say what he means by that?*

**Student 18:** "Not really. People should be allowed to grow and sell tobacco. And people should be allowed to smoke cigarettes. That is all he says."

**Student 17:** "That's not much."

**Student 18:** "No, it's not."

**Student 19:** "We found two reasons, though. One is that tobacco is grown by family farmers."

**Student 20:** "And the other is that some smokers enjoy smoking."

**Student 21:** "The evidence he offered is pretty thin, don't you think? Both pieces of evidence he offers are not very believable."

**Student 22:** "Yes. He paints us a picture of a family farm that grows tobacco. That's nice, but…"

**Student 23:** "How do we know that most tobacco is grown that way? It could be grown on huge plantations and picked by machine, for all we know."

**Student 24:** "And he also shows a young woman whose only pleasure is her cigarette and her cup of coffee."

**Student 25:** "That's silly! She should find some other pleasures, like reading a good book. Going roller skating. Feeding the birds."

**Teacher:** *You all are very perceptive! Good for you! Did you find anything missing from the arguments?*

**Student 26:** "Well, they didn't say anything about the cigarette manufacturers. It's easier to sympathize with the family farmer than it is with the big corporations that make billions of dollars off cigarettes."

**Student 27:** "And when the author described the young smoker, he failed to mention that four smokers out of five want to quit—but they can't, because they are addicted to cigarettes. I read that somewhere."

**Student 28:** "There was no mention of the damage smoking causes. Cigarettes cost a lot of money, and if you're addicted you have to keep buying them. And they cause lung cancer and heart disease—they kill hundreds of thousands of people every year."

**Student 29:** "We marked some loaded words. They were the ones that we worked with at the beginning: 'zealot,' 'fanatic,' 'moral tyrant.'"

**Teacher:** *In what way were they 'loaded'?*

**Student 29:** "Well, we really don't know anything about people who are opposing smoking. They may not be zealots or fanatics or tyrants. They may be people who don't want to work in a tiny office with someone who smokes all day. They may be public health workers who are concerned about their patients. We can't call them zealots or tyrants without knowing something about their motives."

**Student 30:** "That's right. There are good reasons why people might oppose cigarette smoking—even if this author doesn't admit any of them."

**Teacher:** *One more question. Do you think the reasons the author gave justify his conclusion?*

**Student 31:** "That's tricky! If you read this article quickly and thoughtlessly, you might say, "Yes." But the reasons given don't have good evidence to back them up…"

**Student 32:** "And we found so many important things that weren't said in the paper. You might agree with it if you didn't think of the things that weren't said. So, no. We don't think his conclusion is justified."

 **CONSOLIDATION**

In this lesson, the students are exploring argumentation, and ways to detect and argue back against inadequate or dishonest arguments. The teacher now asks the students to consider two questions designed to reinforce polite skepticism about arguments.

**Teacher:** *Given all the gaps we found in this argument, we're getting a little bit suspicious about this author's motives, aren't we? Here is a question to think about with your partner:* **Whose voices, and whose interests, do you think are represented in this article? Whose voices and whose interests are left out?** *[The students are given time to consider and discuss the question.]*

**Student 1:** "Well, it's certainly the voice of someone who is in favor of smoking. It could even be the tobacco industry, the cigarette companies, that's behind this article."

**Teacher:** *We don't know, do we? But whose voices are left out?*

**Student 2:** "All kinds of people. The other workers in the office with that woman, who don't want to breathe her smoke."

**Student 3:** "The public health people, who have to deal with all those people who get sick from smoking.

**Student 4:** "Taxpayers. Because they end up paying the hospital costs of people who can't afford to pay.

**Teacher:** *Okay. One final thing. I'd like you to construct a counter-argument to what you've just read. Remember to state the question, then give your **own** answer. Make sure you provide reasons to support your answers to the question. And evidence to support your reasons. Write these out in the next 15 minutes, and then we will share some of them.*

After the students write, a few of them share.

<u>**the lesson ends here**</u>

## REVIEWING THE LESSON

At the beginning of this lesson, you were invited to think about the lesson in two ways. First, you would focus on your experiences as *a student in the class*, and then, as *the teacher*.

Take a moment and reflect on how it would have felt to be a student participating in this lesson. It may help to write down your thoughts on a piece of paper.

**How did you feel**—interested, engaged, important, detached, controlled, or bored?

**What kind of thinking did you do**—did you accept ideas at face value, or did you look below the surface at the quality of arguments? Were you the passive recipient of ideas or arguments, or were you inclined to exercise skepticism and argue back?

**What will you carry away from the lesson**—information, important ideas, or thinking skills?

Now think back over this lesson as if you had been the teacher. Recall the steps to this lesson. They were the following:

**Think-Pair-Share:** A question is discussed individually and in pairs.

**Terms with M-Charts:** A method for exploring the connotations of key terms, to look for loaded words.

**Focused Lesson on Argumentation:** The teacher introduces and explains terms about argumentation.

**Text Coding:** The students mark parts of the texts where they find elements of argumentation.

**Writing Counter-arguments:** Students write out their own positions and arguments on the question.

Now you may want to learn exactly how you would conduct each activity. Here are the steps to each one.

# METHODS

 **M-CHARTS**
Persuasive writing is not a single method or strategy. In this lesson, several activities were combined to help students write persuasively.

M-Charts on terms are a device for bringing to light "loaded words," terms that make what are called "descriptive assumptions." Descriptive assumptions are value judgments that are built into the words themselves, as you can see in the difference between words like "freedom fighter" and "terrorist."

 **RATIONALE:** Students need to develop strategies to protect themselves from manipulative uses of language.

 **GROUP SIZE:** Unlimited

 **TIME REQUIRED:** Can be completed in 10 minutes.

 **ACTIVITY:**
**Step 1:** Begin by sharing a passage in which a loaded term or terms are introduced.

**Step 2:** Call the students' attention to the term, and ask them what they think the author's disposition is toward the item in question.

**Step 3:** Ask the students to think of terms they would use for that item if they felt the opposite way from the author.

**Step 4:** Now ask students to think of a neutral term for the item in question.

**Step 5:** Write all three groups of terms in a chart with three columns. The positive terms can go on the left, the neutral terms in the middle, and the negative terms on the right.

 **REFLECTIONS ON THE METHOD:** The M-Chart is a graphic organizer for making clear the different stances authors take toward an item by their choice of words. Using this device frequently induces a certain skepticism toward manipulative language and cultivates a spirit of independence in the students.

## FOCUSED LESSON ON ARGUMENTS

A critical discussion is one in which students approach a text with systematic skepticism, identify its arguments, and subject them to scrutiny. This focused lesson introduces students to different elements of arguments, as well as tricks that are commonly used as shortcuts in arguments. (Browne 2000)

**RATIONALE:** Students need to understand the structure and components of arguments so that they can tell when an argument is fairly or badly made, and so that they can develop strategies to protect themselves from manipulative uses of language.

**GROUP SIZE:** Unlimited

**TIME REQUIRED:** There are many ideas to be learned here. An introduction can be done in a class period, but these ideas should be revisited and practiced many times over.

**ACTIVITY:**
**Step 1:** Share a list of the elements of an argument, in the form of questions.

*What is the main question posed by this piece?*
*What answer does it offer?*
*What reasons are offered in support of that answer?*
*What evidence is offered in support of each reason?*
*What "facts" are we asked to accept on faith?*
*What has been left unsaid?*
*What loaded terms must we accept in order to reach the same conclusion as the author? That is, has the author conveyed value by means of her or his choice of words that have positive or negative connotations?*
*Do the reasons the author offers justify the conclusion she or he draws?*

**Step 2:** Explain and give examples of each element.

**Step 3:** Share an argumentative essay with the students. Show the students a set of codes that can be used to mark each element, and ask the students in pairs to mark the text according to the elements they find in it.

**Step 4:** Review the elements the students find.

**REFLECTIONS ON THE METHOD:** There are many ideas being introduced in this lesson. It may be preferable to introduce these elements more slowly, spreading them over several lessons. One way to do so would be to begin with a text that has a well-formed and straightforward argument. After introducing a few of the elements, you would have the students look for the **question**, the author's **answers** to the question, and the **evidence** that is given to support each reason. Then you would ask if the author's **conclusion** was justified. After having the students practice using these elements several times, you would then introduce other elements: so-called **facts** that must be taken on faith, **missing information or arguments**, and **loaded words**.

# VARIATIONS AND RELATED METHODS

 **CRITIQUING NARRATIVE TEXTS**

**Critiquing narrative texts** (Luke 2000, Temple 2001) calls for a slightly different set of questions from those used with argumentative texts. In a sense, any work of fiction is an argument for a certain view of the world, and that argument may be challenged. For example, in traditional stories from many cultures, males are usually portrayed as active heroes and females are depicted as passive "prizes" to be won by the males as rewards for their valor. Old people may be depicted as infirm and useless, and possibly sinister. Stereotypes like these deserve to be questioned.

 **TIME REQUIRED:** You can conduct a discussion in a class period, but critical discussions of this kind will gain power if students have repeated practice with them.

 **ACTIVITY:** Students should be introduced to the dynamics of "reading against the grain" of fiction through one or more focused lessons. Then you can ask them to address questions like the following to works of fiction:

- *Who "won" in this story? What did he or she do to win? Who lost? Why did he or she lose? What lesson do we draw from this?*
- *With whom does the author of this work want us to identify? Whom do you think the author wants us to emulate? What is it about the way characters are portrayed that leads you to those conclusions?*
- *Suppose this character had been of a different sex: Would events have played out the same or differently? Suppose she or he had come from a different social class or a different age group. Would things have been the same or different? How do the answers to these questions square with our contemporary views of male and female, rich and poor, young and old, people from this ethnic group versus that ethnic group?*
- *What things about our lives or our culture or our society does this work set out to defend? What things does this work set out to challenge? What things does it seem to take for granted?*
- *What alternative readings can you suggest for this story?*
- *Who is the intended audience for this story? What sort of reader could accept the premises of this story unproblematically?*

# ABC CHART

Let's see how the preceding methods, variations, and related methods fit into the Anticipation/Building Knowledge/Consolidation rubric. The chart on the following page will help you use the methods in this guide to make your own lesson plans using the ABC rubric.

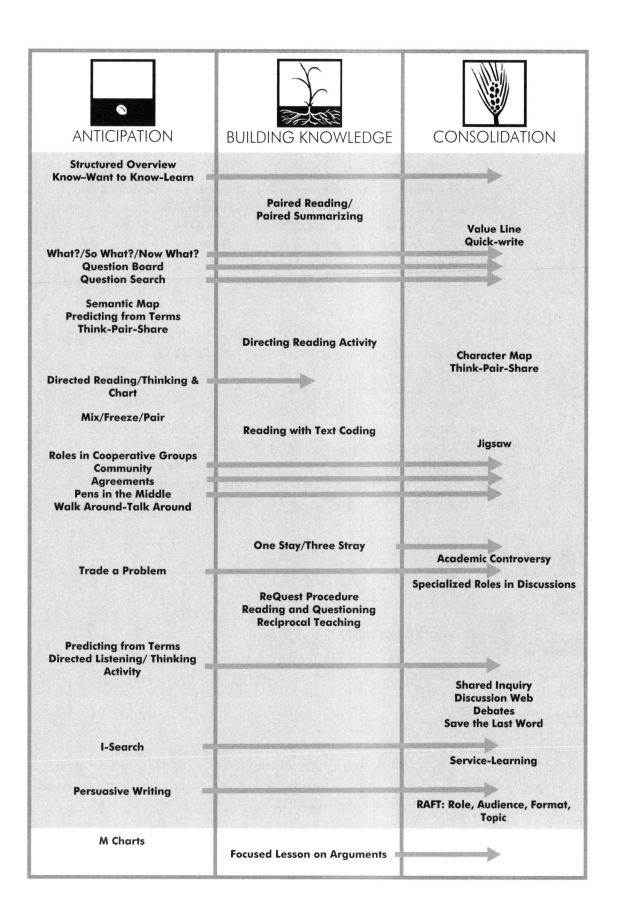

| ANTICIPATION | BUILDING KNOWLEDGE | CONSOLIDATION |
|---|---|---|
| **Structured Overview**<br>**Know–Want to Know-Learn** | | |
| | **Paired Reading/**<br>**Paired Summarizing** | |
| | | **Value Line**<br>**Quick-write** |
| **What?/So What?/Now What?**<br>**Question Board**<br>**Question Search** | | |
| **Semantic Map**<br>**Predicting from Terms**<br>**Think-Pair-Share** | | |
| | **Directing Reading Activity** | |
| | | **Character Map**<br>**Think-Pair-Share** |
| **Directed Reading/Thinking &**<br>**Chart** | | |
| **Mix/Freeze/Pair** | | |
| | **Reading with Text Coding** | |
| | | **Jigsaw** |
| **Roles in Cooperative Groups**<br>**Community**<br>**Agreements**<br>**Pens in the Middle**<br>**Walk Around-Talk Around** | | |
| | **One Stay/Three Stray** | |
| | | **Academic Controversy** |
| **Trade a Problem** | | |
| | | **Specialized Roles in Discussions** |
| | **ReQuest Procedure**<br>**Reading and Questioning**<br>**Reciprocal Teaching** | |
| **Predicting from Terms**<br>**Directed Listening/ Thinking**<br>**Activity** | | |
| | | **Shared Inquiry**<br>**Discussion Web**<br>**Debates**<br>**Save the Last Word** |
| **I-Search** | | |
| | | **Service-Learning** |
| **Persuasive Writing** | | |
| | | **RAFT: Role, Audience, Format,**<br>**Topic** |
| **M Charts** | | |
| | **Focused Lesson on Arguments** | |

# EIGHTH CORE LESSON: CRITICAL LISTENING

Critical listening is the application of critical thinking skills to the process of listening to someone orally present a position on a topic. It is very closely related to critical reading, but with one important exception. When one reads critically, it is possible to read several times. When one listens critically, it is often necessary to capture all of the meaning in a single event. In a political speech or a debate, for example, there may be no repetition of what was said.

## HOW TO READ THIS LESSON

As you read the following demonstration lesson, please bear in mind that its purpose is to demonstrate teaching methods (and not to teach you about the Kyoto Protocol). Think about this lesson in two ways.

1. First imagine that you are *a student* who is participating in this lesson. What is your experience? What kind of thinking are you doing? What are you learning?
2. Then think yourself into the role of *the teacher* who is leading the lesson. What are you doing? Why are you doing it? How are you handling the three phases of the lesson: anticipation, building knowledge, and consolidation?

## LESSON

 **ANTICIPATION**

The anticipation phase is the art of the lesson that activates prior knowledge, prepares the students for learning, and sets out the purposes of the lesson. Here we use the **Fishbowl with Enhanced Lecture and M-Chart**.

The teacher explains to the students that he will present a brief oral argument about a controversial issue, the Kyoto Treaty on Global Warming. The teacher selects six students to serve as the audience in the Fishbowl. The other students will surround and observe them as they listen to the oral argument and then as they evaluate it among themselves.

The teacher reminds the Fishbowl group about the M-Chart and the questions presented in the Seventh Core Lesson on Understanding Arguments: he should provide this in a handout or write it on the chalk board for reference:

| Source | Positive | Neutral | Negative |
|---|---|---|---|
| Anti-smoking from Lesson 7 | Campaigners for clean air; Health guardians. | Anti-smoking activists | Zealots, fanatics, moral tyrants |
| Kyoto Protocol from Lesson 8 | | | |

The teacher begins the lesson by giving a short talk about the topic—just enough to frame the students' thinking about it and to raise their curiosity. The talk goes like this:

**Teacher:** *Today we will be talking about the Kyoto Protocol. Remember that in the last lesson we talked about how language can be used to influence opinions, as you can see in the M-Chart above. I will present a brief lecture about the Kyoto Protocol to our Fishbowl group while the rest listen. See if you can identify the following:*

- *the main question the piece asks*
- *the answer it offers*
- *the reasons it offers in support of that answer*
- *the evidence it offers in support of each reason*
- *the reasons or facts it leaves out that might support a different answer to the question*
- *the "facts" it expects us to accept on faith*
- *the loaded words it uses (words carry value judgments)*

The teacher then reads the following brief enhanced lecture on the Kyoto Protocol to the small group in the Fishbowl with enthusiasm and emotion. In an enhanced lecture listening, questioning, and discussion are introduced in a lecture format. He tries to convince the participants in the Fishbowl of the point of view that they hear.

### BRIEF ENHANCED LECTURE IN OPPOSITION TO THE KYOTO PROTOCOL ON REDUCING GREENHOUSE GAS EMISSIONS

Countries that sign the Kyoto Protocol accept mandatory targets on greenhouse gas emissions. These targets range from –8% to +10 % of each country's 1990 levels. This will result in a reduction of 5% below 1990 levels in the period from 2008 to 2012. The called-for reductions are 8% in the European Union and most of Europe. They are 7% in the United States and 6% in Canada. New Zealand, Russia, and Ukraine are to stabilize their emissions. Some countries, such as Norway, may increase emissions up to 1%.

There are many reasons why this protocol should not be accepted by the international community. Most scientists have concluded that recent increases in surface and atmospheric temperatures of the earth are part of a natural trend. These kinds of changes have occurred many times in the earth's history, and they will occur again in the future. In addition, the changes are very gradual, providing time for more research and consultation among nations.

We must stop listening to the minority of scientists and far-out environmentalists who tell us that the sky is falling. Their research is not scientifically based, and we should instead listen to those who advocate a cautious approach. Some of those crazies even claim that sea levels will rise and that many island nations and coastal areas will be inundated by the sea. This is nonsense. It has not happened yet, and it won't happen.

This brief enhanced lecture contains several examples of weak argumentation, lack of evidence, and other areas of concern. Ask the participants in the Fishbowl to identify those weaknesses at the end of the presentation, and write them on a chart or chalk board. They should use the M-Chart and the questions from the previous lesson to form their responses.

Finally, ask all participants to discuss how understanding these weaknesses helps them listen critically.

**Teacher:** *Now that those of you in the Fishbowl have heard the brief lecture, what was its purpose?*

**First student:** "You tried to convince us that the Kyoto Protocol was not a good thing."

**Teacher:** *Yes. What did I advocate instead?*

**Second student:** "You said that nations should move forward slowly and carefully because these changes in climate might not happen."

**Teacher:** *What evidence did I give for that?*

**Third student:** "You said that these kinds of changes have happened before and that it will happen again, but we are still here."

**Teacher:** *What evidence did I provide?*

**First student:** "You said that most scientists say that this is a natural trend."

**Teacher:** *Are you satisfied with that evidence?*

**Fourth student:** "No, because you also said that some crazy scientists were worried about global warming. But you never said who the scientists were on either side."

**Teacher:** *What about loaded words?*

**Fifth student;** "You talked about 'the sky falling,' 'crazies,' and 'nonsense.'"

**Teacher:** *And what was my evidence for those statements.*

**Sixth student:** "It was just your opinion. You didn't give any evidence."

**Teacher:** *Where would you place those statements in the M-Chart?*

**Third student:** "As Negative."

**Teacher:** *Good. You have noticed many weaknesses in my lecture. Now let's continue to the second part of the lesson.*

 ## BUILDING KNOWLEDGE

The building knowledge phase is the one in which students explore new knowledge about the topic. The students are exposed to new **critical listening** issues and have an opportunity to listen to a speech and identify examples of issues from it.

**Teacher:** *Now you are going to learn about some new critical listening issues to watch for in this lesson. Look at the issues and questions in the graphic organizer on this sheet of paper that I am passing to each of you. You can ask yourself these questions about what you are going to hear in the complete enhanced lecture about the Kyoto Protocol.*

*First, let's arrange ourselves in groups of four.*

*Now that you are in groups, each group will listen to the complete enhanced lecture and try to find examples of their assigned critical listening issues. Some groups have more than one question with their issue.* (The teacher assigns each group to one issue on the sheet).

*Now let's look at the issues and the questions. What do we mean by "bias"?*

**A student:** "When someone has already made up his or her mind."

**Teacher:** *Good. What would be an example?*

**Another student:** "Like if someone says to buy a big car, and they work for a company that makes big cars."

**Teacher:** *Yes. Now, what about sources in the next one?*

**Another student:** "We already saw that in the brief lecture—you talked about scientists, but you didn't tell us who they were."

**Teacher:** *Excellent. And emotionalism or personal attack in the next one?*

**Another student:** "Calling someone a name or talking about their intelligence."

# GRAPHIC ORGANIZER: CRITICAL LISTENING

| ISSUE | Questions to Ask | What the Speaker Said | Notes |
|---|---|---|---|
| Emotionalism, Personal Attack | Are appeals based on emotion, or evidence? | | |

| ISSUE | Questions to Ask | What the Speaker Said | Notes |
|---|---|---|---|
| Sources | Who is cited as an autority? | | |

| ISSUE | Questions to Ask | What the Speaker Said | Notes |
|---|---|---|---|
| Bias | Who is talking? | | |
| | What is the speaker's point of view? | | |
| | What organization does the speaker represent? | | |
| | Does the speaker have a conflict of interest? | | |
| | Does the speaker present alternative points of view? | | |

| ISSUE | Questions to Ask | What the Speaker Said | Notes |
|---|---|---|---|
| Body Language, Inflectional Clues | How does the speaker's body language and inflection reveal his or her biases? | | |

| ISSUE | Questions to Ask | What the Speaker Said | Notes |
|---|---|---|---|
| Currency of Information | How current is the speaker's information? | | |

| ISSUE | Questions to Ask | What the Speaker Said | Notes |
|---|---|---|---|
| Selective Reporting | Are there other data that support an alternative point of view? | | |

| ISSUE | Questions to Ask | What the Speaker Said | Notes |
|---|---|---|---|
| Improper Use of Statistics | Are percentages given without total sample size? | | |

**Teacher:** *What about currency of information?*

**Another student;** "Sometimes someone might use information that is out of date."

**Teacher:** *Yes, good. What do we mean by body language and inflectional cues in the next one?*

**Another student:** "It's not what the speaker says, but how they say it. You can tell how the speaker feels about the topic."

**Teacher:** *Very good. Each group should now listen for their assigned critical listening issue and write down what the speaker says if they hear an example. There is space in the second column to write what the speaker said. You can make a note of any critical thinking issues that have been identified in the last column.*

The teacher reads the lecture below with much expression and in a very persuasive manner.

### REVISED ENHANCED LECTURE IN OPPOSITION TO THE THE KYOTO PROTOCOL ON REDUCING GREENHOUSE GAS EMISSIONS

Countries that sign the Kyoto Protocol accept mandatory targets on greenhouse gas emissions. These targets range from –8% to +10 percent of each country's 1990 levels. This will result in a reduction of 5% below 1990 levels in the period from 2008 to 2012. The called-for reductions are 8% in the European Union and most of Europe. They are 7% in the United States and 6% in Canada. New Zealand, Russia, and Ukraine are to stabilize their emissions. Some countries, such as Norway, may increase emissions up to 1%.

Countries can make up for not meeting their targets by increasing "sinks." These are forests that remove $CO_2$ from the atmosphere. They can do this in their own countries, or they can pay for projects that have the same result in other countries.

The protocol will take effect when 55 countries have ratified it. Many of those must include the industrialized countries that account for most emissions. The United States and Australia have already indicated that they will not support the treaty.

There are many reasons why this protocol should not be accepted by the international community. Most scientists have concluded that recent increases in surface and atmospheric temperatures of the earth are part of a natural trend. These kinds of changes have occurred many times in the earth's history, and they will occur again in the future. In addition, the changes are very gradual, providing time for more research and consultation among nations.

There is no need to make drastic changes to decrease the emissions of greenhouse gases. There is no evidence that this will alleviate the situation. We should take a wait-and-see point of view before rushing into something that scientists don't support.

There is also the danger of severe economic decline. Prominent economists have predicted a 20% decline in economic activity, especially in the industrialized countries most impacted by the protocol.

We should also consider that there are benefits to global warming. Growing seasons in northern climates, such as the Russian Federation, Canada, and the Scandinavian and Baltic countries would be lengthened, permitting them to increase agricultural production.

The protocol is not fair to western industrialized nations. They would be placed at a severe economic disadvantage to newly industrializing nations, such as China and India, which would not be subject to the Kyoto Protocol. They would have to reduce emissions, while developing and least-developed countries could increase their emissions without penalty. The net result would be more greenhouse gas emissions than before the Kyoto Protocol.

We must stop listening to the minority of scientists and far-out environmentalists who tell us that the sky is falling. Their research is not scientifically based, and we should instead listen to those who advocate a cautious approach. Some of those crazies even claim that sea levels will rise and that many island nations and coastal areas will be inundated by the sea. This is nonsense. It has not happened yet, and it won't happen.

We must also protect ourselves against the bogus claims of rabid environmentalists, who would take us back to the Stone Age. Once we begin to limit greenhouse gas emissions, the world will begin a slide backwards in development that will cause millions of people to starve all over the world. As the world economy degrades, what we all know as a middle-class lifestyle will disappear, with everyone shivering in the cold and without employment.

**Teacher:** *Now that you have heard the lecture, have you been able to find some examples of critical listening issues?*

**A student from one group:** "Yes, our group found an example of personal attack when you talked about the 'bogus claims of rabid environmentalists.'"

**Teacher:** *Good, did you hear any evidence to support my argument? By evidence, I mean verifiable data or information that might serve to support conclusions in my lecture.*

**Another student from the same group:** "No, you just said it."

**Teacher:** *What other groups found an example?*

**A student from another group:** "We found an example of negative body language when you talked about the 'nonsense' of islands being covered by the sea. You were not very nice in the way you said that."

**Teacher:** *Yes, I tried to sneer when I said that. What other examples did you find?*

**A student from a new group:** "You never told us who you were in making the speech. We don't know what organization you were representing."

**Teacher:** *Very good. Would you predict that I was from the coal industry or an environmental organization?*

**The same student:** "The coal industry."

**Teacher:** *Of course. Now, what else did you hear when you listened critically?*

**A student from another group:** "You said that economists predicted a 20% decline in economic activity, but you didn't give details."

**A student from another group:** "We noticed the same thing, and you didn't say who the economists were or where they came from."

**Teacher:** *Excellent. You have listened critically and identified many weaknesses in my presentation.*

 **CONSOLIDATION**

The consolidation phase is the one in which students summarize, interpret, and test main ideas; share opinions and make personal responses; and assess their learning. In this lesson they apply their new understandings of critical listening issues to the writing process.

**Teacher:** *Now let's use some of our new skills in critical listening to prepare positions on the Kyoto Protocol. Half of the groups should take my speech in opposition and try to strengthen it by eliminating some or all of the weaknesses. The other half of the groups will write a speech in support of the Kyoto Protocol. Both sets of groups should carefully examine their completed speeches for weaknesses that we might identify when they are read out loud.*

**A student:** "We may need information to strengthen our speeches."

**Teacher:** *If you don't have information that you need, describe what you need and where you might find it.*

The students in each group prepare their speeches. They present them to each other. A group on the other side analyzes each presentation using the criteria for critical listening. Then the groups change roles.

**Teacher:** *Now that you have listened critically to speeches on both sides of the issue, which side has been most successful in avoiding weaknesses in their presentations?*

<u>**the lesson ends here**</u>

REVIEWING THE LESSON

At the beginning of this lesson, you were invited to think about it in two ways: as *a student in the class*, and as *the teacher*.

Take a moment and reflect on how it would have felt to be a student participating in this lesson. (It may help to write down your thoughts on a piece of paper.)

**How did you feel**—interested, engaged, important, detached, controlled, or bored?

**What kind of thinking did you do--**memorize details, find main ideas, look below the surface at important issues, or make interpretations and support interpretations with reasons?

**What will you carry away from the lesson**—information, important ideas, or thinking skills?

Now think back over this lesson as if you had been the teacher. Recall the steps to this lesson. They were:

**Fishbowl and Critical Listening:** A brief lecture in a Fishbowl setting to review skills learned in the Seventh Core Lesson and to set the stage for advanced critical listening skills in this lesson.

**Critical Listening in an Enhanced Lecture:** A set of issues that help students focus on critical listening.

**Writing Activity:** A writing activity that emerges naturally from the construction of new meaning.

## METHODS

 **FISHBOWL AND ENHANCED LECTURE WITH M-CHART**
The teacher presents a brief enhanced lecture to a small group within the class. They are in the Fishbowl, and the other students gather around them and observe how they listen to the lecture and also their discussion about the issues they will record on the M-Chart.

 **RATIONALE:** The purposes of the critical listening activity are to support students' listening comprehension with questions they might ask themselves as they listen, and to prepare them to listen critically when someone speaks to them—politician, salesperson, teacher.

 **GROUP:** The lesson can be done with an entire class.

 **RESOURCES:** Brief enhanced lecture on the Kyoto Protocol on Global Warming; complete enhanced lecture in opposition to the Kyoto Protocol; photocopies of graphic organizer below; easel or chart rack; chart paper; markers

 **TIME:** This type of lesson can be completed in forty to fifty minutes.

 **ACTIVITY:**
**Step 1:** Explain that they will be in a Fishbowl where one group is active and the other groups are observing their activity. Review the critical questions and the M-Chart from the Seventh Core Lesson.

- *What is the main question posed by this piece?*
- *What answer does it offer?*
- *What reasons are offered in support of that answer?*
- *What evidence is offered in support of each reason?*
- *What reasons or facts are left out that might have supported a different answer to the question?*
- *What "facts" are we expected to accept on faith?*
- *What loaded words are used—what words carry value judgments?*

- *Given all we have considered, do the reasons justify the conclusion?*
- *What examples of emotional labeling have you found in this brief lecture? Where would you place them in the M-Chart?*

**Step 2:** Ask the group in the Fishbowl to think about these questions as they listen to the brief enhanced lecture. Read the brief enhanced lecture on the Kyoto Protocol with enthusiasm and emotion. Try to convince the participants in the Fishbowl of the point of view that they hear. This brief enhanced lecture contains several examples of weak argumentation, lack of evidence, and other areas of concern. Ask the participants in the Fishbowl to identify the weaknesses at the end of the presentation, and write them on a chart or chalk board. They should use the M-Chart and the questions from the previous lesson to form their responses. Finally, ask all participants to discuss how understanding these weaknesses helps listeners listen critically.

**Step 3:** Tell the participants that they will learn about some new critical listening issues to watch for in this lesson. Show them the issues in the graphic organizer. They will find questions they can ask themselves about what they have heard. Discuss these issues and questions, ask them for examples, or provide examples, where necessary. There is space in the second column to write what the speaker said. They can make a note of any critical thinking issues they have identified in the last column. Explain that the enhanced lecture is a talk in which listening, questioning, and discussion are introduced in a lecture format.

**Step 4:** Ask all the participants to arrange themselves in groups of four. Provide a copy of the graphic organizer to each group and assign each group to a category of critical thinking issues from the graphic organizer. Each group of four is to listen to the complete enhanced lecture for the purpose of identifying examples of their assigned critical listening issue. Other groups will be listening for examples of the other issues. Encourage them to take rapid notes and to classify on the graphic organizer the problems in their assigned area that they identify in the oral presentation.

**Step 5:** Read the complete enhanced lecture to them slowly and with emotion. Try to persuade them to adopt your point of view. You may read it a second time if they request it. They should *not* have a written copy. This is a *critical listening* lesson.

**Step 6:** After the lecture, ask the participants to meet in their groups of four to share the problem or problems in their category that they have identified. With respect to each problem, they should describe what the speaker said and what critical listening issue arose.

**Step 7:** After five to ten minutes, ask each group to share with the larger group. Have someone record each issue on a larger version of the graphic organizer (on chart paper or a chalk board). Try to find an example of each type of critical listening problem. Ask the students to share their ideas about how useful it was to have criteria and issues to listen critically for during the enhanced lecture.

**Step 8:** Ask the participants to gather into their groups of four again. Ask the participants in half of the groups to rewrite the enhanced lecture in such a way that they avoid all the weaknesses identified in the previous activity. They will need written copies of the lecture. They may not need factual information at hand, but they can describe the kind of information they might need and where they might find it. Ask the participants in the other half of the groups to construct an enhanced lecture in favor of the Kyoto Protocol. Have them use the issues and questions in the graphic organizer to avoid or overcome problems found in the lecture in opposition to the Kyoto Protocol. They may not need factual information at hand, but they can describe the kind of information they might need and where they might find it.

**Step 9:** Ask one of the pro-Kyoto groups to present their enhanced lecture. The anti-Kyoto groups should criticize their lecture using the criteria from the graphic organizer. Ask one of the anti-Kyoto groups to present their revised enhanced lecture. The pro-Kyoto groups should criticize their lecture using the criteria from the graphic organizer. Ask all participants to discuss the effectiveness of the two messages. They may find that the anti-Kyoto message is much less effective when critical listening criteria are applied.

# VARIATIONS AND RELATED METHODS

 **SOCRATIC QUESTIONING**

 **RATIONALE:** According to Richard Paul (1993), Socratic questioning is concerned with clarifying ideas, examining context, considering foundations, identifying assumptions, and defining point of view. Socratic questioning provides an additional set of critical listening issues to apply to oral presentations

 **GROUP SIZE:** Entire class

 **RESOURCES:** Taped or written copies of an oral presentation, paper, pencils and pens

 **TIME REQUIRED:** A class period

**ACTIVITY:**
Some examples of Socratic questioning from Paul include the following:

**Questions that clarify**
- What do you mean when you say…?
- What point are you trying to make…?
- What example can you provide?
- Why did you say…?
- What is the relationship of this to…?

**Questions about assumptions**
- What assumption are you making?
- Why would you make that assumption?

- Are you assuming that…?

**Questions that probe perspective and point of view**

- Is it your perspective that…?
- How do you view…?

**Questions that probe facts, reasons, and evidence**

- What is your evidence for this?
- Why do you believe this?
- How certain are you about this?

**Questions that examine implications and outcomes**

- What is your implication?
- What would be the outcome if that happened (*reductio ad absurdum*)?
- What would be the effect of that (slippery slope)?

These types of questions could be used to supplement the issues raised in the Seventh and Eighth Core Lessons.

# ABC CHART

Now that the eight core lessons are complete, the ABC chart can be seen in its entirety on the following page.

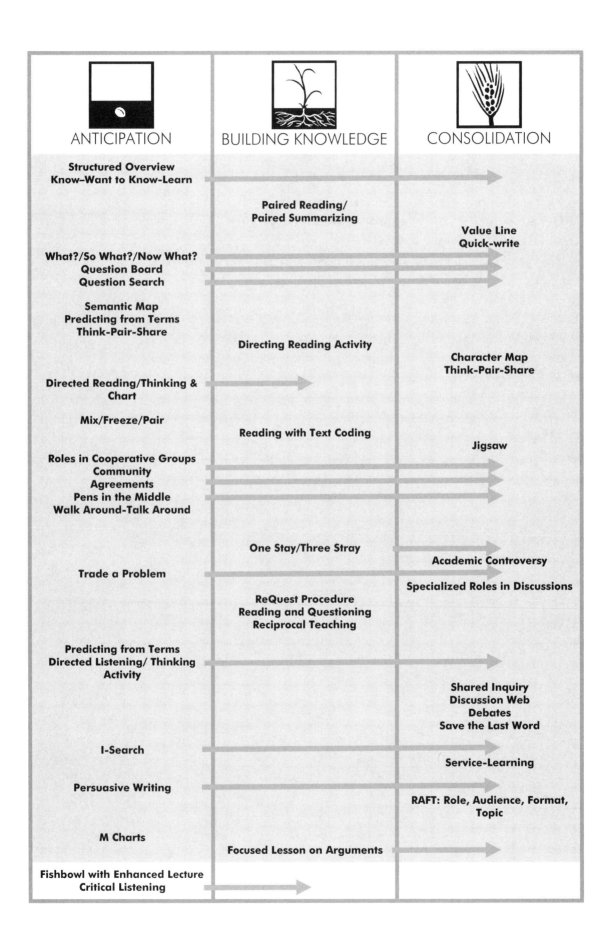

| ANTICIPATION | BUILDING KNOWLEDGE | CONSOLIDATION |
|---|---|---|
| **Structured Overview**<br>**Know–Want to Know-Learn** | | |
| | **Paired Reading/**<br>**Paired Summarizing** | **Value Line**<br>**Quick-write** |
| **What?/So What?/Now What?**<br>**Question Board**<br>**Question Search** | | |
| **Semantic Map**<br>**Predicting from Terms**<br>**Think-Pair-Share** | **Directing Reading Activity** | **Character Map**<br>**Think-Pair-Share** |
| **Directed Reading/Thinking &**<br>**Chart** | | |
| **Mix/Freeze/Pair** | **Reading with Text Coding** | **Jigsaw** |
| **Roles in Cooperative Groups**<br>**Community**<br>**Agreements**<br>**Pens in the Middle**<br>**Walk Around-Talk Around** | | |
| | **One Stay/Three Stray** | **Academic Controversy** |
| **Trade a Problem** | | **Specialized Roles in Discussions** |
| | **ReQuest Procedure**<br>**Reading and Questioning**<br>**Reciprocal Teaching** | |
| **Predicting from Terms**<br>**Directed Listening/ Thinking**<br>**Activity** | | |
| | | **Shared Inquiry**<br>**Discussion Web**<br>**Debates**<br>**Save the Last Word** |
| **I-Search** | | **Service-Learning** |
| **Persuasive Writing** | | **RAFT: Role, Audience, Format,**<br>**Topic** |
| **M Charts** | **Focused Lesson on Arguments** | |
| **Fishbowl with Enhanced Lecture**<br>**Critical Listening** | | |

# SECTION 3:

# LESSON PLANNING AND ASSESSMENT

# 1. LESSON PLANNING

Planning to teach in a way that encourages reading and writing for critical thinking is not a simple thing. Most teachers who come to workshops that demonstrate active teaching methods worry a little or a lot about the demands of "fitting it all in": covering the curriculum, but allowing time for students' creativity to flourish and for their ideas to come forth.

This section approaches planning in two ways. It describes the task of planning individual lessons that encourage reading and writing for critical thinking at the same time it covers the content of the curriculum. It also describes the planning of interdisciplinary units, because these often lead students into genuine real-life inquiry. The discussion begins by considering the fundamental principles a teacher should keep in mind when planning for teaching that elicits deep learning.

## AUTHENTICITY, CHOICE, AND COMMUNITY

How do you decide if your own classroom encourages critical thinking and active learning? How do you set guideposts for yourself and your students?

Here are three important indicators that you can consider as you plan, enact, and assess lessons. These indicators are also important for considering the "feel" of the classroom, what might be called the classroom atmosphere.

### Authenticity
When we teach students about language, we need to think about what people who are competent or masterful users of language go about their work. What they view as valuable? We ask similar questions about scientists or artists. How do they go about their work? What do they view as valuable? In short, we need to foster in students the kind of thinking that people who are good at and love their field of study engage in. How do they ask questions? How do they evaluate their own work? And the work of others?

A general understanding of the authentic processes used by those who work with the information or ideas that students are studying should, ideally, be brought to bear in our planning for student activities.

Authenticity is also an issue for students. Are the problems they encounter in the classroom personally meaningful and engaging to them? Are the challenges sensible? Lucy Calkins, the author of *The Art of Teaching Writing* (2000), talks about the kind of assignments she had as a girl: write about your life as a pencil, or your journey as a postage stamp. Since we will never (nor do we aspire to) be a pencil or a postage stamp, this kind of writing, Calkins suggests, will not be useful to students learning the craft of writing.

Similarly, in choosing reading assignments, our goal is to help students see that what they read has relevance to their lives. Though they will never be Alexander the Great, the choices made by a nation's leader are important to consider and evaluate. Reading and writing both help us better understand how the world and the people in it work; not to use it for that end is frankly foolish.

Authenticity is also evident in the way classroom teachers and students interact. When students' ideas are respected and credited, they are encouraged to take risks and to make their thinking public. Teachers who ask students to do little more then repeat, end up with a classroom of parrots. On the contrary, teachers who ask questions that require thought, questions that the teacher often ponders, finds herself working in a room filled with interesting minds, a room where the experience of individuals enriches the learning of all.

## Choice

Students working in a classroom that values critical thinking and active learning need both the freedom and responsibility of their professional counterparts. If they are to be made responsible for producing excellent work, they have many decisions to make: how will I use my time? With whom do I wish to work? Why? How do I know when I'm doing a good job? What will help me when I am having trouble producing excellent work?

Choice is central to critical thinking. Without choice, there is really no reason to think. Teachers would do well to consider the places in their curriculum where choices might be made available. Here are a few of the variables worth considering:

> Time
> Variations in answers that receive high marks
> Resources, e.g., books, magazines or web sites to be used
> Project ideas
> Grading strategies (have them work with you to create rubrics)
> Topics for writing assignments
> Methods of presentation

## Community

In the classroom, teacher and students work as a unique community of thinkers. One year looks and feels different than the next, not just because a new textbook or strategy is being used, but also because each year students come with different experiences and thoughts to share. To get the most from classroom life, students and teachers must be aware of the resources available within the classroom community: who writes fantasy and who reads biography? Who spells well and who never forgets to bring in her homework? In the real world, we benefit from the talents of others and we help those who need our help. The classroom provides a perfect laboratory for learning those same skills.

## PLANNING FOR INSTRUCTION

When teachers attend workshops where they see new methods for active learning demonstrated, they often wonder how they can work these methods into their short class periods. We will attempt to answer that question here. We recognize, however, that in different places teachers use different lesson plans, and sometimes the form is firmly dictated by local policies. If that is the case, consider the following as a guide to thinking through a lesson, rather than a prescription for a formal lesson plan.

## PLANNING AN INDIVIDUAL LESSON

Teachers report that planning lessons that invite active learning takes more care than planning traditional lessons. That is because the teacher is not simply writing down pages of a book to be covered or a lecture to be delivered. Instead, the teacher is choreographing the activity of many students at once. And this means thinking through what the lesson is meant to achieve and what students must do to gain the most from it.

The planning procedure that is laid out below is deliberately elaborated to show what a teacher thinks about at each phase of a lesson: before, during, and after. With practice, much of this will become second nature, and the plans will not need to be thought through in such detail.

When I teach reading and writing for critical thinking, it is true that I spend more time planning my lessons, because I now think of ways for students to "mine" their own knowledge, instead of thinking of students only as places to "deposit" more knowledge. As a result, the students are taking more risks in learning and communicating, and they are assuming more responsibility for learning in the classroom.

(Secondary-school teacher, Kyrgyzstan)

## PRELIMINARY CONCERNS

**What is the topic or question?** Lesson planning usually begins with the topic. It is preferable to state the topic in the form of a question, because questions raise curiosity and encourage inquiry. For example, instead of setting as the topic "The Amazon River," we might instead frame the study around the question "How has the Amazon River affected the lives of people who live along it?" The students will study the same content either way, but in the latter case they will be invited from the very beginning to look for answers.

**Why is this lesson worthwhile?** It is a good idea to ask why the lesson is valuable: how the lesson in itself helps the students, or how it functions as an important step in the sequence of understandings, or as an opportunity to practice thinking and communication skills.

**What are the objectives? That is, what do you expect students to understand and be able to do by the end of the lesson?** Objectives guide your teaching—but only if they are detailed, only if they describe observable behaviors so clearly that you could tell if the student had or had not achieved the objective. Having objectives for understandings and abilities means that the focus should not just be on what is learned but on what the students can do with the learning: what kind of thinking, interacting, and communicating they do. Objectives should address not only the content students should learn, but also the nature of their learning, and the strategies of thinking, investigating, and communicating they will learn to use. For example, an objective for a lesson might be "Students will learn the geography of the Amazon River and its resources." But a better objective would be "Students will be able to contrast the effects of the Amazon River on the lives of the peoples who live along different stretches of it."

## ACTIVITIES

**Anticipation Activities:** What will you do at the beginning of the lesson to remind the students of what they already know, or give them preliminary information, or lead them to ask questions or set purposes for learning? These include activities like **brainstorming, free writes, think/pair/share,** or **semantic maps.**

**Building Knowledge Activities:** What will you do to help students encounter the material, especially in such a way that they are actively inquiring, exploring, and discovering? Activities for this phase include **text coding, reciprocal teaching,** and **paired reading.**

**Consolidation Activities.** What will you do to help students to think back over what they have learned, and think of its implication? How can they be led to apply it, interpret it, debate it? Activities for the consolidation phase include **shared inquiry**, the **discussion web**, and the **jigsaw.**

**Extension Activities.** What will students do after the lesson to practice new skills, apply new ideas, and otherwise to extend their learning?

## MANAGEMENT CONCERNS

 **RESOURCES:** What materials or space will you need?

**TIME REQUIRED:** With student-centered activities, it can be a challenge to fit all of the activities into a limited amount of time. It helps to write down the amount of time you want to allow for each part of the lesson, so you can speed up or slow down as necessary. It also helps to plan a lesson over more than one instructional period. A lesson might begin with the anticipation activity during the last 10 minutes of one class period. Then the students can carry out the "building knowledge" activity outside of class, by reading or writing something on their own, interviewing someone in the community, or otherwise collecting data. The **consolidation activity** can take place at the beginning of the next class period.

 **GROUP SIZE:** Perhaps you have 30 nine-year-olds in your class. Or you have 100 seven-year-olds. Or you have 10 eight-year-olds, 12 nine-year-olds, and 11 ten-year-olds. In each case, you should decide how you will work with the students:

> As a whole group?
> As individuals?
> Working with a small group while individuals work on their own, independently, or in small groups?
> In small cooperative groups?
> Sharing students with another teacher?
> Having parent volunteers or older students helping out as tutors or small group proctors?

**ASSESSMENT:** How you assess the students depends upon what the objectives for the lesson are. Objectives relating to the mastery of content will require that students demonstrate that they learned the content. Objectives related to the practice of a skill will require that you observe that practice. Assessment is treated at length in a later section.

Here is a sample lesson plan, written to the format just described.

## SAMPLE LESSON PLAN

## PRELIMINARY CONCERNS

| | |
|---|---|
| **What is the topic or question?** What question and information should students investigate during this lesson? | What are the effects of the Amazon River on people who live along different parts of it? |
| **Why does it matter?** Why is this knowledge worth having? What opportunities for thinking and communicating does this lesson afford? | The Amazon River is a major river, worth knowing about in its own right. The class will be studying the history of Brazil, and the river is central to understanding that. The lesson allows students to conceptualize relationships between geography and human activities. |
| **What are the objectives?** What knowledge should the students gain? What should they be able to do with that knowledge? What strategies for thinking, investigating, and communicating will they learn? | **Content objective:** Students will be able to explain the effects of the Amazon River on the lives of the peoples who live along different stretches of it. **Process objective:** Students will be able to read a text to find information about the Amazon River. Students will be able to present information graphically. Students will work cooperatively and share responsibility for a task. |

## ACTIVITIES

**Anticipation.** What will you do at the beginning of the lesson to remind the students of what they already know, or give them needed information, or lead them to ask questions, or set purposes for learning?

**Advance Organizer.** Teacher will tell two short stories to orient students to the topic of the Amazon River.
**K-W-L.** Teacher will ask students what they know and what they want to know about life along the Amazon River.

**Building Knowledge.** What will you do to help students encounter the material, especially in such a way that they are actively inquiring, exploring, and discovering?

**Paired Reading/Paired Summarizing.**
**Reading with Text Coding.** Students will read a monograph about the Amazon River and code information about:
1. Geography of the river
2. History of settlements
3. Economic activity

**Consolidation Activities.** What will you do to help students to think back over what they have learned, and think of its implication? How can they be led to apply it, interpret it, debate it?

**Presentation with Graphic Organizers.**
Students will display their learning about the river using graphic means. Students will critique each other's presentations using a rubric (see below).

**Extension Activities.** What will students do after the lesson to practice new skills, apply new ideas, and otherwise extend their learning?

Students will prepare promotional brochures for chosen sections of the river.

## MANAGEMENT CONCERNS

**Time Required:** How will time be allocated to each part of the lesson?

The lesson will be conducted over three class periods:
1st day: Advance Organizer.
2nd day: Reading and coding, and preparing displays.
3rd day: Presenting displays

**Resources:** What materials or space will you need?

Students will need copies of the monograph "The Story of the Amazon," one for each pair. They will need big sheets of paper and charcoal for writing. They can work on top of their desks to create the displays.

**Group size:** In what groups will students work? Individuals? Pairs? Home groups and expert groups? Whole class?

Pairs will read. They will join other pairs to pool their information and make the displays.

**Assessment:** How will the students learning of the content and of the thinking and communicating strategies be assessed?

Students will be evaluated by means of a paper-and-pencil test about the Amazon River. They will also use these rubrics (they will be shared and discussed in advance):
a. Rubrics for the graphic presentation. (One is for self-assessment, and the other for assessing one other group's project).
b. Rubric for self-assessment of each student's participation in the group.

## THEMATIC UNITS OF INSTRUCTION

A government agency is charged with protecting the environment. A team of experts in that agency is asked to write a law to protect children from the effects of lead poisoning. This cannot be done by a single person. A good solution will draw on many kinds of expert knowledge.

- A physician can explain the harm done by different amounts of lead that people take into their bodies, but she can't tell you all the ways people are exposed to lead originally.
- An environmental scientist can identify sources of lead in the environment, but he cannot say how products can be made differently to eliminate lead pollution.
- An engineer can tell us ways to substitute safer ingredients for lead in many products, but she cannot tell if the companies that produce those products could make those substitutions without losing money.
- An economist can calculate how much it will cost to take lead out of the products that cause lead pollution, but he would not know how to write a law acceptable to everyone.
- A political scientist can suggest ways to write the law that will satisfy most of the people who are affected by it, but she will rely on all of the others for the information she needs.

In fact, it will take all of these people—a physician, an environmental scientist, an industrial engineer, an economist, and a political scientist—working together for many months to write a bill that will protect children from lead pollution.

Inquiry in the real world is often like that: people divide a problem into its parts, find information from different disciplines, and work together to find a solution. As teachers prepare students for productive citizenship in the real world, many make use of thematic units of instruction.

**Thematic units** are usually extended lessons or a series of lessons that approach a topic from different viewpoints. They usually reflect the framework of more than one discipline. Thematic units go beyond lectures and books, and they employ a rich variety of learning resources. They may have students researching different aspects of the topic at the same time, and they almost certainly involve students in making choices of what they will study, in deciding how they will pursue that study, and in carrying out the study.

The thematic unit consists of an interdisciplinary framework for organizing the work of several days or weeks as a set of related and sequenced lessons. The components of a thematic unit usually include:

> **Goals and objectives**—What are the desired outcomes?
> **Activities**—What activities and strategies will lead to success in learning?
> **Instructional materials and resources**—What is needed to implement the unit?
> **Assessment**—How will the teacher assess the effectiveness of the unit?

The thematic unit provides an opportunity for the teacher who teaches all subjects to integrate reading and writing across the curriculum. The unit can incorporate information from social science, science, literature, mathematics, and other subject areas. Teachers can augment the text in the classroom and library with text on the theme from the Internet, from magazines, and from newspapers. Other sources of information include observations, experimentation, field trips, and other direct experiences both in and out of the classroom.

In a departmentalized secondary school, teachers of different subjects may team together to plan and present a thematic unit. A social studies teacher gives lessons on content related to the theme. A literature teacher gives lessons from novels that reflect the theme, and so on. Students can sometimes be involved in planning thematic units with guidance and direction from a teacher or from several teachers in different disciplines.

Thematic units of study offer several advantages to students.

1.  They may follow the course of the students' and teacher's curiosity across disciplinary boundaries. Like real-life inquiries, they demonstrate the integrated nature of knowledge and make natural connections to what students know and what they want to know.
2.  They actively engage students as learners in many levels of activity:
    *   Framing questions
    *   Organizing inquiry
    *   Finding resources
    *   Collecting information
    *   Organizing their findings
    *   Presenting and teaching their findings to others
3.  They allow students to go beyond the limited perspectives of textbooks and use the fullest available range of resources available on a topic.
4.  They offer opportunities for students to work cooperatively on meaningful tasks. Teachers can provide reading materials on different levels to meet the needs of students with different abilities.
5.  Capable students and less capable students can work together effectively.

Thematic units also pose several challenges to the teacher and the students alike. They require:

1.  careful planning; the teacher must locate in advance the resources needed by the students.
2.  the teacher to coordinate the activities of several groups of students working together for many days or even weeks.
3.  the teacher to pay attention to the skills students will need. The teacher may need to conduct "Just in Time" lessons on the skills of research, data processing, writing, and presentation that the students will need to employ, including some or all of the following:

    *   Using a library to find resources
    *   Etiquette and safety issues when arranging and carrying out an interview
    *   Note taking and transcription
    *   What to do when sources disagree
    *   Conducting a survey
    *   Using graphs for tabulating and reporting data from surveys
    *   Writing outlines and first drafts of reports

- Revising reports to make them informative and clear
- Editing reports for correctness
- Making oral presentations to share outcomes

4. that the teacher be ready to assess learning in many different ways; much of the learning will be richer that what can be captured in a paper-and-pencil test.

## STEPS IN DEVELOPING A THEMATIC UNIT

Teachers often plan their own thematic units. A more advanced form of planning involves students at the earliest stages. Below is an example of the steps in this process.

### Step 1: The topic for the unit is decided on.

The teacher identifies a range of possible topics for a unit before bringing the idea to the students. A good topic may come from the curriculum, students' interests or a problem the class is having, or a story in the news.

Before suggesting the topic to the class, the teacher should ensure that there are sufficient resources to support several strands of inquiry suggested by a topic.

### Step 2: The topic is introduced.

The teacher may tell a story or read an essay and ask students what they already know about the topic and what they want to know in a K-W-L mode.

The teacher may make some observations and ask a question.

### Step 3: The students brainstorm subtopics.

The teacher asks the students to list subtopics of a large topic, or questions that invite students to investigate aspects of the topic. The class may together make a cluster of subtopics or questions related to the main topic.

The teacher adds questions of his or her own to ensure that key issues in a topic will be covered and also that the questions will lead students to resources that are available.

The teacher raises questions from different disciplinary viewpoints. In order to prepare these questions, the teacher may consider the following: How has this topic been treated in the arts: in literature, drama, dance, and music? How do science and mathematics help us understand this topic? How has the topic been treated in philosophy? In history? What national significance does the topic have now? How does it affect people in this community right now? How does it affect the students in this class? Other teachers and classes may have contributions to make here.

The teacher asks the students to narrow the list of subtopics down to five or six interesting ones, combining some subtopics into new ones if necessary.

**Step 4: The teacher and the students identify resources for learning more about each subtopic.**

The teacher tells the students about possible sources of information on the subtopics and gives examples: newspapers; community experts; works of fiction; surveys; other teachers; the Internet.

**Step 5: Committees are formed to plan the study of their subtopics.**

Students assign themselves or are assigned to groups to research each subtopic. (Teachers use their judgment to form groups that will work well together.)

Group members prepare a written proposal of the work they plan to do. The teacher posts questions on the wall to guide this step:

> What questions will you answer in your report?
> What resources will you use (books, interviews, surveys)?
> What tasks will each person do?
> What is your schedule for completing your work (proposal submitted, research completed, first draft of report, presentation of the report)?
> What help will you need from the teacher or from others?
> How will you ensure that everyone participates?
> Each proposal is presented to the teacher, who reviews it and makes suggestions for improvements.

**Step 6: The teacher conducts "Just in Time" lessons on the skills the students will need.**

The teacher anticipates the skills of research, data processing, writing, and presentation that the students will need to employ, and also stays alert to other skills that become necessary along the way. The teacher makes short, well-planned lessons to teach each skill. Ideas for such lessons can include some of the following:

- Using a library to find resources
- Etiquette and safety issues when arranging and carrying out an interview
- Note taking and transcription
- What to do when sources disagree
- Conducting a survey
- Using graphs for tabulating and reporting data from surveys
- Writing outlines and first drafts of reports
- Revising reports to make them informative and clear
- Editing reports for correctness
- Making oral presentations to share outcomes

In a typical lesson, the teacher demonstrates and perhaps even role-plays the skill in question, and immediately asks the students to practice the skill themselves, if possible.

## Step 7: The students carry out their research working in their groups.

Time is set aside in class or outside of school for the students to plan together and do their work. The teacher may assign cooperative learning roles within the groups: questioner, checker, timekeeper, active listener, and summarizer.

The teacher meets frequently with each group to ensure that each person has a clear role and direction, that the work is going ahead on schedule, and that obstacles are being overcome.

The teacher arranges a time for each group to make a preliminary presentation of their findings. The teacher may suggest further research at this stage.
Representatives from each group may meet in a plenary committee, with the teacher in attendance, to make sure that the reports will fit together to give adequate coverage of the whole topic.

## Step 8: The groups make their presentations.

The presentations may be made in many media: oral reports, a magazine or class book, a poster discussion (each group displays a poster and uses it as a basis for their talk about their topic), a radio show (real or fictional), or a bill to be introduced in parliament (fictional).

The presentations may be made to different audiences. They may first present their findings to one another, but they also may share them with other classes in the school or with adult citizens' groups. They may write them in book form and put the book in the school library. They may send them to a newspaper.

## Step 9: The class decides on follow-up actions.

The students follow the presentations with a discussion about what they should do next.

There are probably thank-you letters to write, and there may be other actions they can take. For example, if the topic was conflict resolution, how can the class or the whole school incorporate the lessons they learned into their daily conduct? If the topic was waves, how can they send help to the victims of a typhoon they studied?

They may decide what related topic they want to study. A study of waves might lead to a study of the sea. A study of conflict resolution may lead to a study of ethnic group relations.

## Step 10: The students' learning is evaluated.

Evaluation of a thematic unit usually focuses on three aspects:

1. The content the students learned.
2. The skills and processes they used.
3. Whether or not the lesson expanded students' understanding of the topic under consideration.

## EXAMPLE OF THEMATIC UNIT

A typical integrated thematic unit can be seen on the facing page. The teacher has assembled expository text, authentic literature, video, and other resources that reflect the theme of the unit, *Endangered Condors*, and the activity therefore fits into the genre of critical literacy as well. There is a video to initiate the unit and motivate students, one of news accounts of condor kills and another about condors in general. The unit includes expository text about condors and other avian scavengers, trade books in multiple copies, related selections of text from the science textbook used in the classroom, and a book on drawing birds so that students can illustrate their written work.

Over a period of about four weeks, the students will read the texts, building background knowledge and vocabulary related to the theme. Writing activities will also emerge from them, resulting in social action, posters urging students to protect condors and other endangered birds.

| GOALS | ACTIVITIES | ASSESSMENT | TEXT SOURCES | INTERVAL |
| --- | --- | --- | --- | --- |
| formulate questions about condors and their environment | view video or read aloud from magazine or enhanced lecture with illustrations | quality of student questions generated | video about condors | 1 day |
| read with fluency | paired reading | accuracy of oral reading | book about condors | periodic, 3-4 days |
| read silently with comprehension | guided reading in small groups, discuss findings in literature circles | observation, quality of discussion | Andean folk tale about condors | 4 days |
| listening comprehension | listen to music that suggests cultural aspects of condors | quality of discussion | *El Condor Pasa* | 1 day |
| read silently with comprehension | guided reading during science lesson | observation, quality of discussion | science textbook | 2 days |
| find information on the internet or in newspapers; interest groups formed to work together | select them to research condors as scavengers; where condors live; efforts to save condors | criteria: use of descriptors, refinement of descriptors, appropriateness of selected text | Google.com | periodic, 4 weeks |
| write informational and persuasive text about protecting endangered condors; illustrate posters | RAFT (role/audience /format/theme) | rubrics | research from Internet, newspapers | 3 days following research activities |
| illustrate informational writing accurately | illustrate informational and persuasive writings | relationships of illustrations to text written by students | illustrations and photographs of birds | 1 day following writing activities |
| read silently with comprehension | silent sustained reading of self-selected narrative and expository books about condors and related scavenger birds | motivation, conferences | various books about condors and other endangered species | periodic over 4 weeks |

# 2. ASSESSMENT

## ASSESSMENT OF CRITICAL THINKING AND ACTIVE LEARNING

One of the first questions teachers ask when they begin to teach for active learning and critical thinking is, "What do we do about assessment?" After all, when the task is as simple as giving back the right answer, assessing students' learning and assigning marks are straightforward matters. But what if teachers want to assess both content that students have learned and their ability to work together cooperatively in groups, or pose original and logical answers to problems? These are worthwhile aims, but assessing them is not such a simple matter.

In classes that promote active learning and critical thinking, teachers do assess students' mastery of the content of the curriculum, and they may do this by means of traditional paper-and-pencil tests, by oral recitations, or by observations as students discuss topics related to a lesson. But they also look at two more things. They assess students' learning processes. That is, they observe carefully to see how well students can carry out the learning activities that they have been taught, and to find ways to improve their learning. They also assess the quality of students' thinking. At the same time, teachers take care to assess in such a way that they teach students how to perform. We will explain what we mean by this below.

Given the complexity of assessing content and skills learned in lessons that apply active learning and critical thinking strategies, we have included some common questions and problem areas and ideas that teachers have devised to overcome those problems. In addition, we have provided an example of one way to organize for assessment during active learning (Figure 1). This example is from a chem-istry lesson but could as easily be applied to history, biology, or any of a wide range of other content areas.

We also present a rubric for assessing students' skills as they complete a Directed Reading-Thinking Activity (Figure 2). The rubric allows the teacher to assess skills specific to a particular learning activity. Next we have developed a model for marking a particular product—in this case an essay based on a piece of literature (Figure 3). Finally, we have included a set of standards for students and teachers developed around critical thinking and oral and written communication. These standards and rubrics can be applied to a wide variety of lessons and grade levels.

## ASSESSMENT IN ACTIVE LEARNING ENVIRONMENTS

As teachers who use active learning strategies, we are faced with challenges when we are asked to mark the work of individual students. What are some of the challenges and how have some teachers met those challenges?

### With so much activity during lessons, how can a teacher know what to mark?

Many times teachers in this situation will make a checklist of particular skills to be marked. These checklists are frequently used as rubrics to mark each pupil's mastery of those skills. These can include types of questions that pupils ask (high level or low level), whether or not a pupil provides evidence for some claim, or how a pupil responds to a challenge by another pupil. We have included a set of rubrics as an example.

### How can we mark individual pupils when they are working in groups?

Teachers who are faced with this problem sometimes pick one pupil to observe for a period of time and then move on to another pupil. While the teacher is observing the individual, that pupil's contribution to the group's work can be marked. Again, the rubrics we present can be used for individual students. Teachers frequently have folders for individual students and date each entry so that they can observe pupils development across the school year.

### With several pupils working in a group, how can the teacher keep track of which pupils are contributing?

One solution is to make a seating chart of which pupils are seated in groups. As individual pupils contribute, the teacher can make a note of their contribution. This is often used in conjunction with the checklist we described above to mark the contributions of each member of a group. Once the teacher is satisfied that members of a group have been observed adequately, the teacher then moves on to another group.

### Active learning does help us teach pupils how to interact and how to think critically, but how can teachers evaluate knowledge of the content of the lesson?

As in the assessment of skills, some teachers make charts of major concepts or facts covered in the lesson. Then, as pupils use the concepts or facts in their discussions or in their presentations, the teacher can make notes of the use of the information by individual pupils. This often provides a more in-depth assessment of learning than does a test of memory. This style of assessment tells the teacher whether or not the pupil knows how to apply the knowledge, and goes beyond memory tests.

Teachers might also find that the pupils' written products are helpful. These products are frequently in the form of notes or outlines to prompt the presenter or in the form of charts, illustrations, or other display for use as an aid to the presentation or discussion. The products can be assessed for the content of the lesson and for evidence of critical thinking. Several of the rubrics that we present focus on written products.

### Assessment after the activity:

For content assessment, the teacher might prepare a post-debate examination on the content of the debate or other active learning experiences. However, care must be exercised to construct an examination that poses high-level questions in which knowledge of the content and the ability to apply the content are assessed. These examinations are frequently essay examinations that require the pupil to know and apply the content.

Since one way to encourage and assess learning at deep levels is to provide opportunities for students to reflect on their experiences, teachers might ask students to free-write about their thoughts on an activity. This could include thoughts on the progression of the activity, the most effective strategies used during the activity, the least effective, and the content information most important to the activity (e.g., most persuasive points, new points encountered, points that went against individual student's beliefs).

For post-activity assessment, the teacher can refer to the rubrics as a way to evaluate pupils' knowledge and skills. We have included rubrics that are designed to assess written reflections and pupils' motivation and cooperation. Pupils' own reflections about the active learning process can give the teacher insight into how the lessons are progressing.

Following the activity, the teacher might ask participants to write a brief summary of the major points in the lesson and how those points are related to each other. The summaries can then be examined for key content points as well as evidence of critical thinking (see Rubrics in Appendix 1 for examples).

### Self-assessment and peer assessment by the pupils:

Pupils can use the rubrics and checklists to assess their own perceptions of their work in active learning situations. As teachers compare pupils' perceptions with teacher perceptions, differences between teachers' and pupils' views of performance can be discussed and clarified.

Pupils who are working in groups might assess each other's performance in the groups. However, prior to peer assessment, care must be given to pupils' understanding of constructive and helpful feedback.

## STEPS TO SIMPLIFY ASSESSMENT DURING ACTIVE LEARNING

1. Before the lesson, the teacher creates checklists or rubrics based on goals and objectives of the lesson. Assessment is most reliable and valid when teachers clearly state the goals and objectives of the lesson in ways that can be communicated with pupils, parents, and school administrators and in ways that support observations during the lesson.

2. In order to develop rubrics for assessing students' work, the teacher first decides on the criteria that describe a good job of the task. The criteria do not state simply that the students should get the "right answer" to the question, but rather they set out the kind of reasoning and communicating that the student should do (See Figures 2 and 3 for examples). As rubrics and checklists are developed, teachers typically take time to explain them to the pupils. For some active learning strategies, pupils might be included in development of the rubrics and checklists. This provides an opportunity for teaching pupils as well. As the teacher explains and discusses the rubrics with the pupils, pupils' understanding of concepts such as higher order questions or active listening can be checked and reinforced as needed.

3. If individual pupils are to be assessed, checklists that include pupils' names, dates of observations, and the lesson theme can be quite helpful. If rubrics are used for individual pupils, then space for the name, date, and theme are easily included.

4. For each lesson using active learning strategies, select a group (if group work is used) or individuals who will be assessed in advance. This will allow the teacher to plan who and what skills will be assessed on a particular day.

## FIGURE 1: SAMPLE LESSON GOALS AND ASSESSMENT OPPORTUNITIES

Students will be able to describe similarities and differences between hydrogen and helium, explain why hydrogen, given a spark and sufficient oxygen, will explode and why helium will not. In reaching their conclusion, they will require an understanding of the concept of level of activity of each element based on electron activity, and the necessary and sufficient conditions for explosive ignition of a gas.

In the process of the lesson, students will engage in active learning strategies that require listening actively, reporting orally, questioning peers' assertions, identifying sources for information, and engaging in discussions and deliberations with group members to reach consensus on their conclusions.

In order to reach conclusions necessary to achieve the goals of the lessons, students will demonstrate critical thinking skills of comparing, evaluating, identifying cause-effect relationships, and composing presentations (written and oral) that are logically consistent and contain support for assertions.

| CONTENT GOALS: | INSTRUCTIONAL ACTIVITY | PRODUCT OR BEHAVIOR FOR ASSESSMENT |
|---|---|---|
| 1. Characteristics of Hydrogen | Modified Lecture DRTA Jigsaw | Observation:<br>• Discussion during group work<br>• Presentations to home groups<br>Products:<br>• Written notes for reports to home groups<br>• Reports by home groups<br>• Individual papers composed as post-activity reports<br>• Unit examination |
| 2. Characteristics of Helium | Modified Lecture DRTA Jigsaw | Observation:<br>• Discussion during group work<br>• Presentations to home groups<br>Products:<br>• Written notes for reports to home groups<br>• Reports by home groups<br>• Individual papers composed as post-activity reports<br>• Unit examination |
| 3. Valence or Electron Activity Level | Modified Lecture DRTA | Observation:<br>• Discussion during group work<br>• Presentations to home groups<br>Products:<br>• Written notes for reports to home groups<br>• Reports by home groups<br>• Individual papers composed as post-activity reports<br>• Unit examination |
| 4. Conditions for Ignition/Explosion of Gases | Modified Lecture DRTA | Observation:<br>• Discussion during group work<br>• Presentations to home groups<br>Products:<br>• Written notes for reports to home groups<br>• Reports by home groups<br>• Individual papers composed as post-activity reports<br>• Unit examination |

| CRITICAL THINKING SKILL GOALS: | PRODUCT OR BEHAVIOR FOR ASSESSMENT |
|---|---|
| 1. Compare-Contrast attributes of two members of a set (chemical elements) | Observation:<br>• Oral presentations<br>Products:<br>• Written notes for reports to home groups<br>• Written reports by home groups<br>• Individual papers composed as post-activity reports<br>• Unit examination |
| 2. Evaluate propositions to support or refute arguments | Observation:<br>• Discussion during group work<br>• Oral presentations<br>• Questions posed during discussions and presentations<br>Products:<br>• Written notes for reports to home groups<br>• Written reports by home groups<br>• Individual papers composed as post-activity reports<br>• Unit examination |
| 3. Identify and explain cause-effect relationships | Observation:<br>• Discussion during group work<br>• Presentations to home groups<br>Products:<br>• Written notes for reports to home groups<br>• Written reports by home groups<br>• Individual papers composed as post-activity reports<br>• Unit examination |
| 4. Compose a persuasive text presenting a logically consistent cause-effect relationship, including evidence to support assertions. | Observation:<br>• Presentations to whole class<br>Products:<br>• Written reports by home groups<br>• Individual papers composed as post-activity reports<br>• Unit examination |

**FIGURE 2: RUBRIC FOR A DIRECTED READING-THINKING ACTIVITY**

| RUBRIC FOR A DIRECTED READING-THINKING ACTIVITY | NEVER | SOMETIMES | MOST OF THE TIME |
|---|---|---|---|
| Once I know the genre or the type of the story (folktale, tall tale, realistic fiction, or fantasy), I can use it to narrow down my predictions. | | | |
| I look for the main character and the problem in the story and try to predict the solution to the problem from what is said about them. | | | |
| I pay attention to details in the story that may be important, and use them to guide predictions. | | | |
| I read carefully to see if my predictions are coming true or not. | | | |
| I can find the part of the text that confirms or disconfirms my prediction. | | | |
| After reading, I review my predictions and try to see what details guided the correct predictions. | | | |

Note that a rubric such as this should be thoroughly discussed with the students, and should be used frequently so that they will come to know these criteria very well. Once students have internalized the criteria, the rubric may be self-administered by the students.

## ASSESSING THE QUALITY OF STUDENTS' THINKING THROUGH WRITTEN PRODUCTS

Using the principle "assessments that teach" requires that teachers think through what kinds of thought process they want their students to be able to carry out. For example, the teacher who designed the rubric shown in Figure 3 had asked the students to write an essay that answered a question about a short story they had read. Notice that the teacher was not expecting the students to arrive at a particular answer, but rather show qualities of thinking and communicating.

**FIGURE 3: MARKING GUIDE FOR AN ESSAY ON "THE SECRET SHARER" (JOSEPH CONRAD)**

The assignment asks that you respond to this question:

**The captain of the ship in this story is a rigid man. How does his experience with the castaway he hides in his cabin transform him?**

In order to write a good response to this question, you must do these things:

1. Write a statement that clearly answers the question;
2. Furnish convincing arguments that draw on details from the text in order to support your answer;
3. Write an essay that is sufficiently clear that the reader can easily follow your presentation.

**Criterion 1: The essay has a thesis that is expressed by the end of the first paragraph that clearly sets out your answer to the question.**

There is no thesis, or
The thesis is not clearly stated.                                        The thesis is clear.

| 2 | 4 | 6 | 8 | 10 |
|---|---|---|---|----|

**Criterion 2: The thesis is supported by a convincing argument that draws on details from the text.**

The argument is not convincing, or it                    Convincing argument and significant
lacks details from the text                                                          details

| 2 | 4 | 6 | 8 | 10 |
|---|---|---|---|----|

**Criterion 3: The work is clear and correct.**

Paragraphs and transitions:

| 2 | 4 | 6 | 8 | 10 |
|---|---|---|---|----|

Clear sentences:

| 2 | 4 | 6 | 8 | 10 |
|---|---|---|---|----|

Grammatical Correctness:

| 2 | 4 | 6 | 8 | 10 |
|---|---|---|---|----|

Spelling and Punctuation:

| 2 | 4 | 6 | 8 | 10 |
|---|---|---|---|----|

(Source: Bean 1998)

A rubric like this one will be given to students before they begin writing the essay, so that the criteria will guide them as they plan and write the work.

## DEVELOPING RUBRICS

In order to develop rubrics for assessing students' work, the teacher first decides on the criteria that describe a good job of the task. The criteria do not state simply that the students should get the "right answer" to the question, but rather set out the kind of reasoning and communicating that the student should do. The criteria should be clearly and thoroughly explained to the students. It may help to show students examples of some works that do a good job and some that do a poor job of meeting the criteria. The criteria provide excellent teaching tools. If the students know what is important and what is expected, they more effectively listen for important information and instructions from the teacher and ask better questions to help make their learning more personal.

### Using the RWCT Rubrics

Some years ago, teachers in the Reading and Writing for Critical Thinking Project were asked to describe what they observed their students doing when they were learning well. After much deliberation, these teachers, who had for some years been using new teaching methods for reading and writing for critical thinking, arrived at a set of performance standards. The standards can be used to assess how individual students learn. But they can also be used with groups of students to assess the outcomes of the teacher's use of active teaching strategies. The standards for students are listed here.

### Standards for Students:

- The student provides not only answers, but also reasons for their answers to higher order questions.

- The student asks higher order questions of their peers and the teacher.

- The student produces oral and written products that reflect critical thinking.

- The student demonstrates initiative, motivation, and learning within and beyond the classroom by asking questions and initiating activities that go beyond the lesson.

- The student demonstrates self-confidence in learning, questioning, analyzing, and expressing ideas, positions, and opinions by presenting points of view that differ from or extend ideas presented by peers and the teacher.

- The student accesses, analyzes, and synthesizes information.

- The student applies critical thinking in mathematics and science by questioning conclusions drawn by others in response to experiments and by reaching conclusions based on information obtained from observations, measurements, and experiments.

The teachers also developed a set of rubrics for each standard: descriptions of what would be seen in the classroom if students were at beginning, intermediate, and advanced levels of proficiency on each standard. Those performance indicators (rubrics) are found in Appendix 1, at the end of this volume.

## SELF-ASSESSMENT FOR TEACHERS

The group of trainers for the Reading & Writing for Critical Thinking Project next developed a group of standards and performance indicators (rubrics) for teachers who were working new methods of teaching reading and writing for critical thinking into their instruction. These standards and rubrics can be used in at least three ways. First, even before the teachers attend workshops, they give teachers a clear idea of what the outcomes of the training program are intended to be. That is, if they learn everything they can from the training program, these describe what their practices will look like. Second, the teachers can use these standards and rubrics to assess their own performance while they are participating in the training program. They will be able to discern more clearly if their practices are achieving the intended results. And third, the trainers may use these standards and rubrics for evaluating the impact of the training program.

### Standards for Teachers:

The standards for teachers address three domains or aspects of teaching with seven standards:

CLIMATE FOR LEARNING
* Teachers provide student-centered classrooms in which they value students as individuals.
* The classroom environment prepared by teachers reflects content, principles, learning activities, and group strategies appropriate for the lesson.
* Teachers effectively present content from the national curriculum.
* Teachers integrate the crosscutting issues of civics, such as HIV/AIDS education, gender education, environmental education, and children's rights, as they teach the instructional program of their national curriculum.

PLANNING AND INSTRUCTION
* Teachers design instruction to promote active learning.
* Teachers use thoughtful questions to promote higher order thinking.
* Teachers encourage students to assume the roles of questioner, investigator, and civil critic.

ASSESSMENT AND EVALUATION
* Teachers design assessment and evaluation procedures aimed at assessing the content of the curriculum and critical thinking. They use the results of assessment to inform their teaching and enhance student learning.

Performance indicators are found in Appendix 1 at the end of this volume.

# SECTION 4:

# TEACHING IN AND ACROSS THE DISCIPLINES

In the previous sections of this guidebook we have demonstrated teaching methods applied in a range of different subject areas. In this section the focus is on individual disciplines, and also on interdisciplinary teaching.

 # 1. READING AND WRITING FOR CRITICAL THINKING IN LITERATURE STUDY

Of course, by studying literature students gain an appreciation of the forms and history of literature and of the author's craft. But by discussing and interpreting literature, students gain something more. Works of literature bring "slices of life" into the classroom, where students can discuss situations that matter, seen from the outside in and the inside out and described by masters of observation and linguistic craft. They can use works of literature to deepen their understanding of people near and far. As they discuss works with their classmates and hear how others respond to them, they can better understand their classmates and themselves.

In order for literature to contribute to the goal of enhancing students' understanding of human life, active teaching methods must be used. Students rarely gain insights from listening to the teacher's wisdom—they must work for those insights through thinking and discussion. Several teaching methods are especially well-suited for use with works of literature. Some, like **Shared Inquiry**, **Discussion Web**, **Assigning Roles in Discussions**, and **Save the Last Word for Me**, have already been introduced. Below we will introduce several more: **Dramatic Roles**, **Shifting Perspectives**, **Dramatic Interpretations**, and **A Study in Contrasts**.

### VIGNETTE: LITERARY CRITICISM

Mr. Pulin is introducing some analytical tools to an eighth grade literature class. He has deliberately chosen a simple story for this lesson, because his purpose is to show how even an interesting story can yield interesting insights when looked at closely. Sometimes devices from **literary criticism** can help students take a closer look. The story used here is the folktale "Jack and the Beanstalk," which can be found in its entirety in Appendix 2.

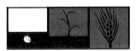 **ANTICIPATION**

**Mr. Pulin:** *Everybody here has been to a sporting event, right?*

**Students:** "Yes, we have."

**Mr. Pulin:** *Who has been to one recently?*

**Student 1:** "I have. It was a football game—the club from our town against the club from the neighboring town."

**Mr. Pulin:** "And did you cheer for one side or the other?"

**Student 2:** "Of course. We cheered for our town."

**Mr. Pulin**: *And what things did you say about the other team, while you were cheering your favorite team."*

**Student 3:** "We said they were clumsy brutes. We wished they would go back where they cam from."

**Mr. Pulin:** *Now tell me honestly.* <u>*Were*</u> *they clumsy brutes?*

**Student 4:** "Maybe not. After all, they won the game!"

**Mr. Pulin:** *You just demonstrated something important. When we are cheering for our own team, we automatically say they are the greatest, and we often think the worst about the other team, even though in reality—if you asked their mothers, at least—the other team may be made up of perfectly nice people. The same thing happens in politics: we assume our side is usually right and the other side is usually wrong. And the same thing even happens in literature. Watch this:*

Mr. Pulin writes these symbols and labels on the board:

> **The Hero**
> **The Goal**
> **The Rival**
> **The Helper**

*Story characters play certain roles, and they want certain things. A French drama critic identified three roles and one object that help orient readers to the characters and actions in a simple story. They are:*

> **The Hero**—*the person whose desires give direction to the actions in the story;*
> **The Goal**—*the object or condition of the protagonist's desires or needs;*
> **The Rival**—*the condition or person that opposes the hero as he or she tries to reach the goal;*
> **The Helper**—*the person or quality that helps the hero reach his or her goal.*

 **BUILDING KNOWLEDGE**

*As you read the story "Jack and the Beanstalk," decide who or what is playing each of those roles.*

The students read. When they have finished, he pairs them up and asks them to share their answers. Then he calls on students to share their answers.

**Student 5:** "We said the hero was Jack." (The class agrees.)

**Student 6:** "We couldn't agree on his goal, though. Was it money? But at first, he didn't know there was money up there. And after he got money, he kept going back."

**Student 7:** "We thought he wanted different things at different times. At first, he wanted just to obey his mother. Then he wanted to escape punishment. Then—"

**Student 8:** "He wanted adventure. And then he wanted money."

**Student 9:** "And then a *source* of money."

**Mr. Pulin:** *And after that?*

**Student 10:** "After he was rich, he wanted to sit back and enjoy the music!"

**Mr. Pulin:** *That's very interesting. Then who do you think Jack's rival was?*

**Student 11:** "Easy. The Giant."

**Mr. Pulin:** *And his helper?*

**Student 12:** "The old man who traded him the beans. After all, without the beans, he couldn't have gone up there."

**Student 13:** "We think it was the Giant's wife. After all, she helped him three times, by saving his life and making it possible for him to steal."

**Mr. Pulin**: *You're saying the Giant's own wife was Jack's helper? Why would she do that?*

 **CONSOLIDATION**

**Mr. Pulin** *Let's stay with the issue you just raised, when you said the Giant's wife was Jack's helper. Why would she help Jack? In your pairs, think about how this story would look if it were told from the Giant's wife's point of view. Suppose the Giant's wife were the hero. What would her goal be? Who would her rival be? Her helper?*

The students deliberate. After four minutes, the teacher calls for responses.

**Mr. Pulin:** *Who has an idea what her goal was?*

**Student 13:** "Here is what we have. If we made the Giant's wife the hero, then her goal was to save the boy's life. Maybe she wants a son because she never had one."

**Mr. Pulin:** *Then who was her rival?*

**Student 14:** "Her husband, the Giant."

**Mr. Pulin:** *And her helper?*

**Student 15:** "She didn't really have one, unless it was Jack. But he didn't seem to give her much thought."

**Mr. Pulin:** *What do you mean?*

**Student 16:** "Well, he didn't. He just left her up there, starving without her husband, for all Jack knew."

**Mr. Pulin:** *Thanks. Interesting answers. Now, can anyone compare what we just did to our earlier conversation about cheering for sports teams? What did it do to your feelings, to your loyalties, once you made the Giant's wife the hero instead of Jack?* [The conversation continues.]

## EXPLANATION AND DISCUSSION

This lesson demonstrates a way of guiding students' inquiry into a work of literature using an analytical tool we call **dramatic roles.** Notice that the use of this tool and the discussion that followed helped students do two things: the first was to better understand the story. The second was to better understand everyday life.

### DRAMATIC ROLES

Story characters play certain roles, and they want certain things. A French drama critic identified three roles and one object that help orient readers to the characters and actions in a simple story. They are:

> **The protagonist**—the person whose desires give direction to the actions in the story;
> **The goal**—the object or condition of the protagonist's desires or needs;
> **The rival**—the condition or the person that opposes the protagonist in getting her or his needs;
> **The helper**—the person or quality that helps the protagonist seek her or his needs.

Although these items are simple, trying to identify them can lead to interesting discussions. In "Jack and the Beanstalk," for example, students will readily agree that the **protagonist** is Jack. But who or what is the **goal**? Early in the story, Jack's goal is to escape punishment. Then it becomes his need for adventure, or to satisfy curiosity. Then it becomes money, then more lasting things. Students will enjoy keeping track of Jack's goal as the story proceeds. Who is the **rival**? Again, students will usually agree that the rival is the Giant. But then who is the **helper**? Some say it is the old man who traded him the magical beans for the cow. But others say it is the Giant's wife, who fed him and hid him from the Giant. If so, then this leads to the question, "Why is the wife of Jack's **rival** also Jack's **helper**?

## SHIFTING PERSPECTIVES

Using dramatic roles allows a class to look at a story from a different character's point of view. Suppose, for example, that the story is told from the point of view of the Giant's wife. She is the **protagonist**.

But what does she want? What is her **goal**? Perhaps it is to protect the boy, Jack. Perhaps her goal is to have companionship. Perhaps her goal is to have peace and harmony in her kitchen.

Who is her **rival**? It must be the Giant. But students will be shocked to see the Giant's wife going against her own husband to pursue the goal of protecting Jack. Why would she do that? Can we think of people in real life who might make the same kind of choice?

Who is her **helper**? She has none. And what happens to her in the end? Students may be shocked to realize that the Giant's wife is abandoned in the sky and left out of our consciousness at the story's end. The author sends our attention following Jack down the beanstalk, and we forget all about the woman who is left alone in the castle.

What does it do to our attention and our sympathy when we identify a character as a protagonist, a rival, or a helper—or don't assign them any role at all? These questions are worth exploring.

## GOALS OF THE DISCIPLINE

When it comes to critical thinking, the goals of the discipline of literature study can be summarized this way:

- Literature gives students templates of experience, plots, characters, situations, and themes that can help them understand similar things when they occur in the students' own experience.
- Literature gives students a common language for referring to and discussing the complex events of human life, including emotions and motives.
- Literature gives students a chance to hear how other people, coming from different sets of background experiences, interpret complex human events. In a sense, literature is a safer place to observe and negotiate different interpretations of events than the family, the neighborhood, or the ballot box.

## HOW READING AND WRITING FOR CRITICAL THINKING MEET THESE GOALS

1. It is important that students have opportunities to make their own interpretations of literary works.

2. They should also participate in discussions so that they will hear and engage other students' interpretations.

## DISCIPLINE-SPECIFIC TEACHING STRATEGIES FOR LITERATURE

Many of the strategies presented throughout this guidebook lend themselves quite well to the study of literature. Virtually all of the discussion techniques do, as well as the strategies for cooperative learning. Here are two additional teaching approaches that work well with literature.

### USING DRAMA TO INTERPRET LITERATURE

Dramatizing a story, or a part of a story, can be a very effective way for children to unpack its meaning. Dramatization should be done after the children have read or heard a story, and have had a chance to air their first thoughts about it. The procedures include these: *immerse* the students in the story, *choose critical moments* to dramatize, do *warm-ups*, invite students to *segment the situation*, *dramatize* the scene, *side-coach*, and *reflect* (The procedures that follow are adapted from Spolin (1988) and Heathcote (Wagner 1976).

**Step 1: Immerse students in the story**. You need to make sure the students get the story on a literal level—that they know what happened. This may mean reading the story to them, or asking them to reread the part you are going to dramatize.

**Step 2: Warm them up to do drama**. There are many warm-up activities that work well to prepare students to act with more expression.

1. *Stretches*. Have the students stand in a circle. Now tell them to stretch their arms as high as they can as they spread their feet apart and make very wide faces. Now tell them to shrink up into tiny balls. Then stretch out big again. Have them do the same with their faces: "Lion face!" (Expansive expression). "Prune face!" (Shrunken expression).

2. *Mirrors*. Have students stand opposite each other. One is the person and the other is her reflection in the mirror. Have the person move (slowly) as the partner mirrors her movements. Then switch roles.

3. *Portraits*. Have students get into groups of four or five. Have them think of something to depict that uses all of them as parts. For example, if they choose **lion tamer**, one student can be the lion tamer, others can be lions, others can be the guards, and others can be the thrilled spectators.

4. *Machines*. Have groups of students think of and dramatize an exotic factory machine in which parts move in relation to each other.

5. *Superactions*. This activity is more complex. Explain to the students that when we do things with other people we often act on two levels: what we are doing, and what we mean by what we are doing. For example, when we pass somebody we know in the hallway, having just seen him a short time before, we may nod and say, "Hi." But when we see a friend in the hallway who has just come back to school after a long vacation, we say "Hi!" In both cases the action is the same: to greet the friend. But the *superaction* is different—In the first case, it's just to show the person we know he's there, but in the second case it's to show that we're surprised and delighted to see him. Now practice dramatizing superactions by setting up brief situations. The **action** can be a waiter taking a customer's order. Write **superactions** on small pieces of paper and give one privately to each actor. They may be: to make the person go away; to make the person stay (you're lonely!); to impress the person. Have different pairs of students act out the same scene, the same actions, with different superactions, leaving time for the other students to guess what they thought the superaction was and say why they thought so.

**Step 3: Choose critical moments to dramatize**. It can be especially useful to dramatize just a few choice scenes from the story—especially the turning points: when the most is at stake. In the story of "Jack and the Beanstalk," a critical scene might be the moment when Jack first approaches the Giant's castle, knocks on the door, and is greeted by the Giant's wife.

**Step 4: Segment the Situation**. Now assign students to take the roles of the characters in the scene. Invite other students to join them as they think about the situation from each character's point of view. What must be on Jack's mind when he approaches the huge door? What do the door and the walls of the castle look like? How large are they in proportion to Jack? What does Jack hear around the place? What does he smell? How does the place make him feel? What makes him pound his fist on the door? What's at stake for him? What are his choices? What will he do if he *doesn't* knock on the door? Why does he decide to do it? Do the same for the Giant's wife. How does the knocking sound to her—huge or puny? What does she think when she sees the small but plucky boy at her door? What thoughts go through her mind, knowing what she knows about her husband? What are her feelings as she looks down at Jack?

Ask the actors to focus their minds on a few of these considerations as they prepare to act out the scene.

**Step 5: Dramatize the scene**. Use minimal props and minimal costumes to help students think their way into their roles. Ask the other students to watch carefully and see what the actors make them think of.

**Step 6: Side coach.** As the director, don't be passive, but take opportunities to make suggestions from the sidelines that will help children act more expressively: As Jack, do you feel scared now or brave? How can you show us how you're feeling?

**Step 7: Invite reflection**. Ask the other students what they saw. What did they think was on the characters' minds? It is worthwhile to invite several groups of students to dramatize the same scene, and discuss the aspects of the situation that each performance brings to light.

## A STUDY IN CONTRASTS

Simple stories, folktales especially, have characters and situations that are starkly contrasted with each other. It can be illuminating for students to study the contrasts in stories and use them to explore the "intertextuality" among stories—the similarities that have made some critics suggest that stories partake of each other and recapitulate the same elements.

It helps to start by asking:

**What two characters in the story are most in contrast to each other?** In the story of "Jack and the Beanstalk," those two characters would be Jack and the Giant. Then we ask,

**What words can we use that describe these characters?** We can set up columns like this:

| Jack | The Giant |
|---|---|
| Young | Old |
| Small | Huge |
| Poor | Rich |
| Weak | Strong |
| Seems unlikely to succeed | Seems invincible |
| On his way up in life | On his way down in life |
| Ambitious | Greedy |

Next, we can explore the idea of intertextuality by adding two more columns and asking:

**Who else is contrasted like these two characters?**

| | Jack | The Giant | |
|---|---|---|---|
| David | Younger | Older | Goliath |
| Hansel & Gretel | Small | Huge | The Witch |
| Snow White | Poor | Rich | Stepmother |
| Robin Hood | Weak | Strong | Sheriff of Nottingham |
| | Seems unlikely to succeed | Seems invincible | |
| | One his way up in life | On his way down in life | |
| | Ambitious | Greedy | |

Conversations about these contrasts can begin with characters in literature, and then go on to characters in history and in contemporary life. Why do stories have repeated patterns such as these contrasted characters? Do we ever exaggerate our differences with people we know in real life by assigning ourselves to one of these contrasted roles, and them to the other? What happens when we do?

# 2. READING AND WRITING FOR CRITICAL THINKING IN MATHEMATICS

## VIGNETTE: LONG DIVISION, SUBTRACTIVE METHOD (REPEATED SUBTRACTION)

Ms. Ybarra is going to re-introduce long division to her fifth-grade class. They learned the process the previous year, but they do not understand the mechanical algorithm that they have been using.

 **ANTICIPATION**

Ms. Ybarra divides her 50 students into.10 groups of 5 students. She gives each group 10 dry beans and asks, "How many times can you subtrac 2 beans from the 10?" Each group begins taking out beans 2 at a time, and one group finally shouts out, "5 times!" She then asks how many times they can subtract 5 beans from 10. The quickly respond, "Twice," without even counting. They can visualize the correct answer. She asks them how they know, and they tell her that 2 X 5 = 5 X 2. She asks what that relationship is called. Some remember that it is the **commutative principle of multiplication**.

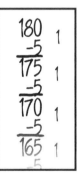

Then she gives each group 170 more beans and asks, "How many do you have now?" They quickly tell her, "180." Then she asks, "How many times can you subtract 5 beans from 180 beans?" They begin to pull out 5 beans at a time while one student records the number of times they do it. Several minutes later, they begin to report. The correct answer is 36, but some groups have different answers because they lost count. She helps them design a recording format by asking questions, but it takes a long time. Each time they subtract 5 beans, they record the number left and repeat by subtracting from the new number of beans that are left. You can see part of their work in the box at the left.

 **BUILDING KNOWLEDGE**

She then asks, "What do you think of this approach?" They respond, "It takes too long. It's boring  It uses too much paper."  She responds, "Let's see if we can solve this problem. How could we do it faster and still find the correct answer?" One student says, "Let's subtract two fives each time." They try it. One says, "It still takes too long. Let's subtract sets of  ten beans at a time."

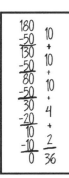

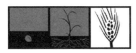

They start subtracting 10 sets of 5 beans. The teacher says, "Look at your table. How could you continue without actually counting the beans?" They continue subtracting sets of 5 beans in the table and push the beans aside. Now, use the commutative principle to check your answer. Each group talked it over, and one group finally multiplied 5 X 36 = 180.

Finally, Ms. Ybarra asked, "How many times, then, can you subtract 5 from 180?" They respond, "36 times."

## CONSOLIDATION

"I have another problem for you, but we can't use beans." "Why can't we?" "We would need a truck filled with beans," says one student. She says, "How would you set up your table?" They prepare the problem.

"Will you use 10 again, or something else?" They respond, "A bigger number." "How do you decide how much bigger," she asks. Each group goes to work.

Each group's work looks different because they subtract different numbers of sets. Ms. Ybarra notices that one group will finish quickly because they subtract 1000 sets of 30 at a time. One group may never finish because they are subtracting 10 sets of 30 at a time. She then uses a jigsaw strategy by asking one student in each group to move to the next group to share strategies. Finally, all groups finish.

She asks them, "What did we do with these numbers?" Several respond, "Division." She asks, "What is division?" They say, "Subtracting, over and over." She says, "Yes, this is a method of long division called 'repeated subtraction,' or the subtractive method. How do you feel about this compared to the other way?" Their responses indicate that it takes a little longer, but it is easy to understand.

## EXPLANATION AND DISCUSSION

In her anticipation phase, Ms. Ybarra forms her large class into cooperative learning groups and provides concrete materials for them to manipulate. She begins by reviewing with a simple division problem that they could solve by inspection. They review multiplication and the commutative principle of multiplication that is part of their background knowledge: 2 X 3 = 3 X 2.

In the building knowledge phase, she provides a more difficult problem that cannot be solved by inspection, and they need a system to record their activities. She never tells or explains, but rather asks questions to lead them to what will be the new subtractive algorithm. They recognize it as a very tedious process in her first application for them, but her questions lead them to shortcuts that they share with each other. She uses a jigsaw cooperative learning technique to move some students to another group so that they can bring new information about strategies.

She leads them from the concrete to the semi-concrete and finally to the abstract, where they can manipulate the numbers based on their concrete understandings from counting the beans. She forces this transition by providing a problem with numbers too large to manage concretely or even semiconcretely. She also provides another opportunity to apply the commutative principle.

In the consolidation phase, Ms. Ybarra provides a problem that must be solved with the new subtractive algorithm. Each small group makes its own decisions about how to solve the problem. She finally has them state in their own words what they have done, and she then tells them the name of it.

## GOALS OF THE MATHEMATICS TEACHING

- Learn mathematics concepts and problem-solving strategies
- Gain new knowledge through problem solving in authentic contexts
- Learn in student-directed, experiential, active, and collaborative setting
- Use inquiry and discovery. (NCTM 1994)

## HOW READING AND WRITING FOR CRITICAL THINKING MEET THESE GOALS

- Students construct their own meaning.
- Students work from concrete, manipulative materials to abstract representations.
- Students solve problems in natural contexts using their own strategies, with guidance from the teacher in the form of questions.
- The teacher poses problems and asks questions to guide student learning without telling or explaining.

## READING AND WRITING FOR CRITICAL THINKING IN MATHEMATICS

Teachers of mathematics often believe that because there is little text to read in their discipline, it is not a field that lends itself to reading and writing for critical thinking. To the contrary, the same general principles apply in mathematics as in literature or the social sciences. The ABC model is highly effective, providing for the activation of background knowledge and the introduction of new vocabulary, not to mention creating interest in the anticipation phase.

There is assuredly less reading of text in the building knowledge phase than in other disciplines, but this is accomplished in mathematics through other ways of presenting new concepts and ideas. The consolidation phase involves less writing and more application in new problems, but writing still has an important, if not frequent place, in mathematics.

# DISCIPLINE-SPECIFIC TEACHING STRATEGIES

## ANTICIPATION STRATEGIES FOR MATHEMATICS

| Strategy | Example |
|---|---|
| Quick-write | Write a description of a circle. |
| Semantic map | Construct a semantic map for the concept "graph." |

| Strategy | Example |
|---|---|
| Think-pair-share | "Think of three other ways to write 15; pair with another student; share and compare your responses." |
| Walk-around, talk-around | Share your favorite geometric shape; explain why you like it. |
| T-graph | Compare and contrast triangle and rectangle. |

## BUILDING KNOWLEDGE STRATEGIES FOR MATHEMATICS

| Strategy | Example |
|---|---|
| K-W-L | What do we know about the quadratic equation?<br>What do we want to know about it?<br>What did we learn about it? |
| Venn diagram | Use a Venn diagram to categorize numbers: ordinal, natural, imaginary, etc. |
| Jigsaw (cooperative learning) | After 10 minutes of small group work, one person from each small group goes to the next group to share insights from the original group. Sometimes more than one leaves. |
| Semantic feature analysis | Construct a semantic feature analysis chart of geometric shapes. Features might include the following:<br>    angles<br>    sides<br>    opposite angles<br>    right angles<br>    and others |
| T-graph | Compare and contrast triangle and rectangle. |

## CONSOLIDATION STRATEGIES FOR MATHEMATICS

| Strategy | Example |
|---|---|
| New problem | Show another way to multiply 16 X 21 application. |
| RAFT | Assume the role of a geometric figure; write to another figure and explain why you are more aesthetically attractive. |
| Semantic map | Expand a semantic map from the anticipation phase with new learned information. |

# 3. READING AND WRITING FOR CRITICAL THINKING IN SCIENCE

## VIGNETTE: EXPLORING DIFFERENCES IN PLANT BIODIVERSITY

Mrs. Valedzic is providing her students with an opportunity to learn about species diversity, one aspect of the larger concept of biodiversity. She chose to investigate two areas on the school grounds because they are convenient, but also will enable the students to see how different habitats and levels of disruption can result in different levels of species diversity.

 **ANTICIPATION**

Mrs. Valedzic asks her students to spend five minutes writing about anything they can think of related to the term *biodiversity*. "What does it mean to you?" she asks them.

The students write as much as they can. Some students seem to have a lot more to say than others. After five minutes have passed, Mrs. Valedzic asks if any of the students would like to share some of what they wrote. Several of the students share their ideas. One talks about biodiversity referring to "the types of animals that live in a particular place."

Another student adds, "It makes me think of environments that need to be protected."

"Good," says Mrs. Valedzic. "So biodiversity is a term that is used to describe an area that might be important in some way."

Other students share there ideas and Mrs. Valedzic listens to their responses; validating what they say at times, but not going into any great detail about any one idea.

Mrs. Valedzic then tells the students that they are going to investigate one component of biodiversity on their own. She divides her 24 students into groups of 4 and gives each group a sampling square and some paper. The sampling square is made out of 4 sticks tied together at each end so they form a square that is 1 meter on each side. She tells the students to bring something to write with and leads them outside.

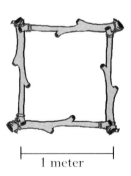
1 meter

 **BUILDING KNOWLEDGE**

Once outside, Mrs. Valedzic says "We are going to assess the species diversity of plants in two different areas here behind our school. In front of you is a field that the school mows on a monthly basis. The grass is a little tall, but you can see that there are a number of different plant species living in this particular habitat. The other area we will sample is the wooded area on the other side of the playground."

She points to a spot about 25 meters beyond the playground. "Here is what you need to do. Find a place where you can drop your sampling square on the ground within each designated habitat. Your goal is to then count and keep track of how many different types of plants you find in each square. You don't need to identify the plant. You only need to keep track of which plants are which and determine how many you have of each type. Any questions?"

The students ask a few clarifying questions about what they should be doing.

"Okay", she says, "please split your groups in two. Two students should work here and the other two students will work in the forested area." "When you are done with your counts, each group should come together and make at least two graphs that represent your results."
She reminds the students that their data might best be organized in a table. The students get to work and begin counting the plants in each habitat.

Mrs. Valedzic rotates from group to group and answers questions that they have about the process. When finished, the students get back in their groups and talk about how to best graph the data they've collected. As class ends, Mrs. Valedzic asks the students to have their graphs ready for class tomorrow.

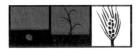 **CONSOLIDATION**

Mrs. Valedzic begins the next class by asking the students to describe what they noticed in general about each of the habitats.

Cecilia says she was surprised to find so many of the same plants in the field. "I would have expected more different types of plants."

Another student says that he was surprised to see so many different types of plants in the forested area.

Mrs. Valedzic tells the students how pleased she is with their observations. "Now lets see how you've chosen to represent those ideas in the graphs you've created as well."

The students share their graphs. One group ended up with the following two graphs.

**FIELD SITE**

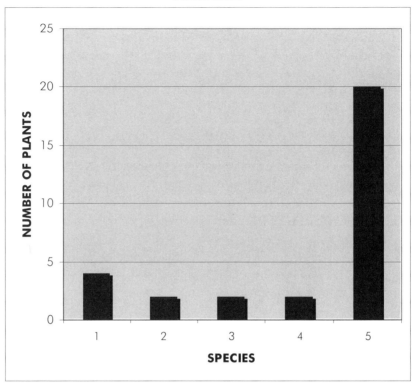

**FOREST SITE**

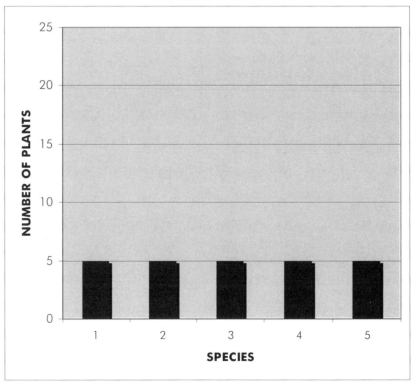

"The first graph," says Cecilia, "is our data from the field site. We had 20 plants of species 5, so we decided to make the graph so it could represent that species as well as enable us to see the differences among the other species that we found. The second graph is our data from the forest site. Surprisingly, we found exactly five plants of each type."

Mrs. Valedzic asks, "So which site would you consider to be more diverse?"

Cecilia responds "I'm not sure?"

Lars, one of Cecilia's group members, responds, "I think that the field site is more diverse because we had the same number of species, but had lots of species 5. I think the number that you have of each species is really important."

"Good," says Mrs. Valedzic, "but the field site only had relatively small numbers of species 2, 3, and 4. Does species diversity mean having large numbers of individuals or large numbers of species?"

"I think it means both!" says Anthony.

"Correct!" says Mrs. Valedzic. "*Species diversity* represents the total number and variety of organisms present in a given area. There is no distinction between organisms of different size or importance. Most importantly, people think of species diversity in two parts. First, is simply the number of species that exist in a particular area. This is also known as *species richness*. Second, is the different number of each species in a particular area. This is called *species evenness*. Evenness describes how many individuals of each species are present in a particular area. This component indicates whether or not one of the species is more or less abundant than the others. Keep these distinctions in mind. We'll use these as a basis for exploring exactly what is meant by biodiversity."

Mrs. Valedzic then leads the students in a discussion about how the more frequent levels of disruption in the field site (it is mowed on a regular basis) probably led to the dominance of one particular species in that area. "This species of grass may be more tolerant to semifrequent cutting than the other species found in this area." She answers some clarifying questions before the end of class.

## EXPLANATION AND DISCUSSION

In the anticipation phase, Mrs. Valedzic ask the students to do a free write on biodiversity. This serves as a good opportunity for students to reflect on and write about what they know about this concept. These writings will also enable Mrs. Valedzic to assess the prior knowledge her students have about this subject, as it will be a focus for the next several lessons. The students share their ideas about biodiversity and Mrs. Valedzic uses their ideas to lead into their focus for the day on species diversity.

In the building knowledge phase, Mrs. Valedzic provides the question of focus for their investigation. She has given them certain materials and basic directions, but the manner in which students choose to graph their data is up to each individual group. Mrs. Valedzic circulates among the groups as the students collect their data. She suggests that they organize the data they are collecting in a table, but, again, does not specify the format. This strategy puts the responsibility on the student and thereby provides them with a sense of ownership about their work.

In the consolidation phase, Mrs. Valedzic asks the students to share what they noticed in general about the two sites. She asks one group to present the graphs they made as a way of representing the differences between the two sites. As the students present their graphs, Mrs. Valedzic engages them in a discussion about their meaning. She questions the students in ways that help them to construct their own informal understandings of what their graphs represent. When a student points out that both the number of species and how many individuals there are of each species are important, Mrs. Valedzic uses this circumstance as an opportunity to provide the students with more formal definitions for each component of species diversity (richness and evenness). The teacher reminds the students that these concepts fall under the larger concept of biodiversity and that they will explore that concept in more detail. Her brief explanation about why the diversity is different in the two habitats is intended to lead to more student questions and future investigations.

## GOALS OF THE DISCIPLINE

- Engage students in meaningful science investigations
- Gain new knowledge through investigations in authentic contexts
- Learn in student-directed, experiential, active, and collaborative settings
- Use inquiry-based teaching strategies
- Help students see science as a way to view and understand the world

## HOW READING AND WRITING FOR CRITICAL THINKING MEET THESE GOALS

- Students construct their own meaning.
- Students ask questions, collect relevant data or evidence, analyze the data or evidence, and develop logical explanations for the outcomes.
- Students solve problems in natural contexts using their own strategies, with guidance from the teacher.
- The teacher provides various levels of support, guidance, and structure to the problem or question being investigated.

## READING AND WRITING FOR CRITICAL THINKING IN SCIENCE

Scientific inquiry is a way of communicating scientific knowledge to students that actively engages the students in investigations around larger ideas and central themes. This perspective requires teachers to serve as guides in supporting student investigations. Students are provided various levels of ownership over the questions at hand, the methodology, and how they choose to make sense of the data. This type of experience enables students to "do science" and construct their understandings of scientific phenomena through hands-on investigations.

# DISCIPLINE-SPECIFIC TEACHING STRATEGIES

## ANTICIPATION STRATEGIES FOR SCIENCE

| Strategy | Example |
| --- | --- |
| Quick-write | Write a definition of biodiversity. |
| Semantic map | Construct a semantic map for the concept of biodiversity. |

## BUILDING KNOWLEDGE STRATEGIES FOR SCIENCE

| Strategy | Example |
| --- | --- |
| K-W-L | What do we know about biodiversity? What do we want to know about it? What did we learn about it? |
| Venn diagram | Use a Venn diagram to categorize numbers: ordinal, natural, imaginary, etc. |
| Jigsaw (cooperative learning) | After 10 minutes of small group work, one person from each small group goes to the next group to share insights from the original group. Sometimes more than one leaves. |

## CONSOLIDATION STRATEGIES FOR SCIENCE

| Strategy | Example |
| --- | --- |
| New problem | Design a procedure to assess the species diversity within local stream or pond. |

# 4. READING AND WRITING FOR CRITICAL THINKING IN THE ARTS

## VIGNETTE: USING DRAMA TO TEACH LITERARY INTERPRETATION

 **ANTICIPATION**

Ms. Martinez began by asking her students to take out a piece of paper and list several characters, real or imagined, who scare them or their friends.

Then Ms. Matinez read "The Three Billy Goats Gruff," a Norwegian folktale by Aarne Thompson (and edited/translated here by D. L. Ashliman) to her eighth grade students. She has several copies of the story available in case students want them.

### THE THREE BILLY GOATS GRUFF
Aarne Thompson, Translated by D. L. Ashliman

Once upon a time there were three billy goats, who were to go up to the hillside to make themselves fat, and the name of all three was "Gruff."

On the way up was a bridge over a cascading stream they had to cross; and under the bridge lived a great ugly troll, with eyes as big as saucers, and a nose as long as a poker.

So first of all came the youngest Billy Goat Gruff to cross the bridge. "Trip, trap, trip, trap! " went the bridge.

"Who's that tripping over my bridge?" roared the troll.

"Oh, it is only I, the tiniest Billy Goat Gruff , and I'm going up to the hillside to make myself fat," said the billy goat, with such a small voice.

"Now, I'm coming to gobble you up," said the troll.

"Oh, no! Pray don't take me. I'm too little, that I am," said the billy goat. "Wait a bit till the second Billy Goat Gruff comes. He's much bigger."

"Well, be off with you," said the troll.

A little while after came the second Billy Goat Gruff to cross the bridge. "Trip, trap, trip, trap, trip, trap," went the bridge.

"Who's that tripping over my bridge?" roared the troll.

"Oh, it's the second Billy Goat Gruff, and I'm going up to the hillside to make myself fat," said the billy goat, who hadn't such a small voice.

"Now I'm coming to gobble you up," said the troll.

"Oh, no! Don't take me. Wait a little till the big Billy Goat Gruff comes. He's much bigger."

"Very well! Be off with you," said the troll.

But just then up came the big Billy Goat Gruff . "Trip, trap, trip, trap, trip, trap!" went the bridge, for the billy goat was so heavy that the bridge creaked and groaned under him.

"Who's that tramping over my bridge?" roared the troll.

"It's I! The big Billy Goat Gruff," said the billy goat, who had an ugly hoarse voice of his own.

"Now I 'm coming to gobble you up," roared the troll.

> *Well, come along! I've got two spears,*
> *And I'll poke your eyeballs out at your ears;*
> *I've got besides two curling-stones,*
> *And I'll crush you to bits, body and bones.*

That was what the big billy goat said. And then he flew at the troll, and poked his eyes out with his horns, and crushed him to bits, body and bones, and tossed him out into the cascade, and after that he went up to the hillside. There the billy goats got so fat they were scarcely able to walk home again. And if the fat hasn't fallen off them, why, they're still fat; and so,

> *Snip, snap, snout.*
> *This tale's told out.*

(Source: Asbjørnsen n.d., no. 37, 275–276)

 **BUILDING KNOWLEDGE**

Students then moved into groups of five. "We are going to re-enact the story of the "Three Billy Goats Gruff," she began, "but in our case, we will give the story a more modern twist. Discuss among yourselves the characters you have listed as somehow fearsome and together decide on which character you wish to see serve as the troll in your group's drama. You have about ten to fifteen minutes to figure out who will be the narrator, who will play the three goats and who will be the troll. You may also wish to modify the dialogue between troll and goats or change the ending to suit your purposes. If you have any time left, practice your lines."

The students begin to discuss the characters and decide on which will produce the best mini-play. One group has an alluring drug dealer serve as the troll, another has a bully from the school yard, another uses a historical figure, a fourth has the football coach as the troll, and a fifth group has a greedy corporate troll.

Each group presents its mini-drama and is greeted with applause.

 ## CONSOLIDATION

The teacher then calls the class back to their regular seats and in pairs they list the variations different groups employed. These insights are then brought back to a total class. Students recognized that changes were made in character, setting, outcome, and props. A lively discussion ensued about whether there were changes in theme with both sides arguing with evidence for their position, though no conclusion was reached. One student also introduced the notion of "rhythm"—were there differences in the rhythm of the mini-productions. Ms. Martinez said that she wanted to think more about this and that tomorrow they would continue their discussion.

Assessment in the arts is based largely on level of participation/involvement and originality, i.e., if students come up with interesting or surprising responses to a prompt. In this way, a student who sat on the sidelines and another who made a joke about another's ideas were given a negative mark, and a student who made up a short rap song and sang it in her role as the troll, got extra credit.

In the case of this lesson the teacher was also able to gather information on how well the students were able to analyze the artistic productions of others, a different skill than engaging in an artistic event.

## EXPLANATION

In the anticipation phase the teacher sets the stage for the building activity by (1) asking them to identify people whom they fear and (2) reading them a story that they will use as background for the building activity. In the consolidation phase she looks to see if students were able to apply what they had learned about elements of story as they discussed the various mini-dramas.

## GOALS OF ARTS TEACHING

As Howard Gardner, among others, has suggested, we as a species exhibit many different kinds of "intelligences." Schools need to celebrate more of these ways of learning and being in the world.

The goal of arts education is to allow for personal expression, but to do so in a way that benefits from exposure to the performances of others and an analysis of the decisions made by other artists and audiences. In this sense, a good arts program

- Supports students in taking risks
- Values craft, but not at the expense of creativity

- Encourages discussion of artistic products and production
- Helps students recognize the knowledge they have gained in the process of engaging in artistic activities
- Provides opportunities for growth within an arts-oriented community

## HOW READING AND WRITING FOR CRITICAL THINKING MEET THESE GOALS

- Students are given choices.
- Choices and decision making are discussed.
- Students are encouraged to assess their own development.
- Students learn to discuss the work of others in constructive and meaningful ways.
- A teacher supports student growth by modeling the aforementioned qualities.
- All concerned realize that similarity of product is not desirable.
- In the arts, closure is not necessarily valued.

## DISCIPLINE-SPECIFIC STRATEGIES

The arts are broadly defined here and include music, graphic arts, drama, and creative writing, The three-part lesson model functions extremely well in arts education. What differs most from other fields is the assessment. Whereas replicability, for instance, is essential to a good science experiment, we know that a painting is not considered good because others can make one exactly like it. The arts involve both craft and creativity. One common mistake made by teachers is to insist that knowledge of the craft must precede creativity. Our position is that creativity and craft can be developed together—sometimes one leads and the other follows—but the teacher must keep both aspects in mind at all times and make sure that an encouraging balance is available to students. (Note that *craft* in this sense is used as meaning something other than safety. A student might be encouraged to make a basket without having perfected his or her weaving skills, but you would not let someone use a power tool without being carefully supervised.)

Like scientists or historians, artists actively work to solve problems. Helping students to make explicit the problems they are trying to solve and the possible solutions they are considering is surely a part of reading and writing for critical thinking.

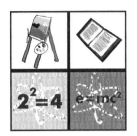

# 5. READING AND WRITING FOR CRITICAL THINKING IN INTERDISCIPLINARY TEACHING

## VIGNETTE: ESTIMATING STREAM DISCHARGE COMBINING MATH AND SCIENCE

Mr. Berde is going to have his students estimate the stream discharge of a local stream. The students have studied basic trigonometry in math this year and are now able to apply what they've learned in their science class.

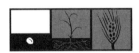 **ANTICIPATION**

Mr. Berde asks his students "Can anyone tell me what they think 'stream discharge' refers to?" One of the students guesses that it refers to how much water runs through a particular stream. Mr. Berde exclaims, "Yes!" "But why would such a number be important? Who might use or need such information?"

The students begin to share their ideas. Their ideas range from the local water company, to fisherman, to the factory that pumps water out of the stream for use in manufacturing.

Mr. Berde listens to their answers, providing positive feedback and explaining specific examples of how specific local industries rely on some of the rivers and streams in the area. Eventually the class decides that stream discharge would be measured in a particular volume of water passing a particular location in the stream during some period of time.

Mr. Berde divides the students into five groups of four students and poses the following challenge to the class. "Today we will go outside to the stream across the street from our school. The goal for each team is to choose a location on the stream and measure or estimate the amount of water passing that location for a particular time interval. Each team will be given a meter stick, string, and an orange. Can anyone tell me what they think the two pieces of data are that you will need?"

A student in the back says, "You'll need to know how fast the water in the stream is flowing and how big the cross-sectional area of the stream at that location might be."

"Correct!" says Mr. Berde. However, how you choose to find out each of those pieces of information is up to you. I have given you the necessary information, but each group will have to come up with its own procedure for solving the problem. Any questions? Ok, lets head out."Mr. Berde leads the students out of the building and across the street toward the stream.

## BUILDING KNOWLEDGE

The student groups arrive at the stream and each group begins to assess the materials they were given. Each group has a meter stick, some string, and an orange.

Denis, Maria, Mya, and Franz begin to talk about what they can do with these materials. "Well, we know we need to measure how fast the stream is flowing and then do something to measure the cross-sectional area," says Maria.

Mya says, "Why don't we focus on figuring out how fast the stream is flowing to begin with."

"Okay", states Denis, "I'm guessing we should use the orange since it certainly can't have much to do with figuring out area."

Franz says, "Well, the speed of the stream is going to be measured in something like a particular distance traveled in a particular amount of time. I remember doing something in class where we looked at the speed of miniature cars traveling in meters per second."

"Okay", says Denis. "Why don't we throw the orange into the water and measure how long it takes to travel a particular distance. First we'll have to choose a certain distance."

"Alright," says Maria. "Lets use a certain amount of string to mark off the distance. How about 4 meters? Does that sound okay?"

"Sure," states Mya. "Why don't you and Denis hold the string, I'll release the orange, and Franz can keep track of the time using his watch."

Denis and Maria use the meter string to measure out four meters. Mya stands upstream of Denis and Maria, and Franz positions herself on the bank of the stream so she can clearly see both Denis and Maria. Mya tells Franz that she is ready and Franz tells her to go ahead. Mya releases the orange into the water about two meters above where Denis is standing. When the orange reaches Denis, Franz begins to count off the number of seconds that pass, "One, two, three, four, etc...." When the orange reaches Maria, Franz says the last number and stops counting.

$$
\begin{array}{r}
9 \text{ seconds} \\
8 \text{ seconds} \\
+ \ \underline{9 \text{ seconds}} \\
27 \text{ seconds}
\end{array}
$$

27 / 3 trials = 8.7 sec.

$$\frac{4 \text{ meters}}{8.7} \Big/ \frac{8.7 \text{ seconds}}{8.7} =$$

0.5 meters / second

"9 seconds! Okay, let's try it again." Franz remembers from science class that they should always measure or test something multiple times in order to test the accuracy and precision of their outcome. The students repeat the process 2 more times, getting very similar answers (8 seconds and 9 seconds).

"Alright, if we average the 3 measurements," says Maria, "we get about 8.7 seconds. Therefore, if the speed for 4 meters is 8.7 seconds, then our speed in meters per second," she does the necessary calculations on a piece of paper, "would be 0.5 meters/second. Okay, we have half of the puzzle solved!"

The students now focus their attention on determining the cross-sectional area of a particular location in the stream. They have an overall estimate of how quickly the water is traveling, but they don't know how much water (in volume) passes a particular point during a particular period of time. The students decide to sketch their cross section out on a piece of paper. The first measurement they take is the width of the stream. Again, Denis and Maria hold the string at each bank and Mya uses the meter stick to measure the distance from one side to the other. They come up with a value of 5.5 meters.

Mr. Berde walks over to the students and asks them how things are coming. Denis asks the teacher whether they can just measure the depth of the stream and multiply it by the width.

Mr. Berde says "Well, why might that not give you the best estimate?"

Maria responds by saying "Because the bottom of the stream is very uneven. It might be very shallow in one section and very deep in another."

"So how might you account for those differences?" says Mr. Berde. The students decide that they can measure the depth of several points across the stream and use those measurements to determine the area. Mya and Franz decide to measure the depth at 5 locations from one bank to the other at 1 meter intervals. Their depths range from 0.5 meters to 1.2 meters.

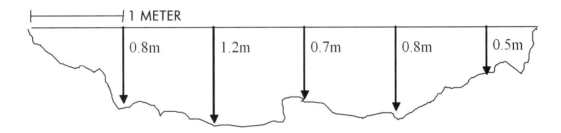

Franz sketches out their results and the students discuss how they can use these results to estimate the area of this section of stream.

Mya says, "We could break everything into either rectangles or triangles, calculate the areas of each of those, and then add them all up."

Denis asks whether or not they need to use triangles. "What if we only use rectangles?"

"Wouldn't we end up overestimating the area?" asks Franz.

"No, we could overestimate some sections and underestimate others. Let me show you." Denis adds lines to the drawing to make each section into a rectangle of some size.

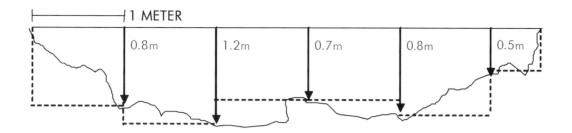

1m X 0.8 m = 0.8 m²
1m X 1.2 m = 1.2 m²
1m X 0.7 m = 0.7 m²
1m X 0.8 m = 0.8 m²
0.5m X 0.5 m = 0.25 m²

He says, "This means that each section can be calculated by multiplying the appropriate height by its width, which is going to be 1 meter for the first 5 sections and 0.5 meters for the last."

$$0.8m^2 + 1.2m^2 + 0.7m^2 + 0.8m^2 + 0.25m^2 = 4.45m^2$$

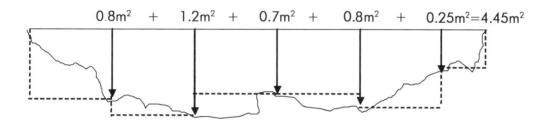

"Great! We have the second piece of the puzzle! Now how do we combine these pieces to get one answer?" asks Franz.

"Well," says Maria, "we have 0.5 m/s for the speed of the stream and 4.45 m² for the cross-sectional area. And, we want to end up with a volume, which means the units will be something that includes cubic meters."

"I think that means that we should multiply the two." says Mya.

0.5 m / sec. X 4.45 m² = 2.23 m³ / sec.

Franz gets out his pen and paper and does the calculation. "It's 2.23 cubic meters per second!" says Franz.

The students are very pleased with their result and ask Mr. Berde if their result seems reasonable. Mr. Berde tells them that their calculations look reasonable, but they'll have to compare their results with the other groups to see if they each arrived at a similar answer. The other groups begin to finish their work and eventually the class heads back to the school.

 **CONSOLIDATION**

The next day, Mr. Berde tells the class what a good job they did working at the stream. "Now I would like each group to share the strategies they used to calculate the stream discharge and their final result." As the groups share their results, Mya's group becomes more and more pleased with their result. Most of the groups obtained answers between nine and ten cubic meters per second. One group had a much lower answer, but through discussing their results with the class, they realized that they should have used a greater distance between their two time points when estimating the flow speed of the stream. Their distance was so short, only one meter, that the potential for error or underestimating the time was much greater.

Mr. Berde asked the class why there was variability among the answers that different groups obtained. Michelle, a student from another group, stated, "I think each group approached the problem a little differently. For example, we calculated the area of both triangles and rectangles in our cross section. We felt that this would give us a more accurate answer. Whether or not that is the case, we don't know, but I still think it is."

"Well, we would have to do additional tests to find out if that was indeed the case, wouldn't we? Okay, what if we went out and repeated our investigation tomorrow? Do you think we would get the same results?" asked Mr. Berde.

"No!" said Maria. "It's raining outside today. Our results would probably be higher."

"Good point!" said the teacher. "We might get very different results. So to have a better understanding of a stream or river, we would have to monitor the stream discharge over time." Mr. Berde talks to the students about how scientists use stream discharge to monitor water availability within a watershed and provides some specific examples of how much water levels can change due to rainfall or seasonal snowfall and subsequent melting.

## EXPLANATION AND DISCUSSION

In his anticipation phase, Mr. Berde asks the students to share what they know about stream discharge and who might use or rely on such information. He then establishes the context for the investigation and asks the students to identify what they will need to determine or calculate. Finally, he puts the responsibility for the investigation on his students, provides them with the materials they need and give them a well defined goal.

In the building knowledge phase, the students engage in a series of problem-solving sessions. The teacher has provided a tangible problem and the students develop ideas and potential explanations based on prior experiences. When the students ask their teacher about the methods they are using, Mr. Berde responds with questions, rather than specific suggestions. Even when they have arrived at a final conclusion, Mr. Berde affirms their approach, but withholds judgment as to the accuracy of their answer. He wants them to compare their results with the rest of the class, giving more credibility to the consensus of their classroom community, rather than a single predetermined answer.

In the consolidation phase, Mr. Berde facilitates the presentation and discussion of the results. He asks questions of the students who are presenting and helps students explain their calculations or results in more detail. The different groups are able to determine the extent to which their results are reasonable by comparing their results to those of the other groups. Such an experience shifts the focus of success from the teacher to the entire class. Mr. Berde then asks the students to extend their experience to future circumstances and apply what they have learned.

## GOALS OF INTERDISCIPLINARY TEACHING

- To learn interrelated concepts and principles through problem solving
- To create authentic contexts in which students can apply new knowledge
- To help students see and experience tangible connections among disciplinary topics and concepts
- Gain new knowledge through hands-on investigations in authentic contexts
- Learn in student-directed, experiential, active, and collaborative settings
- Use inquiry-based teaching strategies (NRC 1996; NRC 2001)

## HOW READING AND WRITING FOR CRITICAL THINKING MEET THESE GOALS

- Students construct their own meaning.
- Students ask questions, collect relevant data or evidence, analyze the data or evidence, and develop logical explanations for the outcomes.
- Students solve problems in natural contexts using their own strategies, with guidance from the teacher.
- The teacher provides various levels of support, guidance, and structure to the problem or question being investigated.

## READING AND WRITING FOR CRITICAL THINKING IN INTERDISCIPLINARY TEACHING

Interdisciplinary lessons and units can be developed from any perspective or emerge out of any specific discipline. Ideally, most units are interdisciplinary in nature to some extent. However, being very explicit about combining two or more subjects or disciplines in a single unit is a good way to create meaningful contexts for learning.

The anticipation phase helps students make connections among concepts and topics learned previously. Students must integrate and apply knowledge from different disciplines in the building knowledge stage. Problem solving is often at the center of student activity. The consolidation phase is an opportunity for the teacher to make connections among the various concepts explicit for the students and help them to understand the relevance of their investigation.

# 6. ACTIVE LEARNING ON YOUR OWN: STUDY SKILLS FOR STUDENTS

There are times when students are expected to study and learn on their own, without a teacher present. At those times, they need **study skills**, so they can learn from written text on their own or with a partner.

It is best if the teacher begins with an **anticipation** activity, and to set purposes for learning. Then they can do the reading and studying on their own. Later, back in class the students may take part in discussions and other **consolidation** activities, so that they can make the new learning fully their own.

## READING AND QUESTIONING

This is a study strategy that can be practiced individually or in groups.  It has the following steps:

1. The students read the chapter in sections. They read from heading to heading. As they read these sections, they should write down key terms in the margins.

2. Using the key words in the margins as cues, the students next review the material by asking test questions like those they think might appear on an examination covering the material.

3. Now they should say aloud the answers to the questions.

4. Remind them that if they were studying the material for the test to be taken some time in the future, they would repeat this question-and-answer process every few days to provide an ongoing review of the material.

5. An excellent way to review the questions is this: Students prepare small slips of paper, 20 cm by 50 cm. On one side of each piece of paper they write down the questions they derived from the words in the margins. On the other sides, they write down answers to the question. They use these papers later, when they study for the exam. They should review the questions and answers

## SURVEY-QUESTION-READ-RECITE-REVIEW (SQRRR)

This technique is a self-guided directed study procedure intended for use by students working individually. **SQRRR** is perhaps the world's best known study technique. It guides students in making a careful analysis of text, followed by repeated reviews, so that they can learn the material well enough to recall the key points later. Note that recall is not the same thing as critical thinking, however. Students should take part in consolidation activities after studying the materials, if the goal is for them to think about the material.

SQRRR follows these steps:

1. **Survey.** Survey a chapter before reading it closely:
   a. Read the title and think about what it says or implies.
   b. Read the headings and subheadings.
   c. Read the summary, if there is one.
   d. Read the captions under the pictures, charts, graphs, or other illustrations.
   e. See if there is a bibliography or a list of books related to the content of the chapter.

2. **Question.** Ask yourself questions about what you are going to read:
   a. What does the title of the chapter mean?
   b. What do I already know about the subject?
   c. What did the teacher say about this chapter when it was assigned?
   d. What questions do the headings and subheadings suggest?
   e. Read the review questions in the chapter. What answers can I offer to them now, before reading?

3. **Read.** Read Actively:
   a. Read to answer the questions you raised while doing the survey/question routine.
   b. Read all the study aides included in the chapter (maps, graphs, tables, and other illustrations).
   c. Read all the underlined, italicized, or boldface words or phrases extra carefully.

4. **Recite.** Go over what you read in step 3 by either summarizing what you just read or making notes.

5. **Review.** At intervals later on, repeat to yourself what you read and learned:
   a. Use your notes or text marks to refresh your memory.
   b. Review immediately after reading.
   c. Review again periodically.
   d. Review again before taking an exam on the subject.

(Source: Manzo 1994).


## PAIRED STUDY: JUICE

**JUICE** is a study procedure for two students who are working without a teacher. JUICE is an acronym that stands for the five steps of the procedure: *job, understand, instruct, critique, and exchange*:

1. **Job:** Both readers decide on a part of the text to read and a time line for reading it. (The part may be a few pages or a whole chapter of a book).

2. **Understand:** The readers read the same section of the material. They concentrate on general understanding rather than memorizing. They mark the important parts and the difficult parts of the text. They decide which partner will teach that section to the other. Here the steps of JUICE are explained.

3. **Instruct:** One partner is assigned the role of instructor for that section of the text. That partner explains the material in that section to the other and asks the other questions about it.

4. **Critique:** The other reader, playing the role of student, listens to the instructor, searches for mistakes, and also asks questions about the material. This role is difficult because the instructor must be challenged to be very clear if the process is to work well.

5. **Exchange:** After the instructor finishes teaching, the student summarizes what the instructor taught. Both students exchange what they have learned as they discuss the material and create test questions about it. They agree what the important points are in the material. The process continues as they go on to succeeding sections, exchanging roles as they go.

# APPENDIX 1: STUDENT AND TEACHER PERFORMANCE STANDARDS AND RUBRICS

# 1. STUDENTS STANDARDS AND RUBRICS

## FIRST STANDARD

Student responds appropriately to and asks higher order questions.

| INDICATOR | NEEDS IMPROVEMENT | SATISFACTORY | OUTSTANDING |
|---|---|---|---|
| student responds to higher order questions from teacher and peers with relevant and informed responses | responds mainly to recall and memory-type questions from teacher and peers | sometimes able to respond to higher order questions from teacher and peers | consistently responds to higher order questions from teacher and peers |
| students asks higher order and open questions of teacher and peers that reflect relevance and active listening | asks mainly recall and memory-type questions of teacher or peers | sometimes asks higher order questions of teacher or peers | consistently asks higher order questions of teacher or peers |

# SECOND STANDARD

Students produce oral and written products that reflect critical thinking.

| INDICATOR | NEEDS IMPROVEMENT | SATISFACTORY | OUTSTANDING |
|---|---|---|---|
| works reflect coherence and cohesion in structure appropriate for narrative and expository text | unfocused, reflecting a lack of coherence and cohesion in structure | generally coherent and cohesive in structure | highly focused, reflecting coherence and cohesiveness in structure |
| final/published works reflect excellence in mechanics, spelling, and syntax | contain numerous age-inappropriate errors in mechanics, spelling, and syntax | contain some age-appropriate errors in mechanics, spelling, and syntax | contain few errors in mechanics, spelling, and syntax |
| final/published works include clearly stated main ideas or themes logically and coherently connected to supporting information | lack clearly stated main ideas and themes are not logically and coherently connected to supporting information | include main ideas, with themes generally connected to supporting information | include clearly stated main ideas or themes logically and coherently connected to supporting information |
| supporting information reflects valid and reliable sources | lacks valid and reliable sources | often supported by valid and reliable sources | consistently supported by valid and reliable sources |
| final/published works reflect attention to audience, rich and appropriate vocabulary, and readable style | do not address the planned audience and lack appropriate vocabulary | often address the planned audience, with appropriate vocabulary and a readable style | consistently address the planned audience, with appropriate vocabulary and a very readable style |
| final/published works reflect evidence to support premises and conclusions | lack evidence supporting premises and conclusions | often reflect evidence to support premises and conclusions | consistently reflect evidence to support premises and conclusions |
| work demonstrates use of prewriting strategies (e.g., brainstorming, clustering, story mapping) | demonstrates use of prewriting strategies | demonstrates use of prewriting strategies | consistently demonstrates use of prewriting strategies |

# THIRD STANDARD

The student demonstrates initiative, motivation, and learning within and beyond the classroom.

| INDICATOR | NEEDS IMPROVEMENT | SATISFACTORY | OUTSTANDING |
|---|---|---|---|
| student initiates projects or activities related to but beyond classroom assignments | fails to initiate projects or activities beyond classroom assignments | sometimes initiates projects or activities related to but beyond classroom assignments | often initiates projects or activities related to but beyond classroom assignments |
| student demonstrates learning beyond the classroom by discussing classroom-related issues with peers, teachers, and others outside classroom environment | rarely demonstrates learning beyond the classroom by discussing classroom-related issues with peers, teachers, and others outside classroom environment | sometimes demonstrates learning beyond the classroom by discussing classroom-related issues with peers, teachers, and others outside classroom environment | often demonstrates learning beyond the classroom by discussing classroom-related issues with peers, teachers, and others outside classroom environment |
| student seeks resources beyond those of the school (e.g., libraries, Internet, newspapers, museums) | rarely seeks resources beyond those of the school (e.g., libraries, Internet, newspapers, museums) | sometimes seeks resources beyond those of the school (e.g., libraries, Internet, newspapers, museums) | often seeks resources beyond those of the school (e.g., libraries, Internet, newspapers, museums) |
| student responds appropriately to teachers' and peers' questions and statements with no prompting | rarely responds appropriately to teachers' and peers' questions and statements without prompting | sometimes responds appropriately to teachers' and peers' questions and statements with no prompting | often responds appropriately to teachers' and peers' questions and statements with no prompting |
| student engages in new strategies without prompting | rarely engages in new strategies without prompting | sometimes engages in new strategies without prompting | often engages in new strategies without prompting |

# FOURTH STANDARD

The student demonstrates self-confidence in learning, questioning, analyzing, and expressing ideas, positions, and opinions.

| INDICATOR | NEEDS IMPROVEMENT | SATISFACTORY | OUTSTANDING |
|---|---|---|---|
| student initiates requests for feedback on ideas, positions, and opinions from teachers and peers | rarely initiates requests for feedback on ideas, positions, and opinions from teachers and peers | sometimes initiates requests for feedback on ideas, positions, and opinions from teachers and peers | often initiates requests for feedback on ideas, positions, and opinions from teachers and peers |
| student recognizes and responds appropriately to weaknesses in content or structure in own reasoning | rarely recognizes or responds appropriately to weaknesses in content or structure in own reasoning | sometimes recognizes and responds appropriately to weaknesses in content or structure in own reasoning | often recognizes and responds appropriately to weaknesses in content or structure in own reasoning |
| student examines authoritative statements for consistency of logic and validity of content | rarely examines authoritative statements for consistency of logic and validity of content | sometimes examines authoritative statements for consistency of logic and validity of content | often examines authoritative statements for consistency of logic and validity of content |
| student asserts and maintains well reasoned and validly supported position or decision when faced with majority opposition | rarely asserts or maintains well reasoned and validly supported position or decision when faced with majority opposition | sometimes asserts and maintains well reasoned and validly supported position or decision when faced with majority opposition | often asserts and maintains well reasoned and validly supported position or decision when faced with majority opposition |

# FIFTH STANDARD

The student accesses, analyzes, and synthesizes information and own biases.

| INDICATOR | NEEDS IMPROVEMENT | SATISFACTORY | OUTSTANDING |
|---|---|---|---|
| student demonstrates the ability to locate and evaluate information from multiple data/information sources | rarely demonstrates the ability to locate or evaluate information from multiple data/information sources | sometimes demonstrates the ability to locate and evaluate information from multiple data/information sources | often demonstrates the ability to locate and evaluate information from multiple data/information sources |
| student recognizes own biases and accounts for those biases in own work | rarely recognizes own biases or accounts for those biases in own work | sometimes recognizes own biases and accounts for those biases in own work | often recognizes own biases and accounts for those biases in own work |
| student monitors own comprehension and recognizes errors in content and reasoning | rarely monitors own comprehension or recognizes errors in content and reasoning | sometimes monitors own comprehension and recognizes errors in content and reasoning | often monitors own comprehension and recognizes errors in content and reasoning |
| student classifies and categorizes data/information in multiple categories or classification schemes | rarely classifies or categorizes data/information in multiple categories or classification | sometimes classifies and categorizes data/information in multiple categories or classification | often classifies and categorizes data/information in multiple categories or classification |
| student demonstrates use of background knowledge and newly constructed knowledge to formulate, express, and defend new ideas and opinions | rarely demonstrates use of background knowledge or newly constructed knowledge to formulate, express, and defend new ideas and opinions | sometimes demonstrates use of background knowledge and newly constructed knowledge to formulate, express, and defend new ideas and opinions | often demonstrates use of background knowledge and newly constructed knowledge to formulate, express, and defend new ideas and opinions |
| student summarizes new ideas and opinions in reasoned oral and written arguments | rarely summarizes new ideas and opinions in reasoned oral and written arguments | sometimes summarizes new ideas and opinions in reasoned oral and written arguments | often summarizes new ideas and opinions in reasoned oral and written arguments |

# SIXTH STANDARD

The student applies critical thinking in mathematics and science.

| INDICATOR | NEEDS IMPROVEMENT | SATISFACTORY | OUTSTANDING |
|---|---|---|---|
| student demonstrates ability to construct own informed hypotheses | rarely demonstrates ability to construct own informed hypotheses | occasionally demonstrates ability to construct own informed hypotheses | frequently demonstrates ability to construct own informed hypotheses |
| student gathers, organizes, where appropriate, quantifies, and appropriately presents data | unable to gather, organize, quantify, or appropriately present data | sometimes able to gather, organize, where appropriate, quantify, and appropriately present data | consistently able to gather, organize, where appropriate, quantify, and appropriately present data |
| student summarizes and analyzes new data in relation to prior knowledge | unable to summarize or analyze new data in relation to prior knowledge | often able to summarize and analyze new data in relation to prior knowledge | consistently able to summarize and analyze new data in relation to prior knowledge |
| student draws reasoned and defensible conclusions from results of analyses | rarely draws reasoned and defensible conclusions from results of analyses | sometimes draws reasoned and defensible conclusions from results of analyses | often draws reasoned and defensible conclusions from results of analyses |
| student interprets results of analyses in reasoned and defensible arguments | unable to interpret results of analyses in reasoned and defensible arguments | often able to interpret results of analyses in reasoned and defensible arguments | consistently able to interpret results of analyses in reasoned and defensible arguments |

# 2. TEACHER STANDARDS AND RUBRICS

## FIRST STANDARD

Teachers provide student-centered classrooms in which they value students as individuals.

| INDICATOR | NEEDS IMPROVEMENT | SATISFACTORY | OUTSTANDING |
|---|---|---|---|
| teacher encourages diverse interpretation of subject matter | requires formal recitation of correct response | accepts some divergent responses | consistently encourages and accepts divergent responses |
| teacher encourages students to express and support their ideas and opinions | rarely encourages students to express or support their ideas and opinions | often encourages students to express and support their ideas and opinions | consistently encourages students to express and support their ideas and opinions |

## SECOND STANDARD

The classroom environment prepared by teachers reflects content, principles, learning activities, and group strategies appropriate for the lesson.

| INDICATOR | NEEDS IMPROVEMENT | SATISFACTORY | OUTSTANDING |
|---|---|---|---|
| teacher adapts the physical arrangement of the classroom to reflect lesson needs and to facilitate the grouping of students for effective interaction | arranges classroom seating in straight rows; does not adapt the arrangement for different activities | often changes the classroom arrangement for different activities | consistently changes the classroom arrangement, as needed, for different activities |
| teacher ensures that the learning environment and wall displays show student work | rarely encourages students to express or support their ideas and opinions | often encourages students to express and support their ideas and opinions | consistently encourages students to express and support their ideas and opinions |

# THIRD STANDARD

Teachers effectively present content from the national curriculum.

| INDICATOR | NEEDS IMPROVEMENT | SATISFACTORY | OUTSTANDING |
|---|---|---|---|
| teacher approaches curriculum content in more than one way to ensure that students learn with understanding | always teaches every lesson in the same way, regardless of content or student needs | sometimes uses active learning strategies and cooperative learning techniques | frequently uses active learning strategies, such as K-W-L, reciprocal teaching, and cooperative learning techniques |

# FOURTH STANDARD

Teachers integrate the crosscutting issues of civics, HIV/AIDS education, gender education, environmental education, and children's rights into the instructional program.

| INDICATOR | NEEDS IMPROVEMENT | SATISFACTORY | OUTSTANDING |
|---|---|---|---|
| teacher raises crosscutting issues in classroom discussions | rarely includes crosscutting issues in classroom discussions | sometimes includes crosscutting issues in classroom discussion | frequently integrates lessons on crosscutting issues into the daily program |
| teacher provides reading and writing opportunities for students to express themselves about crosscutting issues | rarely provides opportunities for students to read and write about crosscutting issues | sometimes provides opportunities for students to read and write about crosscutting issues | frequently provides opportunities for students to read and write about crosscutting issues |

# FIFTH STANDARD

Teachers design instruction to promote active learning.

| INDICATOR | NEEDS IMPROVEMENT | SATISFACTORY | OUTSTANDING |
| --- | --- | --- | --- |
| teacher uses active learning teaching methods | uses lecture style almost all of the time | uses lecture style often; students ask some questions | rarely uses lecture style; frequently redirects student responses to other students |
| teacher uses a mixture of independent, paired, small group, and whole class lesson activities | students participate as a whole class in all lessons | students sometimes work in pairs and small groups | students frequently work in pairs and small groups |
| teacher develops careful time management for each activity | does not manage time; does not consider nature of lesson or needs of students | often manages time according to nature of lesson and needs of students | consistently plans time according to nature of lesson and needs of students |

# SIXTH STANDARD

Teachers use thoughtful questions to promote higher order thinking.

| INDICATOR | NEEDS IMPROVEMENT | SATISFACTORY | OUTSTANDING |
| --- | --- | --- | --- |
| teacher asks thought-provoking, higher order questions | consistently asks low level, recall questions | often asks higher order questions | consistently asks higher order questions |
| teacher encourages students to express and support their ideas and opinions | rarely encourages students to express or support their ideas and opinions | often encourages students to express and support their ideas and opinions | consistently encourages students to express and support their ideas and opinions |

# APPENDIX 2:
# TEXTS FOR DISCUSSION

## ELEPHANTS AND FARMERS

The elephant population continues to dwindle in many African countries. In others, however, long-standing conservation measures have been so successful that elephants are more numerous than at any time in recorded history.

Wildlife experts are calling this a victory, but to the struggling African farmer, it is yet one more example of how the forces of nature threaten her precarious livelihood. Elephants foraging for food that their expanding population has made scarce can destroy an entire plantation in a matter of hours. Profits on the larger farms, already under threat from rocketing seed and fertilizer prices and the effects of globalization, are plummeting. For the subsistence farmer and her family, a single act of trespass by an elephant herd can mean the loss of a season's work, the destruction of house and home, and possible destitution.

It is these facts which have led many farmers to call for a revival of the right to shoot elephants and to trade their meat, hides and ivory. The price of a single tusk can be equivalent to many years' income for an impoverished farmer. In a world where the livelihoods of poor people are more at risk than those of elephants, this is an increasingly persuasive argument. In addition to this, legalization would reduce the need for the expensive, military style policing currently used to control the violent behavior of ivory smugglers.

However, many conservationists have reacted with horror to this proposal. Legalizing the shooting of elephants, even on a controlled basis, will, they argue, lead to a free for all which will drive the elephant back to the brink of extinction. The corruption and exploitation linked to the trade in ivory will return. And to many, the very idea of killing an animal as majestic, noble and intelligent as the elephant is every bit as abhorrent as killing a whale.

## THE SHILLING
Liam O'Flaherty

Three old men were sitting on the splash wall of Kilmillick Pier with their backs to the sea and their faces to the village and the sun. A light breeze came from the sea behind them, bringing a sweet salt smell of seaweed being kissed by the sun. The village in front was very quiet. Not a movement but the lazy blue smoke curling slantwise from the cabin chimneys. It was early afternoon, Sunday, and all the young men and women were in Kilmurrage at a football match. The three old men were telling stories of big fish they had caught in their youth.

Suddenly there was a swish of canvas and a little white yacht swung around the corner of the pier and came alongside. The three old men immediately got to their feet and advanced through the turf dust to the brink of the pier looking down at the yacht. Patsy Conroy, the most active of the old men, seized the mooring rope and made the yacht fast. Then he came back and joined the other two watching the yachtsmen getting ready to go ashore. "She's a lovely boat," said old Brian Manion, the old fellow with the bandy right leg and the bunion behind his right ear. "Heb," he said, scratching the small of his back, "it must cost a lot of money to keep that boat. Look at those shiny brasses and you can see a carpet laid on the cabin floor through that hatchway. Oh boys! I'd like to have her for a week's fishing," said Mick.

Feeney breathed loudly through his long red nose. His big red-rimmed blue eyes seemed to jump in and out. He gripped the top of his stick with his two hands and looked down at the yacht with his short legs wide apart.

Patsy Conroy said nothing. He stood a little apart with his hands stuck in his waist-belt. Although he was seventy-two, he was straight, lithe and active, but his face was yellow and wrinkled like old parchment and his toothless red gums were bared in an old man's chin. His little eyes beneath his bushy white eyebrows roamed around the yacht cunningly as if they were trying to steal something. He wore a yellow muffler wound round and round his neck up to his chin, in spite of the heat of the day.

"Where is the nearest public-house?" drawled a red-faced man in a white linen shirt and trousers from the yacht deck.

The old men told him, all together.

"Let's go and have a drink, Totty," said the red-faced man.

"Right-o," said the other man.

When the red-faced man was climbing the iron ladder on to the pier, a shilling fell out of his hip pocket. It fell noiselessly on a little coil of rope that lay on the deck at the foot of the ladder. The red-faced man did not notice it, and he walked up the pier with his friend. The three old men noticed it, but they did not tell the red-faced man. Neither did they tell one another. As soon as the shilling landed on the little coil of rope and lay there glistening, the three of them became so painfully conscious of it that they were bereft of the power of speech or of coherent thought. Each cast a glance at the shilling, a hurried furtive glance, and then each looked elsewhere, just after the manner of a dog that sees a rabbit in a bush and stops dead with one paw raised, seeing the rabbit although his eyes are fixed elsewhere.

Each old man knew that the other two had seen the shilling, yet each was silent about it in the hope of keeping the discovery his own secret. Each knew that it was impossible for him to go down the iron ladder to the deck, pick up the shilling and ascend with it to the pier without being detected. For there was a man who wore a round white cap doing something in the cabin. Every third moment or so his cap appeared through the hatchway and there was a noise of crockery being washed or something. And the shilling was within two feet of the hatchway. And the old men, except perhaps Patsy Conroy, were too old to descend the ladder and ascend again. And anyway each knew that even if there were nobody in the cabin, and even if they could descend the ladder, the others would prevent either one from getting the shilling, since each preferred that no one should have the shilling if he couldn't have it himself. And yet such was the lure of that glistening shilling that the three of them stared with palpitating hearts and feverishly working brains at objects within two feet of the shilling. They stared in a painful silence that was loud with sound as of a violent and quarrelsome conversation. The noise Mick Feeney made breathing through his nose exposed his whole scheme of thought to the other two men just as plainly as if he explained it slowly and in detail. Brian Manion kept fidgeting with his hands, rubbing the palms together, and the other two heard him and cursed his avarice. Patsy Conroy alone made no sound, but his very silence was loud and stinking to the other two men, for it left them in ignorance of what plans were passing through his crafty head.

And the sun shone warmly. And the salt, healthy smell of the sea inspired thirst. And there was excellent cool frothy porter in Kelly's. So much so that no one of the three old men ever thought of the fact that the shilling belonged to somebody else. So much so indeed that each of them felt indignant with the shameless avarice of the other two. There was almost a homicidal tendency in the mind of each against the others. Thus three minutes passed. The two owners of the yacht had passed out of sight. Brian Manion and Mick Feeney were trembling and driveling slightly at the mouth.

Then Patsy Conroy stooped and picked up a pebble from the pier. He dropped it on to the deck of the yacht. The other two men made a slight movement to intercept the pebble with their sticks, a foolish unconscious movement. Then they started and let their jaws drop. Patsy Conroy was speaking. "Hey there," he shouted between his cupped hands.

A pale-faced gloomy man with a napkin on his hip stepped up to the second step of the hatchway. "What d'ye want?" he said.

"Beg yer pardon, Sir," said Patsy Conroy, "but would ye hand me up that shilling that just dropped out a' me hand?"

The man nodded, picked up the shilling, muttered "Catch," and threw the shilling on to the pier. Patsy touched his cap and dived for it. The other two old men were so dumbfounded that they didn't even scramble for it. They watched Patsy spit on it and put it in his pocket. They watched him walk up the pier, sniffing out loud, his long, lean, grey-backed figure with the yellow muffler around his neck moving as straight and solemn as a policeman.

They looked at each other, their faces contorted with anger. And each, with upraised stick, snarled at the other: "Why didn't ye stop him, you fool?"

O'Flaherty 1937

# REMEMBERING COLUMBUS
Bucksnort Trout

Twenty thousand years ago the land bridge over what is now the Bering Strait sank too low to be passable, and two halves of the world began to grow up separately. Plants and animals, peoples and cultures, gods and diseases, all went their separate ways—until one sunny morning, 500 Octobers ago, when a skiff bearing Christopher Columbus crunched into the sand on San Salvador Island and brought the two parts of the world together again.

It is amazing to think that one person could have engineered that first contact, however unknowingly. When he did, Christopher Columbus was caught in the glare of world scrutiny forever. Columbus was an Italian map-maker and some-time wool salesman from Genoa. Somehow he persuaded Isabella, the Spanish queen of Castilla (but not her husband Ferdinand, the king of the neighboring province of Aragon), into giving him three ships to command on his improbable trip to China. But the queen made him wait until Spanish soldiers pried the last of the Moors, the Muslims from the south, loose from their 800 year occupation of Spain. What a year that was, 1492. The Moors were pushed out of Spain. The Spanish Inquisition was established, and all religions but Christianity were outlawed. And in August, Columbus embarked on his famous journey. For Spain, 1492 was a bizarre combination of fanaticism, intolerance, and  discovery.

The powers that flowed through Columbus' point of contact changed the whole world profoundly and rapidly. The plants that the Indians offered to the Europeans—plants that they had bred carefully and improved through many, many generations—potatoes, corn, long-staple cotton—soon reversed the Old World's cycles of famine and led to population explosions—and changed everything from economies to cooking. Who can imagine Italian food without tomatoes? Or Indian food without hot peppers? Or an Irish meal without potatoes? (Or Sherlock Holmes without pipe tobacco?) All came from the New World. Without long-staple cotton, Europe wouldn't have had a textile industry. Without long staple cotton and the example of the sugar mills of the Caribbean—which were arguably the world's first factories—Europe may not have had an Industrial Revolution.

Going the other way, who can imagine "the Wild West" without cattle, or cowboys and Indians without cows and each other to chase or horses on which to chase them? The Spanish brought both cows and horses to the New World in 1493, and they quickly adapted, multiplied, and spread. In the 1580s, the Spanish explorer Cabeza de Vaca was blown across the Gulf of Mexico and shipwrecked on the Texas coast. He was the first European to see Texas, but Spanish cattle already had beat him there, and they looked so wild, so much at home, that he assumed they were native to America. The Lakota Sioux, Indians of the American Great Plains, have legends about the coming of wonderful animals that improved their lives. The Elk Dogs were said to have been brought up from a magical land at the bottom of a deep lake. They were horses, of course.

But the diseases Columbus and his followers brought with them wiped out whole civilizations within a few decades. The Taino people who lived on the Caribbean island of Hispaniola (the location of present day Haiti and the Dominican Republic), for example, were reduced from perhaps half a million souls to virtually none within a space of only 50 years. And even though European explorers didn't arrive on the seaboard of North America until many years after Columbus' voyage, the diseases introduced by the Spanish are believed to have spread rapidly northward, so that by the time Captain James Smith reached Jamestown in Virginia in 1607, the indigenous population was already in disarray because at least a fourth of them had died from a plague of smallpox that had originated with the Spanish explorers far to the south, and had been passed northward from tribe to tribe.

Back a century earlier in the Caribbean, when the Taino population began dying off at an alarming rate, the Spanish imported forced workers from Africa, and the troubled heritage of slavery, as well as the multiracial character of the New World, began to take shape.

All of this happened because of a man who didn't know where he was.

# IVAN AND THE SEAL SKIN

A Traditional Scottish Tale, Retold by Bucksnort Trout

Along the north coast of Scotland, the winter wind howls through dark nights and gray days, and towering waves smash against black rocks. But in summer, the sea calms, and the days lengthen, so that daylight lasts through twenty-four hours. Then the few fishermen who live on that remote coast may dare to throw their nets out into the sea, and try to catch their livelihood. Even in summer, a sudden storm may overtake them; or a silent fog may creep upon them and make them lose their way. Then their loved ones go down to the shore, and gaze for some sign at the mute waves, perhaps to see a seal stare back with big sad eyes. The people see the seals, and they wonder...

On a little cove by the sea lived a fisherman and his wife, and their one son, Ivan Ivanson. It was the longest day of the year: Midsummer's Eve. Close to midnight, with the sky still a radiant orange, young Ivan, barely seven years old, was exploring the rocks by the shore, searching for shells and bits of net and whatever else the waves might have washed up.

Suddenly a strange sound drifted to him on the wind. It was like the singing of unearthly voices, blended in beautiful harmony. He looked up. Away down the shore to his right he could see a tendril of smoke rising from a hole at the base of the rocks, near the point.

Ivan would have explored, but his short legs wouldn't carry him over the large boulders, so when his mother called, he returned to the family cottage without investigating further.

Seven years went by. Ivan, now fourteen, found himself once again down on the shore, right at midnight, on Midsummer's Eve. Once again he thought he heard strange singing, and again he saw smoke rising from a hole at the base of the rocks, down by the point. I don't know why he didn't go to the source this time. Perhaps some emergency called him back to his parents' cottage. His father's health, like as not. For both his parents were growing old.

Seven more years went by. His father had worn out from fishing the cold brine, so his parents had retired to town, leaving their cottage to Ivan. Ivan lived all alone, with only the cries of the shore birds for company. He fished long days, and warmed himself at night by the little peat fire. I imagine he was lonely.

When Midsummer's Eve came again, Ivan remembered the singing, and the smoke. At midnight, he walked down to the shore. The same strange singing reached his ears, woven into unearthly and beautiful harmonies.

This time, no boulders would stop him, and there was no one to call him back. Ivan made his way down the shore toward the point. As he drew closer, he could hear the crackle of a fire, and could see its reflection against the rocks. Beautiful singing came from inside the cave. And there at the cave's mouth lay a pile of sleek and beautiful gray furs: seal skins.

Ivan chose the one he thought the most comely and slowly, carefully, drew it off the pile. He rolled the seal skin into a ball and made straight off for home with it. Once there, he locked the seal skin in a wooden trunk, slipped the key onto a leather thong tied around his neck, and went to bed.

In the morning he took the blanket from his bed and returned to the cave. There he found a sad and beautiful young woman, huddled and shivering, covering her nakedness with her arms and long hair. Without a word, Ivan wrapped the young woman in his blanket and led her home to his cottage.

Ivan treated the woman kindly, and in time they fell in love. They had one son, then another. Ivan was happy enough, and the woman was a good mother. But often Ivan saw his wife staring off at the sea with big, sad eyes. He never told her what was in the wooden box, and he forbade her to open it.

More years passed. One Christmas Eve Ivan readied his family to go to church. The wife said she was feeling poorly, though, and asked Ivan and the boys to go on alone.

Perhaps Ivan was angry at this. In his haste to dress, Ivan left the thong with the key hanging on his bed stead, and went off to church without it.

Ivan and the boys returned from church after midnight. They saw the open door before they reached the cottage. They found the wooden box lying open, and the key still in the lock. The wife was gone.

They say that sometimes when the boys walked along the shore, a beautiful seal with large sad eyes would follow along close by in the cold water. And they say sometimes when Ivan was fishing, the same sad and beautiful seal seemed to herd the herring fish into his nets. Perhaps the seal was Ivan's wife. No one knows. All we know is that Ivan never saw his wife on this earth again.

## JACK AND THE BEANSTALK
Retold by Bucksnort Trout

If you had known Jack, you not would have expected him to get rich so young. With that knee on his left leg sticking through his trousers, and that toe on his right foot poking through his boot, and that piece of rye straw dangling from his mouth, no. You wouldn't have picked Jack for a winner. But here's what happened.

Jack was living alone with his Ma. Poor as dust, the both of 'em. It had come a drought, and scorched the corn. The chickens ran away to a more prosperous home. Then the cow, Milky White, went dry.

"Jack," said his Ma, wringing her hands in her apron. "Take that cow Milky White to the market and see what you can get for her. Go on, now. Bring us back some money."

"Yes,m," said Jack. "Come on, Milky White." And the two of them lumbered off down the road.

They hadn't gone too far 'til they came to a funny-looking old man sitting on a stump.

"Mornin', Jack"

"Mornin', old man."

"You look like a bright young fellow. But I bet you don't know what *five* is."

"Do, too. Two in each hand and one in your mouth."

"Well, well. You *are* right bright. Tell you what. I'll trade you that cow of yourn for these here wonder beans," and he held out a handful of beans with strange colors and odd shapes.

"Go on, you would, too."

"I'm telling you, Jack. They're magical."

Jack rubbed his chin. "All right, then."

When his Ma saw him back without the cow, she shouted for joy.

"Back so soon, Jack? How much did you get for that cow? Not 10 pounds, Jack! 20 pounds? Oh, Jack. You don't mean you got thirty—"

"Look at these beans, Ma!"

Well, his mother took the beans and flung them out the window. Then she whalloped Jack about the head and shoulders so that he had to jump in the bed for cover.

In the morning, there was green where there should have been sunshine. Jack squinted his eyes and looked again. Yep. A *huge bean trunk* was growing up out of sight, just outside his window. Jack got right on it and commenced to climb. He climbed and he climbed and he climbed and he climbed and he climbed and he climbed and he *climbed* until he got up to the sky. He stepped off the bean trunk onto a cloud, found it held his weight, and then pranced across the sky, bouncing from cloud to cloud, until he came to a great big castle. Jack pounded on the door and soon it swung open. There stood the tallest biggest woman you ever saw.

"Morning, ma'am. What you got for breakfast?" And Jack scooted right between that big woman's legs and into the kitchen. He shinnied up a chair leg and onto the table, and commenced to help himself to a big bowl of porridge.

"You—you better not let my husband the giant catch you eating his porridge. He'll soon *eat—you—up!*"

And just then they heard the great front door slam shut.

"Fee, fie, foe, fum!
I smell the blood of an Englishman!
Be he alive or be he dead,
I'll *grind his bones*
To make my bread!"

"Better hide in this copper pot, quick now, Jack!"

Jack crawled up into a big copper cooking pot, and pulled the lid down over himself—*whong!* Now that pot hung on a big iron arm. All anybody had to do was give it a shove and it'd swung over the cooking fire, and that boy was *roasted*.

The giant sat down and ate up the porridge. Then he called for his bag of gold coins. He commenced to counting: "Three, eleven, nine, two, fourteen.... " Now giants don't do too good in math. And soon that giant was nodding off from the strain of all that calculation.

Jack jumped quick out of the pot, snatched the bag of coins, sprinted out of the door, bounced across the clouds, and scrambled down the bean trunk. When he got to the bottom, he and his Ma lived pretty good—

For a while. And then Jack got adventurous again. So, he climbed and he climbed and he climbed and he *climbed* back up the bean trunk, bounced back across the clouds, knocked on that big door again, ate more porridge, barely escaped that giant—

"Fee, fie, foe, fum!"

—and this time, made away with a *hen that laid golden eggs*! Jack sprinted out the door, bounced across the clouds, and scrambled down the bean trunk a second time. When he got to the bottom, he and his Ma lived even better—

For a while. And then Jack got adventurous *again*. So, he climbed, bounced, knocked, ate, and—

"Fee, fie, foe, fum!"

—he almost didn't escape from the giant this time.

Here's what happened. When the giant came into the kitchen, Jack hid in the pot, just like those other times. The giant called for his harp that played music all by itself, and of course, the harp hardly played a few bars before the giant was snoring away. So Jack jumped quick out of the pot and snatched up the harp. But the harp commenced to shriek, "Master, Master!" Who would have thought such a pretty instrument could have such an awful voice? The giant woke right up and gave chase. For all his bouncing and prancing and lugging that screaming harp, Jack barely reached the bean trunk ahead of the giant.

As he climbed and he climbed and he climbed, down and down and *down* the bean trunk, the giant dropped from limb to limb and almost caught him!

"Ma! *Fetch the axe! Fetch the axe,* Ma!" Jack shouted.

Soon as his toes touched the ground he snatched the axe from his Ma and,

"Whunk! Whunk! Whunk! Whunk! *Whunk!*"

—he cut through that bean trunk.

"Ayeeeeeeeeeeeee!!!"

Down came the bean trunk. And the giant. Made a big crater. In a year or two that crater filled up and made a pond, back behind Jack and his Ma's new house. The one with the *two* fine milk cows, the scattering of plump chickens, and the patch of tall corn? I hear they're doing pretty good. If you go by there some time, tell 'em I said Hi.

## LET'S HEAR IT FOR SMOKERS!
Stallmore Dodge

In more and more places in the world there are campaigns against cigarette smoking. Few and far between are the places of work or leisure where smoking is still allowed. In some places cigarette manufacturers are even being sued to pay the medical expenses of people who become ill from smoking. Well, it's time someone stood up for the rights of people who make cigarettes and those who smoke them, and that's what we intend to do here. Let me be clear: many good people are involved in the production of tobacco, and many more good people enjoy their products. Their rights must be respected. Leave them alone!

Picture, if you will, a family farm with a small plot of tobacco, sometimes only two hundred meters on a side. Every day the family walks the rows between the growing plants to tend them, one by one. Even the children can carefully pick off the tassels, so the leaves will grow to their fullest. They harvest the tobacco by hand, and the whole community gathers to pile the broad tobacco leaves carefully on a mule-drawn wagon, and later to hoist racks of leaves up into the barn where they will hang until they are dry. When the tobacco is sold in town at auction, the family makes a tidy profit to spend on its needs. Tell me—would you take that money away from them?

Now picture the smoker. This one is a young woman who's risen before dawn to catch a commuter train to work. In the fifteen minutes she has between arriving at the station and signing in at the office, she can have a cup of coffee—and a cigarette. And in that short space of time, she is truly in charge of her world and fully at peace. The rest of her day may belong to someone else, but for now she is alone with herself, her coffee, and her cigarette. Would you take that joy from her, too?

Those zealots, those fanatics, those moral tyrants who would take away the virtues of family farming, and invade the privacy of smokers like this hard-working young woman—they ought to be ashamed of themselves.

## REVISED ENHANCED LECTURE IN OPPOSITION TO THE
## THE KYOTO PROTOCOL ON REDUCING GREENHOUSE GAS EMISSIONS

Countries that sign the Kyoto Protocol accept mandatory targets on greenhouse gas emissions. These targets range from −8% to +10 percent of each country's 1990 levels. This will result in a reduction of 5% below 1990 levels in the period from 2008 to 2012. The called-for reductions are 8% in the European Union and most of Europe. They are 7% in the United States and 6% in Canada. New Zealand, Russia, and Ukraine are to stabilize their emissions. Some countries, such as Norway, may increase emissions up to 1%.

Countries can make up for not meeting their targets by increasing "sinks." These are forests that remove $CO_2$ from the atmosphere. They can do this in their own countries, or they can pay for projects that have the same result in other countries.

The protocol will take effect when 55 countries have ratified it. Many of those must include the industrialized countries that account for most emissions. The United States and Australia have already indicated that they will not support the treaty.

There are many reasons why this protocol should not be accepted by the international community. Most scientists have concluded that recent increases in surface and atmospheric temperatures of the earth are part of a natural trend. These kinds of changes have occurred many times in the earth's history, and they will occur again in the future. In addition, the changes are very gradual, providing time for more research and consultation among nations.

There is no need to make drastic changes to decrease the emissions of greenhouse gases. There is no evidence that this will alleviate the situation. We should take a wait-and-see point of view before rushing into something that scientists don't support.

There is also the danger of severe economic decline. Prominent economists have predicted a 20% decline in economic activity, especially in the industrialized countries most impacted by the protocol.

We should also consider that there are benefits to global warming. Growing seasons in northern climates, such as the Russian Federation, Canada, and the Scandinavian and Baltic countries would be lengthened, permitting them to increase agricultural production.

The protocol is not fair to western industrialized nations. They would be placed at a severe economic disadvantage to newly industrializing nations, such as China and India, which would not be subject to the Kyoto Protocol. They would have to reduce emissions, while developing and least-developed countries could increase their emissions without penalty. The net result would be more greenhouse gas emissions than before the Kyoto Protocol.

We must stop listening to the minority of scientists and far-out environmentalists who tell us that the sky is falling. Their research is not scientifically based, and we should instead listen to those who advocate a cautious approach. Some of those crazies even claim that sea levels will rise and that many island nations and coastal areas will be inundated by the sea. This is nonsense. It has not happened yet, and it won't happen.

We must also protect ourselves against the bogus claims of rabid environmentalists, who would take us back to the Stone Age. Once we begin to limit greenhouse gas emissions, the world will begin a slide backwards in development that will cause millions of people to starve all over the world. As the world economy degrades, what we all know as a middle-class lifestyle will disappear, with everyone shivering in the cold and without employment.

# THE THREE BILLY GOATS GRUFF

Aarne Thompson, Translated by D. L. Ashliman

Once upon a time there were three billy goats, who were to go up to the hillside to make themselves fat, and the name of all three was "Gruff."

On the way up was a bridge over a cascading stream they had to cross; and under the bridge lived a great ugly troll, with eyes as big as saucers, and a nose as long as a poker.

So first of all came the youngest Billy Goat Gruff to cross the bridge. "Trip, trap, trip, trap!" went the bridge.

"Who's that tripping over my bridge?" roared the troll.

"Oh, it is only I, the tiniest Billy Goat Gruff , and I'm going up to the hillside to make myself fat," said the billy goat, with such a small voice.

"Now, I'm coming to gobble you up," said the troll.

"Oh, no! Pray don't take me. I'm too little, that I am," said the billy goat. "Wait a bit till the second Billy Goat Gruff comes. He's much bigger."

"Well, be off with you," said the troll.

A little while after came the second Billy Goat Gruff to cross the bridge. "Trip, trap, trip, trap, trip, trap," went the bridge.

"Who's that tripping over my bridge?" roared the troll.

"Oh, it's the second Billy Goat Gruff, and I'm going up to the hillside to make myself fat," said the billy goat, who hadn't such a small voice.

"Now I'm coming to gobble you up," said the troll.

"Oh, no! Don't take me. Wait a little till the big Billy Goat Gruff comes. He's much bigger."

"Very well! Be off with you," said the troll.

But just then up came the big Billy Goat Gruff . "Trip, trap, trip, trap, trip, trap!" went the bridge, for the billy goat was so heavy that the bridge creaked and groaned under him.

"Who's that tramping over my bridge?" roared the troll.

"It's I! The big Billy Goat Gruff," said the billy goat, who had an ugly hoarse voice of his own.

"Now I 'm coming to gobble you up," roared the troll.

*Well, come along! I've got two spears,*
*And I'll poke your eyeballs out at your ears;*
*I've got besides two curling-stones,*
*And I'll crush you to bits, body and bones.*

That was what the big billy goat said. And then he flew at the troll, and poked his eyes out with his horns, and crushed him to bits, body and bones, and tossed him out into the cascade, and after that he went up to the hillside. There the billy goats got so fat they were scarcely able to walk home again. And if the fat hasn't fallen off them, why, they're still fat; and so,

*Snip, snap, snout.*
*This tale's told out.*

Ashliman n.d.

# GLOSSARY

**Academic Controversy.** A cooperative activity for discussing issues on which there are divergent opinions.

**Active Learning.** An approach to learning that includes question-posing, inquiry, and self-directed learning. It is the opposite of rote learning.

**Advance organizer.** An anticipation activity at the beginning of a lesson to frame the students' thinking about the topic and to raise their curiosity; it could be a short talk about the topic, a one-sentence written summary of text to be read, or an organizing question.

**Anticipation.** The phase at the beginning of a lesson in which activities done to remind students of what they already know about a topic, encourage them to raise questions about the topic, and set purposes for their learning.

**Assessment.** The activity of finding out what students are learning and how they are learning it. Also, the activity of observing how teachers are teaching, and what the results of that teaching are. Assessment can be **formative assessment** when it looks at the effects of a lesson while that lesson is going on, or **summative assessment** when it is done at the conclusion of a lesson to see what the lesson achieved. Assessment con focus on **content**—that is, the concepts, facts, and attitudes that are learned—and on **processes**—the skills that students learn to perform.

**Best Practices.** Teaching methods whose effectiveness has been demonstrated through wide use, often including research.

**Brainstorming.** A technique of rapid, uncritical thinking. Brainstorming is used to get plenty of ideas out for discussion,. It is often followed by deliberative thinking.

**Building Knowledge.** In an active learning model, the phase toward the middle of a lesson in which students inquire into a topic and pursue answers to their questions.

**Character Map.** A graphic organizer often used as a consolidation activity; it allows readers to record and organize traits of characters for compare and contrast.

**Community Agreements.** A set of agreed-upon behavioral standards used to keep students' activity focused and productive when they work in cooperative groups.

**Consolidation.** In an active learning model, the phase toward the end of a lesson in which students reflect on what they learned, and interpret their new knowledge, critique it, apply it, debate it, and innovate upon it.

**Cooperative learning.** An approach to working in groups that makes students responsible for each other's learning, and each accountable for their own learning. "Collaborative learning" is a synonym for cooperative learning.

**Critical incident journal.** A journal used to lead students to reflect upon experiences they have during experiential learning activities. It focuses on salient experiences and leads the students to examine their responses to them.

**Critical Thinking.** An approach to thinking that emphasizes stating original claims or opinions and supporting them with reasons. Critical thinking is used expressively when students make interpretations and support them verbally or in writing. Critical thinking is used receptively when students critique other people's arguments.

**Directed Listening Thinking Activity (DL-TA).** Similar to the Directed Reading Thinking Activity (DR-TA), except that the teacher reads the text aloud to students. See below.

**Directed Reading Activity (DRA).** A building-knowledge strategy for guiding the silent reading of students with comprehension-level questions; often associated with reading with stops or chunking.

**Directed Reading Thinking Activity (DR-TA).** A building-knowledge strategy in which the silent reading of students is guided by a graphic organizer that asks students to predict, defend their predictions, and then verify them as they proceed through the text.

**Discussion Web.** A graphic organizer and an approach to cooperative discussions that uses it.

**Dramatic roles.** A structuralist means of discussing works of literature by examining the roles characters play in the plot.

**Dual-entry diary.** A format for making written responses to a reading. The page is divided into two columns: one for a quotation from the text and the other for the reader's comment on that quotation.

**Elbow partner.** In group activities, this is the student to the side of you.

**Experiential learning.** A generic term for activities conducted outside of the classroom in which students learn from direct experience. Service-learning (see below) is an example of experiential learning.

**Face partner.** In group activities the face partner is the student in front of you or behind you. If chairs can be moved, they are turned face to face. If the furniture is fixed, one student turns around to talk to the student behind.

**Free Writing.** Timed informal writing focused on a topic, with the emphasis on showing students their own thoughts, rather than making a written statement for public consumption.

**Graphic organizer.** A chart or table used to help students arrange their responses in ways that outwardly demonstrate the arrangement of ideas in the mind. Examples include **semantic webs** and **T-Charts**.

**Jigsaw.** A cooperative learning activity in which students work in **home groups** (relatively long-term groups in which students learn together) and **expert groups** (ad hoc groups in which students prepare to carry out a task) and teach each other the material of the lesson.

**Journals.** Notebooks in which students record their responses to what they are learning. The emphasis is more on personal reactions and associated thoughts, rather than on note taking. (Note taking is valuable, too, of course; but it serves a different purpose from response journals.)

**JUICE.** Job, Understand, Instruct, Critique, Evaluate is a study technique designed for use by pairs of students.

**Just in time lecture.** Especially in workshop classes, this is a brief lesson that teaches students just what they need to know and no more so that they can carry out a task.

**K-W-L.** A graphic organizer that encompasses the anticipation, building knowledge, and consolidation phases of a lesson; students record what they Know, what they Want to know, and what they Learn.

**Learning log.** A written reflection students make to recap the steps they went through in carrying out a learning activity.

**Levels of Thinking.** Refers to the degrees of intellectual challenge and the complexity of the mental tasks involved in different kinds of thinking. It is assumed that simply remembering a fact is easier, and therefore on a lower level, than applying an idea, or comparing and contrasting it to other ideas.

**M-Chart.** A graphic organizer with three columns.

**Mix/Freeze/Pair.** A cooperative activity in which students circulate around the room and stop at the direction of the teacher, pair up with whomever is nearest, and discuss a topic.

**One Stay, Three Stray.** A cooperative learning activity in which students from one home group visit different home groups and report those groups' ideas back to their own home group.

**Paired Reading/Paired Summarizing.** A cooperative activity in which pairs read a text together and question each other about it.

**Pens in the Middle.** A cooperative learning strategy that helps students share group time equitably.

**Predicting from Terms.** A pre-reading cooperative strategy in which students work in pairs or small groups to use several vocabulary words from a piece of narrative text to compose a story that contains all of the vocabulary elements.

**Question board.** A device on which students write questions about things they want to find out—topics that may or may not be related to the materials under study.

**Quick-write.** A brief written response to a question or prompt posed by the teacher.

**Quiet signal.** A silent means of asking for silence and getting students' attention. It is used in workshop settings when several activities are going on at once.

**RAFT.** A writing activity usually used in the consolidation phase of a lesson in which students consider four elements: ROLE (who is writing?), AUDIENCE (who receives it?), FORMAT (what form?), and TOPIC (what is it about?).

**Reading and Questioning.** A cooperative learning and study activity in which pairs of students read a text and write questions about the text and answers to those questions. Later they may use the questions and answers as study aids.

**Reading with Stops.** A strategy in which the teacher has students read silently a specific part of the text, such as a paragraph or a half page, to find the answer to a question; it is often used in DRA and DR-TA.

**Reciprocal Teaching.** A cooperative reading and discussion activity in which group members take turns playing the role of teacher.

**ReQuest.** A cooperative learning activity in which pairs of students read a text and question each other about it. (The name is derived from re-["again"] and *question*).

**Rubric.** A set of descriptors that show students what constitutes adequate performance on a task. Rubrics are developed around several criteria for excellence, and are used because they are a form of assessment that shows students how to perform well.

**Save the Last Word for Me.** A discussion technique in which students take turns guiding discussions of quotations they have chosen from a text. The name is derived from a song that was popular in the 1960s.

**Scaffolding.** Temporary help that is given to students to help them succeed at a task. It is removed once it is no longer needed.

**Semantic map.** A graphic organizer in which ideas are listed and displayed in hierarchical relationships as satellites of a main idea.

**Service-learning**. A way of extending teaching beyond the classroom and out into the community. Students perform useful service work in some domain that is relevant to a subject they are studying in school, and are led to reflect on their service experiences both in terms of academic learning and personal growth.

**Shared Inquiry.** A method for conducting discussions that calls for critical thinking and independent judgments. The discussion uses **interpretive questions**, which are open-ended questions, focused on the text.

**Spec sheet.** Short for "specification sheet," this is a list of items or points that should be included in a written essay.

**SQRRR.** Survey, Question, Read, Reflect, Review is a study technique for use by individual students.

**Structured Overview.** A brief introductory talk given at the beginning of a lesson. Its purpose is to introduce the topic and to present some of the important vocabulary.

**T-Chart.** A graphic organizer with two columns.

**Text coding.** A means of having students read a text, looking for certain features or facts, and making light marks in the margins when they find them.

**Thematic Unit.** A unit of planning that examines a topic from several different perspectives, including different disciplines. It usually engages a range of activities, from reading and writing, to direct observation, to drama and art.

**Think/Pair/Share.** A questioning procedure in which a question is posed to the class and the students (1) think of individual answers, (2) compare their answers with a partner, and then (3) selectively share their ideas with the whole class.

**Three-part journal.** A journal used to lead students to reflect upon experiences they have during experiential learning activities; a means of relating experiences to classroom readings and discussions.

**Trade a problem.** A cooperative learning activity in which students in one group prepare questions about the material under study for students in another group to solve.

**Value Line.** A cooperative activity in which students stand along an imaginary line in relation to their position on a binary ("yes"/"no") question.

**Walk Around/Talk Around.** A cooperative activity for sharing ideas during the anticipatory phase of a lesson.

**Warm-up**. Also called an "ice-breaker," a warm-up, is used before group activities are undertaken in order to relax the participants and prepare them to work together. Particular warm-ups described in this guide include **Scavenger hunt, Secret Talents, I love you, dear, Spider Web, Talk to Me,** and **Look Up Mon.**

**What? So What? Now What?** An activity that usually follows the K-W-L (Know/Want to Know/Learn) teaching method. The point is to pursue the implications of what has been learned. In other words, "Now that we know XXX, why does it matter? What should we do about it?"

**Writing across the Curriculum.** Writing that is used as an aid to learning and thinking. The emphasis is often on short exploratory pieces of writing that may include responses to questions, predictions, and questions for the class to examine.

# REFERENCES

Anderson, L. W. 2000. *Taxonomy for learning, teaching, and assessing: A revision of Bloom's taxonomy of educational objectives,* complete edition. New York: Longman.

Anderson, L. W., D.R. Krathwohl, P.W. Airasian, K. A. Cruikshank, R. E. Mayer, P. R. Pintrich, J. Raths, and M. C. Wittrock. 2000. *A taxonomy for learning, teaching, and assessing: A revision of Bloom's taxonomy of educational objectives.* New York: Pearson Allyn and Bacon.

Atwell, N. 1987. *In the middle: Writing, reading, and learning with adolescents.* Portsmouth, NH: Heinemann.

Ausubel, D. P. 1968. *Educational psychology: A cognitive view.* New York: Holt, Rinehart and Winston.

Baloche, L. 1997. *The Cooperative classroom.* New York: Prentice Hall.

Bean, J. 1996. *Engaging ideas: The professor's guide to integrating writing, critical thinking, and active learning in the classroom.* San Francisco: Jossey Bass.

Beck, I. L., M. G. McKeown, and L. Kucan. 2002. *Bringing words to life.* New York: Guilford.

Bleich, D. 1975. *Subjective criticism.* Baltimore: Johns Hopkins University Press.

Bloom, B. S., ed., et al. 1969. *Taxonomy of educational objectives: The classification of educational goals. Handbook I: Cognitive Domain.* New York: McKay.

Brown, R. 1958. *Words and things.* Garden City, NY: Basic Books.

Browne, M. N., and S. Keeley. 1997. *Asking the right questions: A guide to critical thinking (5th Edition).* New York: Prentice Hall.

Buehl, D. 2001. *Classroom strategies for interactive learning.* Newark, DE: International Reading Association.

Calkins, L. M. 2000. *The art of teaching writing.* New York: Longman.

Campus Compact. 2000. *Introduction to service-learning toolkit.* Providence, RI: Campus Compact.

Daniels, H. 2002. *Literature circles: Voice and choice in book clubs and reading groups.* Portland, ME: Stenhouse.

De Bono, E. 1973. *Lateral thinking: Creativity, step-by-step.* New York: Perennial.

Egan, K. 1992. Teaching as storytelling. In C. Temple and P. Collins, eds., *Stories and readers.* Norwood, MA: Christopher-Gordon.

Elbow, P. 1998. *Writing without teachers,* 2nd ed. New York: Oxford.

Freire, P. 2000. *Pedagogy of the oppressed.* New York: Continuum.

Frye, N. 1968. *The educated imagination.* Bloomington, IN: Indiana University Press.

Gardner, H. 1993. *Frames of mind: The theory of multiple intelligences.* New York: Basic Books.

Gibbs, J. 2001. *Tribes: A new way of learning and being together.* Windsor, CA: Center Source Systems.

Gillet, J.W., C. Temple, and A. Crawford. 2004. *Understanding reading problems: Assessment and instruction.* 6th ed. White Plains, NY: Longman.

Glasser, W. 1993. *The quality school teacher.* New York: HarperCollins.

Graves, D. H. 1982. *Writing: Teachers and children at work.* Portsmouth, NH: Heinemann.

Gunning, T. G. 2000. *Creating literacy instruction for all children.* Boston: Allyn and Bacon.

Halpern, D. 1995. *Thought and knowledge: An introduction to critical thinking.* Mahwah, NJ: Lawrence Earlbaum Associates.

Heimlich, J. E., and S. D. Pittelman. 1986. *Semantic mapping: Classroom applications.* Newark, DE: International Reading Association.

Herrenkohl, L. R., and M. R. Guerra. 1998. Participant structures, scientific discourse, and student engagement in fourth grade. *Cognition and Instruction* 16: 431–473

Herrenkohl, L. R., and J. Wertsch. 1999. The use of cultural tools: Mastery and appropriation. In I. E. Sigel, ed., *Development of mental representation: Theories and applications.* Mahwah, NJ: Lawrence Erlbaum Associates.

Inhelder, B., H. Sinclair, and M. Bovet. 1974. *Learning and the development of cognition.* Cambridge, MA: Harvard University Press.

Kagan, S. 1997. *Cooperative learning.* San Clemente, CA: Kagan Cooperative Learning.

Kermode, F. 1975. *The sense of an ending.* Chicago: University of Chicago Press.

Kurland, D. 1995. *I know what it says…What does it mean? Critical skills for critical reading.* New York: Wadsworth.

Luke, A. 2000. Critical literacy in Australia: A matter of context and standpoint. *Journal of adolescent and adult literacy* 43 (5): 448–461.

Macrorie, K. 1998. *The I-search paper.* Portsmouth, NH: Boynton/Cook.

Manzo, A. 1969. The ReQuest procedure. *Journal of Reading* 31 (11):123–126.

Manzo, A., and U. Manzo. 1994. *Teaching children to be literate: A reflective approach.* Orlando, FL: Harcourt.

Marzano, R. 1992. *A different kind of classroom: Teaching with dimensions of learning.* Washington, DC: Association for Supervision and Curriculum Development.

Marzano, R., D. Pickering, and J. Pollock. 2001. *Classroom instruction that works: Research-based strategies for increasing student achievement.* Washington, DC: Association for Supervision and Curriculum Development.

Mathews, S.R. 2003. Encouraging and assessing spontaneous use of critical thinking strategies. Paper presented at the 13th European Reading Conference, Tallinn, Estonia.

Moss, J. 1998. Planning instructional units. In C. Temple, M. Martinez, J. Yokota, and A. Naylor, *Children's books in children's hands.* Needham Heights, MA: Allyn and Bacon.

Murray, D. M. 2003. *A writer teaches writing,* 2nd. ed. Portsmouth, NH: Heinemann.

Neisser, U. 1976. *Cognition and reality: Principles and implications of cognitive psychology.* New York: Freeman.

O'Flaherty, L. 1937. A shilling. *The short stories of Liam O'Flaherty.* London: Case.

Ogle, D. 1986. K-W-L: A teaching method that develops active reading of expository text. *The Reading Teacher*, 39:564–570.

Palincsar, A. M., and A. L. Brown. 1984. Reciprocal teaching of comprehension fostering and comprehension monitoring activities. *Cognition and Instruction* (1): 117–175.

Paul, R. 1993. *Critical Thinking: What every person needs to survive in a rapidly changing world.* Santa Rosa, CA: Foundation for Critical Thinking.

Pearce, C. 2003. The question board. *The Thinking Classroom*, 4, (1): 43–44.

Pearce, C. R. 1999. *Nurturing inquiry: Real science for the elementary classroom.* Portsmouth, NH: Heinemann.

Pearson, P. D. and R. C. Anderson. 1984. A schema-theoretic view of basic processes in reading. In P. David Pearson. et. al., eds., *Handbook of reading research.* New York: Longman.

Plecha, J. 1992. Shared inquiry. In C. Temple and P. Collins, eds., *Stories and readers*. Norwood, MA: Christopher-Gordon.

Rapaport, R. 1986. Desecrating the holy woman: Derek Freeman's attack on Margaret Mead. *American Scholar*, 55 (3):313–347.

Rosenblatt, L. 1937. *Literature as exploration*. New York: Modern Language Association.

———. 1978. *The Reader, the text, and the poem*. Carbondale, IL: Southern Illinois University Press.

Santa, C. 1988. *Content writing, including study systems*. Dubuque, IA: Kendall/Hunt.

Sims Bishop, R. 1990. Mirrors, Windows, and Sliding Glass Doors. *Perspectives* 6:ix–xi.

Slavin, R. 1994. *Cooperative learning: Theory, research, and practice*. Boston: Allyn and Bacon.

Stauffer, R. G. 1969. *Teaching reading as a thinking process*. New York: Harper and Row.

Steele, J. L., and K. Meredith. 1997. *Reading and writing for critical thinking, Guidebook I*. New York: Open Society Institute.

Temple, C. 2003. *The B/C teachers' upgrade guide*. Dar es Salaam: Tanzanian Ministry of Education and Culture.

———. 2000. *Critical thinking across the curriculum: RWCT in higher education*. New York: Open Society Institute.

———. 2005. Critical thinking and critical literacy. *The Thinking Classroom* 6 (2): 15–20.

Temple, C., R. Nathan, N. Burris, and F. Temple. 1993. *The beginnings of writing*, 3rd ed. Needham Heights, MA: Allyn and Bacon.

Tierney, R. J., M. Carter, and L. Desai. 1991. *Portfolio assessment in the reading-writing classroom*. Norwood, MA: Christopher-Gordon.

Unrau, N. 1997. *Thoughtful teachers, thoughtful learners: A guide to helping adolescents think critically*. New York: Pippin.

Vacca, R. T., and J. L. Vacca. 1996. *Content area reading*, 5th ed. White Plains, NY: Longman.

Valencia, S., W. McGinley, and P. D. Pearson. 1990. *Assessing reading and writing: Building a more complex picture for middle school assessment*. Champaign, IL: University of Illinois, Center for the Study of Reading.

Vaughn, J., and T. Estes. 1986. *Reading and reasoning beyond the primary grades*. Boston: Allyn and Bacon.

Wagner, B. J. 1976. *Drama as a learning medium*. Washington, DC: NEA.

Zohar, A., Y. Weinberger, and P. Tamir. 1994. The effect of the Biology Critical Thinking Project on the development of critical thinking. *Journal of Research in Science Teaching* 31:183